THE ESSENTIALS

of

CONDITIONING

and

LEARNING

Third Edition

Michael Domjan

University of Texas at Austin

THOMSON

WADSWORTH

Australia • Canada • Mexico • Singapore • Spain
United Kingdom • United States

To Deborah

Publisher / Executive Editor: Vicki Knight
Acquisitions Editor: Marianne Taflinger
Technology Project Manager: Darin Derstine
Assistant Editor: Jennifer Wilkinson
Editorial Assistant: Justin Courts
Marketing Manager: Chris Caldeira
Marketing Assistant: Laurel Anderson
Advertising Project Manager: Brian Chaffee
Senior Project Manager, Editorial Production:
  Paul Wells

Art Director: Vernon Boes
Print/Media Buyer: Emma Claydon
Permissions Editor: Sarah Harkrader
Production Service: G&S Book Services
Copy Editor: Christine Gever
Cover Designer: Roger Knox
Cover Image: Philip Rostron/Masterfile
Compositor: G&S Book Services
Printer: Webcom

Printed in Canada
2 3 4 5 6 7 08 07 06 05

Library of Congress Control Number: 2004102950

ISBN 0-534-57434-3

Thomson Wadsworth
10 Davis Drive
Belmont, CA 94002-3098
USA

Asia
Thomson Learning
5 Shenton Way #01-01
UIC Building
Singapore 068808

Australia/New Zealand
Thomson Learning
102 Dodds Street
Southbank, Victoria 3006
Australia

Canada
Nelson
1120 Birchmount Road
Toronto, Ontario M1K 5G4
Canada

Europe/Middle East/Africa
Thomson Learning
High Holborn House
50/51 Bedford Row
London WC1R 4LR
United Kingdom

Latin America
Thomson Learning
Seneca, 53
Colonia Polanco
11560 Mexico D.F.
Mexico

Spain/Portugal
Paraninfo
Calle Magallanes, 25
28015 Madrid, Spain

BRIEF CONTENTS

Contents

CHAPTER FIVE

Stimulus Relations in Pavlovian Conditioning   66

CHAPTER SIX
Theories of Associative Learning 84

CHAPTER SEVEN
Instrumental or Operant Conditioning 101

CHAPTER FOURTEEN
Memory Mechanisms   227

Michael Domjan is Professor and Chair of the Psychology Department at the University of Texas at Austin, where he has been teaching undergraduate and graduate courses in learning since 1973. He served as Editor of the *Journal of Experimental Psychology: Animal Behavior Processes* and Associate Editor of *Learning and Motivation*. He is noted for his research on food-aversion learning and learning mechanisms in sexual behavior. He is recipient of the G. Stanley Hall Award from the American Psychological Association, and his research on sexual conditioning was selected for a MERIT Award by the National Institutes of Mental Health. His textbook, *The Principles of Learning and Behavior*, is now in its fifth edition.

PREFACE

The principles of conditioning and learning are used in many areas of psychology and allied disciplines. The purpose of this book is to provide a concise, current, and sophisticated summary of the essentials of conditioning and learning for students and professionals in those areas.

Concepts from conditioning and learning have been used in the design of behavior therapy procedures and in various educational settings, including special education, rehabilitation training, and elementary education. The principles of conditioning and learning are also important in behavioral neuroscience, physiological psychology, developmental psychology, psychopharmacology, and comparative psychology. Researchers in these areas are interested in how nonverbal organisms learn, process, and remember information. Asking animal and nonverbal human subjects how they learn and think invariably requires using conditioning procedures in some way. Therefore, interpretation of the results of such experiments necessitates understanding the underlying processes and mechanisms that are responsible for conditioning and learning effects.

The basic procedures of habituation, classical conditioning, and instrumental conditioning have not changed much in the past 50 years and are familiar to many students and professionals. However, our understanding of these procedures has changed dramatically, with the result that many common presumptions about learning are no longer valid. Consider, for example, the following claims:

- Learning, just like aggression, maternal behavior, and other important activities, can be directly observed in the behavior of organisms.
- Pavlovian conditioning involves the learning of new conditioned responses to previously ineffective stimuli.
- Extinction is the opposite of conditioning and involves the unlearning of an association.

- Avoidance responses occur because they prevent the delivery of an aversive event.
- Using a larger reinforcer makes instrumental behavior more resistant to extinction.

All of these claims seem reasonable, but none of them is valid in light of contemporary research. The purpose of this book is to summarize contemporary perspectives to enable students and professionals to use concepts from conditioning and learning more effectively in their work.

The book can serve as the primary source for an introductory course on conditioning and learning. It can also serve as a supplemental text for courses in behavior modification, behavioral neuroscience, special education, and related areas. Finally, the book can be used to provide the foundations for an advanced course in which students are required to read a collection of specialized articles.

In preparing this book, I was guided by my students, who have encouraged me over the past 30 years to keep searching for ways to explain concepts more simply and directly. The goals of previous editions were followed in preparing the third edition. The third edition includes two new chapters (Chapter 6, Theories of Associative Learning; and Chapter 10, Extinction of Conditioned Behavior), as well as numerous updates and adjustments of the text. New human examples and procedural tables have been added to improve the accessibility of the information, and each chapter now includes practice questions, in addition to a summary and a list of technical terms. The third edition also includes new references and suggested readings, where appropriate.

I would like to thank Marianne Taflinger of Wadsworth/Thomson Learning, who encouraged me to prepare this revision; the reviewers, who helped keep me on track; and Gretchen Otto, who guided the book through the production process.

Michael Domjan
Austin, Texas

CHAPTER ONE

Basic Concepts and Definitions

DID YOU KNOW THAT:

- Learning can result in either an increase or a decrease in responding.

- Learning is not always evident in the actions of an organism. It can be behaviorally silent.

- Learning may be investigated at the behavioral, neurophysiological, or cellular level.

- Learning is a special type of cause of behavior.

- Learning can be investigated only with experimental methods. Naturalistic observations may provide suggestive evidence but cannot prove that a behavior is due to learning.

- Learning is identified by means of an inference based on a difference in behavior between individuals with a particular type of experience and individuals lacking that experience.

- Control procedures are as important in studies of learning as training or experimental procedures.

Learning is of great interest because it is the means by which organisms adjust to changes in their environment and then retain those adjustments. Learning requires flexibility in the mechanisms of behavior and therefore was considered evidence of intelligence by Darwin and other early comparative psychologists (Darwin, 1897; Romanes, 1884). Contemporary scientists study learning to gain insights into how the mechanisms of behavior are altered by experience. Learning procedures are also often used to study motivation, memory, drug effects, and the neural bases of behavior.

Learning is a pervasive feature of human behavior and is evident in many other animal species as well. It has been found in creatures as diverse as fruit flies, sea slugs, honeybees, rodents, birds, and monkeys. Thus, **learning** is one of the fundamental characteristics of behavior.

Fundamental Features of Learning

People learn to recognize friends as different from strangers. They learn how to hold a telephone, and to pick it up when it rings. They also learn to swim, to ride a bicycle, and to avoid stepping in potholes. In all of these cases, *learning is identified by a change in behavior*. An experienced swimmer or cyclist behaves very differently than someone who has not learned to swim or ride a bike yet.

Learning to swim or ride a bicycle involves learning new hand, leg, and body movements and coordinating these movements to achieve balance and forward locomotion. Many, but not all, instances of learning involve the acquisition of new responses. We also learn to *not* do certain things. Children have to learn to keep quiet during a sermon, to hold still when being examined by a doctor, and to not run into the street when a car is coming. Learning to inhibit or suppress behavior is often as important as learning new responses. Riding a bicycle, for example, requires learning to pedal as well as learning not to lean too much to one side or the other. Thus, *the change in behavior that is used to identify learning can be either an increase or a decrease in a particular response*.

LEARNING AND OTHER FORMS OF BEHAVIOR CHANGE

Although all learning is identified by some kind of change in behavior, not all instances in which behavior is altered are instances of learning (see Figure 1.1). Therefore, it is important to distinguish learning from other sources of behavior change.

A major feature of learning that makes it different from other forms of behavior change is that *learning is relatively long lasting*. This serves to distinguish learning from various short-term or temporary changes in behavior. Physiological factors such as **fatigue** and drowsiness can cause widespread

Sources of Behavior Change

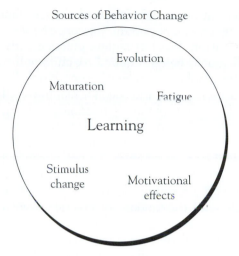

FIGURE 1.1 **Possible mechanisms that can result in changes in behavior.**
Note that learning is only one of several possible sources of behavior change.

and large changes in behavior (many of your actions become slower and less vigorous). However, such changes are temporary and can easily be reversed by a good rest. Major short-term changes in behavior can also be caused by changes in **motivation.** For example, people are much more reactive to stimuli related to food when they are hungry than after a hearty meal. Changes in stimulus conditions can also cause widespread but short-term changes in behavior. Imagine getting a stone in your shoe. The pressure of the stone is likely to change the way you walk and may induce you to stop and empty your shoe. But the disruption is likely to be short-lasting; you will resume your usual gait once the stone is removed. Learning, by contrast, involves longer-term changes. The assumption is that once something is learned, it will be remembered for a substantial period of time. For example, you are not considered to have learned a new concept discussed in class if you cannot remember it the next day.

Although learning involves enduring changes in behavior, not all long-term changes are due to learning. Long-term changes in behavior can also be produced by physical growth or **maturation.** Children become more skillful in lifting heavy objects and reaching a cookie jar on a high shelf as they get older. However, these changes are not due to learning. Rather, they result from physical growth and maturation. Children become taller and stronger as they get older.

Behavioral changes due to learning and changes due to maturation can be interrelated and difficult to distinguish. As a child becomes stronger and taller with age, these physical changes facilitate the learning of new skills. However, one important difference between learning and maturation is that maturation does not require practice with things specifically related to the skill that is being acquired. A child will become better able to reach high shelves as she gets older whether or not she ever practices reaching for cookies. **Practice** is not needed for maturation, but it is required for learning.

Practice is obviously necessary to learn a skill such as swimming or riding a bicycle. One cannot become a good swimmer without spending a lot of time rehearsing various swim strokes, and one cannot become an expert bicycle rider without extensive practice with pedaling, steering, and balancing. In contrast, other things can be learned very quickly. A child will learn not to touch a burning log in a fireplace after just one painful encounter. Regardless of the amount of practice involved, however, all *learning requires some practice or experience specifically related to the acquired behavior*.

Another difference between maturation and learning is that the same maturational process can produce behavioral changes in a variety of situations. As a child grows taller, she will be able to reach taller shelves, climb taller trees, and catch butterflies that are flying higher off the ground. Physical growth and maturation can result in changes in behavior in many different contexts. In contrast, *behavior changes due to learning are more limited to the practiced response*. Learning to operate a kitchen stove will help you cook indoors but will not improve your skill in building a fire for cooking on a camping trip. This is not to say that learning about one thing cannot help you do something else. Some generalization of learning can occur. However, generalization of learning tends to be limited. What you learn about one situation only generalizes to other similar situations. For example, learning to operate a particular gas stove will improve your ability to work other similar stoves but may not help if you are trying to cook with a microwave oven.

Another type of long-term change that has to be distinguished from learning is change due to **evolution.** Evolution serves to shape not only the physical attributes of organisms but also their behavior. Furthermore, evolutionary changes, like learning, are a result of interactions with the environment. However, evolutionary changes occur across generations. In contrast, learning results in behavioral changes within the lifetime of an individual organism.

Although learning is clearly distinguishable from evolution, it is no doubt the product of evolutionary processes. Considering how pervasive learning is in the animal kingdom, it is safe to assume that it has evolved in particular environmental niches because organisms with the ability to learn are more successful in producing offspring in those environments (Hollis, Pharr, Dumas, Britton, & Field, 1997). The greater reproductive fitness of individuals with the ability to learn increases the likelihood that their genes (and the genetic bases of learning) will be passed on to future generations. This evolutionary process produces changes in the mechanisms of behavior from one generation to the next. Learning, in contrast, involves changes in behavior during an individual's own lifetime.

LEARNING, PERFORMANCE, AND LEVELS OF ANALYSIS

That learning has occurred can only be determined by observing a change in behavior; the change, however, may only be evident under special circumstances. A physics student, for example, may not be able to provide an adequate definition of a quark, suggesting that he has not learned the concept. However, the same student may be able to pick out the correct definition from a list of alternative possibilities. Children can learn many things about driving a car by watching adults drive. They can learn what the steering wheel is good for and what are the functions of the gas and the brake pedals. However, they may show no evidence of this knowledge until they are old enough to take driving lessons. These examples illustrate that *learning can be behaviorally silent*—having no visible behavioral manifestation. In such cases, special procedures must be used to determine what the individual has learned.

Learning may not be evident in the actions of an organism for a variety of reasons. One possibility is that what is learned is a relationship between stimuli or events in the environment rather than a particular response. For example, we may learn to associate the color red with ripe apples. The learning of an association between two stimuli is called **stimulus-stimulus learning,** or S-S learning. A learned association between red and ripeness will not be reflected in what we do unless we are given a special task, such as judging the ripeness of apples. S-S learning is usually not evident in the actions of an organism unless special test procedures are used.

The things an individual does, a person's observable actions, are collectively referred to as **performance.** Performance depends on many things, including motivation and the stimulus conditions or behavioral opportunities provided by the environment. Learning is just one of the many factors that determine performance. You may be an excellent flute player, but if you do not have the opportunity or inclination to play the flute, no one will be able to tell what an accomplished musician you are.

I will describe a number of behaviorally silent forms of conditioning and learning in the following chapters. Examples of behaviorally silent learning suggest that learning cannot be equated with a change in behavior. Rather, learning involves a change in the kinds of things an organism could do given the right circumstances. Thus, *learning involves a change in the potential for doing something.*

Where does the change in the potential for action reside? Behavior is regulated by the nervous system. Therefore, learning involves long-lasting changes in the neural mechanisms of behavior. In fact, early neuroscientists, such as Ivan Pavlov, considered behavioral studies of learning to be studies of

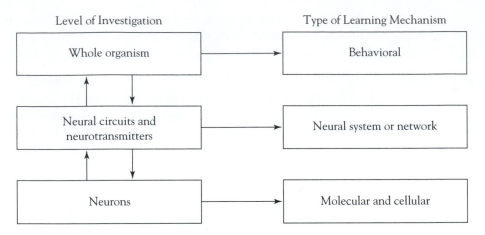

FIGURE 1.2   Levels of analysis of learning.
Learning mechanisms may be investigated at the organismic level, at the level of neural circuits and transmitter systems, and at the level of nerve cells or neurons.

how the nervous system works. They regarded learning procedures as techniques for the investigation of neural function.

Because learning involves changes in the nervous system, it may be investigated at a variety of different levels of analysis (see Figure 1.2). We may study learning at the level of molecular changes within nerve cells, or neurons. We may also study changes in neurotransmitter systems and neural circuits associated with learning. Finally, we may study learning at the level of changes in the behavior of intact organisms.

Historically, studies of learning began at the level of the intact organism, where learning is manifested by changes in observable behavior; and learning has been investigated most extensively at that level. However, with recent advances in the neurosciences, concepts and terms that have been developed for the behavioral analysis of learning have also been applied to investigations at the level of neural circuits and neurotransmitter systems, as well as at the cellular and molecular level. One of the challenges facing the study of learning in the coming years will be to integrate the findings from these diverse levels of analysis. Understanding how learning occurs at the behavioral level is critical for this integration. This book describes the behavioral analysis of learning.

A DEFINITION OF LEARNING

I identified a number of characteristics of learning in the preceding discussion. Learning involves a change in the potential or neural mechanisms of behavior. This change is relatively long-lasting and is the result of experience with environmental events specifically related to the behavior in question. These characteristics are combined in the following definition:

> Learning is a relatively enduring change in the potential to engage in a particular behavior resulting from experience with environmental events specifically related to that behavior.

Naturalistic versus Experimental Observations

Behavior occurs in many ways and in many situations. Basically, however, just two approaches to the study of behavior are available, naturalistic observations and experimental observations. **Naturalistic observations** involve observing and measuring behavior as it occurs under natural conditions, in the absence of interventions or manipulations introduced by the investigator. In contrast, **experimental observations** involve measuring behavior under conditions specifically designed by the investigator to test particular factors or variables that might influence the learning or performance of the behavior.

Consider, for example, activities involved in foraging for food by tree squirrels. Foraging can be investigated using naturalistic observations. One could watch squirrels in a park, for example, and count how often they picked up a seed, how often they ate the seed right away, and how often they buried the seed for later retrieval. Making such observations throughout the day would provide detailed information about the foraging behavior of the squirrels in that park. However, such observations would not reveal why the squirrels did what they did. Observing squirrels undisturbed cannot tell us why they select one type of seed instead of another, why they devote more effort to foraging in one part of the day than another, or why they eat some seeds right away and bury others to eat later. Naturalistic observations cannot provide answers to questions that probe the *causes* of behavior. They may help us formulate questions or hypotheses about why animals do certain things, but naturalistic observations cannot provide the answers.

The causes of behavior can only be discovered using experimental observations. Experimental observations require the investigator to manipulate the environment in special ways that facilitate reaching a causal conclusion. Using naturalistic observations, you may find that squirrels bury more seeds in the fall than in the winter. What might cause this outcome? Naturalistic observations cannot answer this question, because environmental conditions in the fall differ from conditions in the winter in many respects. Food is more plentiful in the fall than in the winter, and the climate is warmer. Daylight gets shorter from day to day in the fall and longer in the winter. And trees have more leaves in the fall than in the winter, making it easier for squirrels to hide seeds without being seen.

To determine what factors encourage squirrels to bury seeds, the environment must be manipulated in order to isolate each possible causal variable. Consider, for example, whether the availability of excess food causes seed burying. We could test this possibility by comparing squirrels under two different conditions. Under one condition, the squirrels would be provided with excess food by spreading lots of store-bought peanuts in the observation area. Under the second condition, only a subsistence food supply would be available. The squirrels would not be provided with extra peanuts, and some of the food growing in their habitat would be harvested by the experimenter to reduce the food supply. In all other relevant respects, the test conditions would be the same. Temperature, changes in daylight from day to day, and extent of foliage in the trees would be identical. Given these identical conditions, if the squirrels buried more seeds when food was plentiful than when food was scarce, we could conclude that excess food encourages or causes the burying of seeds.

Although experimental observations permit us to draw conclusions about the causes of behavior, it is important to realize that the causes of behavior cannot be observed directly. Rather, causes must be inferred from differences in behavior observed under different experimental conditions. When we conclude that excess food causes seed burying, we are not describing something we have actually observed. What we saw in our hypothetical experiment is that squirrels bury more seeds when food is plentiful than when food is scarce. The conclusion that excess food causes seed burying is an inference arrived at by comparing the two experimental conditions. *Causal conclusions are inferences based on a comparison of two (or more) experimental conditions.* Causes cannot be observed directly.

Uncontrolled naturalistic observations can provide a wealth of descriptive information about behavior. We have learned a great deal from naturalistic observations about foraging for food, courtship and sexual behavior, maternal behavior, parental behavior, and defensive and territorial behavior. Considering that learning is ultimately also evident in the behavior of human and other animals, one might suppose that observational techniques can also be useful in the study of learning. In fact, some have advocated that detailed investigations of learning should begin with naturalistic observations of learning phenomena (Miller, 1985). However, naturalistic observations are inherently unsuitable for studies of learning, because they cannot identify causal variables.

The Fundamental Learning Experiment

According to the definition developed in this chapter, learning is a relatively enduring change in behavioral potential resulting from experience with environmental events specifically related to that behavior. A critical aspect of this definition is that learning is a result of past experiences. As such, learning is a causal variable, one that involves past experience with relevant environmental events. To conclude that learning has occurred, we have to be sure that the change in behavior we are seeing is *caused* by past experience.

As I noted above, causes cannot be observed directly. Instead, they have to be inferred from experimental observations. This idea has profound implications for the study of learning. Because learning is a causal variable, it cannot be observed directly. Rather, learning can only be investigated by means of experimental manipulations that serve to isolate a specific past experience as the cause of a change in behavior.

To conclude that a change in behavior is due to a specific past experience, or learning, one has to compare individuals with and without that experience under otherwise identical circumstances. The specific past experience is the independent variable (IV), and the resultant change in behavior is the dependent variable (DV). Consider, for example, the fact that most 8-year-old children can ride a bicycle proficiently, whereas 3-year-olds cannot. A reasonable interpretation is that the older children are expert riders because they have had more time to practice riding a bicycle. That is, the change in behavior from 3 to 8 years of age may be caused by experience with bicycles. To support this conclusion, it is not enough to point to the fact that 8-year-olds are better riders than 3-year-olds. Such a difference could be due to physical growth and maturation. It is also not compelling to point out that 8-year-olds spend more time riding bicycles than 3-year-olds, because this may be an effect rather than a cause of the greater skill of 8-year-olds. Some kind of experiment has to be conducted to prove that proficient riding is a result of past experience or learning.

One way to prove that bicycle riding is a learned skill would be to conduct an experiment with 3-year-old children who have never ridden a bicycle. We could assign the children randomly to one of two treatment groups: an *experimental group* and a *control group*. The experimental group would receive three 1-hour lessons in riding a bicycle. This would be the independent variable (IV). The control group would also receive three 1-hour lessons through which they would become familiar with bicycles. However, the control group would not be taught to ride. Rather, they would be told about the various parts of a bicycle and how the parts fit together. At the end of the lessons, both groups of children would be tested for their skill in riding. Proficiency in bicycle riding would be the dependent variable (DV). If proficient riding is learned through relevant practice, then the children in the experimental group should be more proficient than the children in the control group.

The above example illustrates the *fundamental learning experiment*. To conclude that a behavior change is a result of learning, we have to compare the behavior of individuals under two conditions. In the **experimental condition,** participants are provided with the relevant environmental experience or training. In the **control condition,** participants do not receive the relevant training but are treated identically in all other respects. The occurrence of learning is inferred from a comparison between the two conditions.

One cannot conclude that learning has occurred by observing only individuals who have acquired the skill of interest. Rather, conclusions about learning require a comparison between the experimental and control conditions.

THE CONTROL PROBLEM IN STUDIES OF LEARNING

Are there any special consequences of the fact that learning can only be inferred through a comparison between individuals with a particular training history and others that lack that history? Yes, indeed. One important consequence is that *learning cannot be investigated by means of naturalistic observations*. Under natural circumstances, individuals with a particular training history often differ in a number of respects from individuals that do not have the same history. Therefore, the requirements of the fundamental learning experiment are difficult to satisfy under entirely natural circumstances.

A second important consequence of the fact that learning depends on the comparison of an experimental with a control condition is that the control procedure must be designed with as much care as the experimental procedure. In fact, some landmark contributions to the study of learning have come not from analyses of experimental procedures for producing learning but from analyses of control procedures (e.g., Church, 1964; Rescorla, 1967; see also Papini & Bitterman, 1990). Different training procedures require different control procedures. I will discuss this issue in greater detail as I discuss various types of learning in the following chapters. For now, suffice it to say that the design of a control procedure is dictated by the particular aspect of past experience one wishes to isolate as being responsible for the behavioral change that is of interest.

In the example of children learning to ride a bicycle, we were interested in whether practice riding is critical for becoming a skillful rider. Children who practice riding also learn a lot about how a bicycle works (how the pedals make the wheels turn, for example). That is why we designed the procedure for the control group so that the children in that group got to learn about the parts of a bicycle and how those parts go together. However, the children in the control group were not provided with practice in sitting on a bicycle and pedaling it. Thus, the design of the control procedure allowed us to isolate practice in riding a bicycle as the critical factor involved in learning to ride.

A third important consequence of the fact that learning can only be inferred by means of a comparison between experimental and control conditions is that learning is usually investigated with at least two independent groups of participants, an experimental group and a control group. Thus, traditional studies of learning involve the use of **between-subjects experimental designs.**

An important exception to traditional between-subjects experimental designs was developed in the Skinnerian tradition of learning research (Sidman, 1960). Skinner advocated the extensive investigation of individual subjects rather than groups of participants. However, even **single-subject**

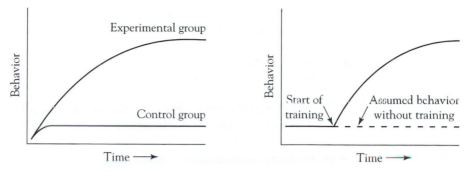

FIGURE 1.3   Two versions of the fundamental learning experiment.
In the left panel, two groups of individuals are compared. The training procedure is provided for participants in the experimental group but not for participants in the control group. In the right panel, a single individual is observed before and during training. The individual's behavior during training is compared to what we assume its behavior would have been without training.

experiments involve comparisons between experimental and control conditions (see Figure 1.3). Basically, single-subject experiments require that the individual's behavior be understood well enough to permit accurate assumptions about how the individual would have behaved if it had not received the training procedure of interest.

Consider, for example, a 4-year-old child who is unable to catch a ball tossed to him. If we spend several hours a day teaching the child how to catch a ball, he will become proficient within a few days. From this we may conclude that the child has learned to catch a ball. Notice, however, that this conclusion is based on our assumption that the child would not have acquired the skill so rapidly if he had not received instruction. Only if we have sufficient knowledge to make this assumption can we infer that the child has learned to catch the ball. Thus, the study of learning in individual subjects also involves a comparison between an experimental and a control condition. The only difference is that the control condition is not provided by an explicit control group but by evidence obtained from other sources that gives us confidence that the behavior would not have changed without the training procedure.

THE GENERAL-PROCESS APPROACH TO THE STUDY OF LEARNING

In addition to relying on experimental techniques, investigators of learning typically employ a general-process approach. Such an approach assumes that learning phenomena are the products of fundamental or basic processes that operate in much the same way in different learning situations.

The general-process approach is common in science and engineering.

For example, in designing cars, engineers assume that the basic principles of how an internal combustion engine operates are pretty much the same whether the engine is used to propel a four-door sedan or a large sport utility vehicle. In an analogous fashion, the basic principles involved in learning are assumed to be the same whether the learning involves rats obtaining food in a maze or children learning to tie their shoelaces. The general-process approach focuses on underlying commonalities across learning situations, with the goal of identifying universal principles.

The assumption that universal, basic laws of association are responsible for learning phenomena does not deny the diversity of stimuli different animals may learn about, the diversity of responses they may learn to perform, and species differences in rates of learning. The generality is assumed to exist in the rules or processes of learning—not in the contents or speed of learning.

If we assume that universal rules of learning exist, then we should be able to discover those rules in any situation in which learning occurs. Thus, an important methodological implication of the general-process approach is that general rules of learning may be discovered by studying any species or response system that exhibits learning. This implication has encouraged scientists to study learning in a small number of experimental situations and in model systems, such as the *Aplysia*. I will describe examples of standard experimental paradigms as I introduce various learning phenomena in future chapters.

THE USE OF NONHUMAN SUBJECTS IN RESEARCH ON LEARNING

Many of the basic principles of learning that I will describe in the course of this book were first established in research with nonhuman animal subjects and were only later extended to humans. There are many advantages to studying learning in nonhuman laboratory subjects. These include (1) better knowledge and control of the prior learning experiences of the subjects, (2) greater precision and control over the learning environment and administration of the learning procedures, (3) the ability to observe the same individuals under precisely the same conditions over repeated training and test trials, (4) knowledge of and ability to control the genetic makeup of the subjects, (5) greater control over motivational variables that might affect learning, (6) better chance to minimize the role of language, and (7) better chance to minimize efforts by the subject to please or displease the experimenter. Without the use of laboratory animals such as rats and mice, scientists would also be unable to develop behavioral tools that are critical to the study of the neurobiology and neuropharmacology of learning and memory. Such studies may someday lead to the discovery of cures for serious maladies such as Alzheimer's disease.

Although nonhuman laboratory animals provide numerous advantages for the study of learning, some have argued in favor of alternatives. Four common alternatives have been proposed: (1) observational research, (2) plants, (3) tissue cultures, and (4) computer simulations. As I pointed out previously, observational techniques do not involve the kind of precise experimental manipulations that are critical for studies of learning. Nor do plants provide a viable alternative, because plants do not have a nervous system, which is critical for learning. Tissue cultures can be useful in isolating the operation of specific cellular processes. However, without behavioral research involving intact organisms, one cannot determine the importance of a particular cellular process for the behavioral changes that characterize learning. Finally, computer simulations do not provide a viable alternative, because detailed observations of learning are required before one can prepare a successful computer simulation.

Summary

Although learning is a common human experience, what it is and how it must be investigated are not obvious. Learning is evident in a change in behavior—either the acquisition of a new response or the suppression of an existing response. However, not all instances of altered behavior involve learning, and not all instances of learning produce immediately observable changes in behavior. The term *learning* is restricted to cases in which there is an enduring change in the potential to engage in a particular behavior that results from prior experience with environmental events specifically related to that behavior.

Learning mechanisms may be examined at the level of intact organisms, the level of neural circuits or systems, or the level of nerve cells or neurons. However, because learning is a causal variable, it can be investigated only with experimental methods. Naturalistic observations may provide suggestions about learning but cannot provide definitive evidence. The basic learning experiment involves comparing an experimental and a control condition. The experimental condition includes the training procedure or experience whose effects are being tested. The control condition is similar but omits the relevant training experience. Learning is inferred from a difference in outcomes between the experimental and control conditions. For this reason, control procedures are as important for studies of learning as are experimental procedures.

Studies of learning have been based on a general-process approach, which assumes that diverse learning phenomena reflect the operation of universal elemental processes. This general-process approach together with other factors have encouraged the use of nonhuman animal subjects in learning experiments. Given the nature of learning phenomena, alternatives to the study of intact organisms are not viable.

Practice Questions

1. What is S-S learning?

2. What is an example of behaviorally silent learning?

3. What is the difference between learning and evolution?

4. What is the difference between learning and maturation?

5. What is the difference between learning and behavior caused by stimulus change?

6. What is the difference between learning and performance?

7. What is the definition of learning?

8. What is the difference between naturalistic observations and experimental observations?

9. What are the main features of the fundamental learning experiment?

10. What types of manipulations serve as independent variables in studies of learning?

11. What types of measures serve as dependent variables in studies of learning?

12. Why are control groups important in studies of learning?

13. What are the basic features of the general-process approach to learning?

14. What advantages do laboratory animals provide for the study of learning?

15. Why are alternatives to laboratory animals inadequate for learning research?

Technical Terms

Between-subjects experiment
Control condition
Evolution
Experimental condition
Experimental observation
Fatigue
Learning

Maturation
Motivation
Naturalistic observation
Performance
Practice
Single-subject experiment
Stimulus-stimulus learning

CHAPTER TWO

The Structure of Unconditioned Behavior

D I D   Y O U   K N O W   T H A T :

- Learning is constrained by the organism's unconditioned behavior.
- Unconditioned behavior is organized in complex and systematic ways.
- Organized elicited behavior can result in well-coordinated social interactions.
- Behavior in a complex environment can be governed by small, isolated stimulus features.
- Species-typical or instinctive behavior is not invariant but modulated by the animal's motivational state.

Learning enables organisms to benefit from experience. Through learning, behavior can be altered in ways that make the individual more effective in interacting with its environment. Animals can forage more effectively by learning where and when food is likely to be available (e.g., Kamil & Clements, 1990). They can defend themselves more successfully by learning when and where they are likely to encounter a predator (e.g., Hollis, 1990). And they can be more effective in reproduction by learning when and where they are likely to encounter a potential sexual partner (Domjan, Cusato, & Villarreal, 2000; Hollis, Pharr, Dumas, Britton, & Field, 1997).

Shaping and Homogeneous versus Heterogeneous Substrates of Behavior

In all instances of learning, the behavior of an organism is modified or shaped by its prior experience. B. F. Skinner introduced the term *shaping* in reference to a particular type of conditioning procedure that I will describe in greater detail in Chapter 6. For our present purposes, it is sufficient to point out that through shaping, an organism's behavior can be gradually changed to enable it to perform new responses. A child's uncoordinated arm and leg movements, for example, can be gradually shaped to enable him to swim rapidly across a pool.

Skinner chose the term *shaping* by analogy with the way in which a sculptor gradually changes and molds a lump of clay into a recognizable object (Skinner, 1953). A sculptor interested in making a statue of a swan, for example, starts with an unformed lump of clay. She then cuts away excess clay here and there and molds what remains in special ways. As this process continues, a recognizable swan gradually emerges. In an analogous fashion, learning can change or shape an organism's behavior, with the result that the individual comes to respond in ways that it did not before.

The analogy with molding a block of clay into a swan captures some of the aspects of how learning is changed through behavior. However, the analogy has a serious shortcoming. Clay is a homogeneous substance that can be molded in any direction with equal ease. Behavior is not like that. Behavior cannot be changed in any direction with equal ease. Changes in behavior occur in the context of genetically programmed predispositions that make certain changes easier to produce than others. For example, it is much easier to train animals to approach and manipulate food-related stimuli (Hearst & Jenkins, 1974) than it is to train them to release or withdraw from stimuli related to food (Breland & Breland, 1961; Timberlake, Wahl, & King, 1982).

Learning procedures do not shape new behavior in the way that a sculptor shapes clay into a new object. A more apt analogy for the behavioral substrate of learning is provided by wood rather than clay (Rachlin, 1976). Unlike clay, wood has a heterogeneous or uneven consistency. It is grainy and has knots. Cutting with the grain is easier and results in a smoother line than cutting against the grain, and cutting around knots is easier than cutting through them. Because of this heterogeneity, if you are carving a statue out of wood, you have to pay close attention to how the statue is oriented in relation to the grain and the knots in the wood. Analogously, learning psychologists must pay close attention to how what they are trying to teach an organism fits with the organism's preexisting behavioral tendencies. Chapter 2 is devoted to a description of these preexisting behavioral tendencies.

All instances of learning reflect an interaction between the training procedures used and the individual's preexisting behavior. Changes brought about by learning are not applied to a homogeneously modifiable substrate. Rather, learning is superimposed on a heterogeneous preexisting behavioral structure. Therefore, understanding how learning occurs requires an appreciation of the heterogeneous behavioral substrate that organisms bring to a learning situation.

The dependence of learning on unlearned aspects of behavior has been emphasized in some areas of learning more than others. The interaction between conditioned and unconditioned aspects of behavior has been the focus of attention in studies of Pavlovian conditioning and avoidance learning (see Chapters 4 and 12). However, we will see numerous examples of how learning effects depend on unlearned behavioral tendencies in analyses of other aspects of learning as well.

The Concept of the Reflex

The smallest unit of unconditioned behavior is the reflex. The concept of a reflex was formulated by the French philosopher René Descartes (1596–1650). Descartes made numerous contributions to Western philosophy, including ideas about behavior that are familiar to most of us today but were innovative in the seventeenth century. Like other philosophers of his time, Descartes believed that important aspects of human behavior were voluntary. However, he was also impressed with the seemingly automatic and involuntary nature of some actions and proposed the concept of the reflex to characterize involuntary behavior.

Descartes based his concept of the reflex on animated statues that he saw in public parks in France. Sophisticated animated characters, such as those created by Disney Studios, were not available in Descartes's time. But some of the parks Descartes frequented had statues whose limbs would move when someone walked by. To enable the statue to move, its limbs were attached by means of joints. Through a series of levers and linkages, the limbs and joints were connected to stepping stones along the walkway near the statue. Whenever someone stepped on one of these stones, the pressure was transferred to the statue, causing its arm or leg to move.

The moving statues appeared lifelike, and it occurred to Descartes that some aspects of human and animal behavior were similar to the behavior of

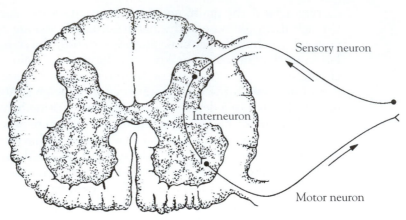

Cross-section of spinal cord

FIGURE 2.1   Neural organization of simple reflexes.
The environmental stimulus for the reflex response activates a sensory neuron,
which transmits the sensory message to the spinal cord. Here the neural impulses
are relayed to an interneuron, which in turn passes the impulses to the motor neuron. The motor neuron activates muscles involved in the reflex response.

the statues. Descartes pointed out that animals and people also perform
certain actions in response to particular environmental stimuli. For example,
we quickly withdraw our finger when we touch a hot stove, we "instinctively"
flinch when we hear a sudden noise, and we extend our arm when we lose
our footing. Such responses to particular stimuli are examples of **elicited
behavior.**

In the statues Descartes saw, the movements were in a sense reflections
of the eliciting stimulus, the force that was applied to the associated stepping
stone. Descartes coined the term **reflex** to capture this idea of behavior being a reflection of an eliciting stimulus. The entire unit from stimulus input
to response output was termed the **reflex arc** (see Figure 2.1).

Reflexes are involved in many aspects of behavior important for sustain-
ing critical life functions. Respiratory reflexes provide us with sufficient air
intake. The suckling reflex provides a newborn's first contact with milk, and
chewing, swallowing, and digestive reflexes are important in obtaining nutrients throughout life. Postural reflexes enable us to maintain stable body
positions, and withdrawal reflexes protect us from focal sources of injury.

For about 250 years after Descartes, investigators of reflexes were primarily concerned with physiological questions. Scientists studied the neural
circuitry of the reflex arc, the mechanisms of neural conduction, and the role
of reflexes in various physiological systems. These investigations continued

at an accelerated pace in the twentieth century. In addition, the idea of elicited behavior was extended to more complex forms of overt behavior. Much of this work was done in the newly emerging field of **ethology,** which is a specialty within biology concerned with the evolution and development of functional units of behavior (Baerends, 1988).

Complex Forms of Elicited Behavior

Ethologists discovered that complex social behavior in various species is made up of response components that are elicited by social stimuli. A male stickleback fish, for example, establishes a small territory and builds a nest tunnel during the mating season. After the territory has been set up, the approach of a male intruder elicits an aggressive defensive response from the resident male. In contrast, if a female enters the territory, the resident male engages in courtship zigzag swimming movements (see Figure 2.2). The courtship zigzag movements stimulate the female to follow the resident male to the nest tunnel. Once the female is in the tunnel, with her head at one end and her tail at the other, the male prods the base of the female's tail. This causes the female to release her eggs. The female then leaves the nest and the male enters and fertilizes the eggs. After that, he chases the female away and fans the eggs to provide oxygen until the eggs hatch (see Tinbergen, 1952).

In this complex behavioral duet, the male and female each has its own special role. Stimuli provided by the female trigger certain actions on the part of the resident male (zigzag swimming); the male's behavior in turn provides stimuli that trigger other responses on the part of the female (following the resident male to the nest); the female's behavior then leads to further responses from the male; and so on. The outcome is a sequence of nicely coordinated social responses. The behavior sequence progresses only if the male's behavior provides the necessary stimulation to elicit the next response from the female, and vice versa. If the response of one participant fails to trigger the next response in its partner, the sequence of actions is interrupted, and the social interaction may come to an end.

MODAL ACTION PATTERNS

Careful observations by ethologists have revealed numerous examples of complex social and nonsocial behavior that are made up of sequences of elicited responses of the sort illustrated by the sexual behavior of sticklebacks. Elicited responses have been shown to be involved in, among other things, nest building, incubation, parental feeding of the young, grooming, foraging, and defensive behavior (Alcock, 2001). Each unit of elicited behavior is made up of a characteristic response and its corresponding eliciting stimulus.

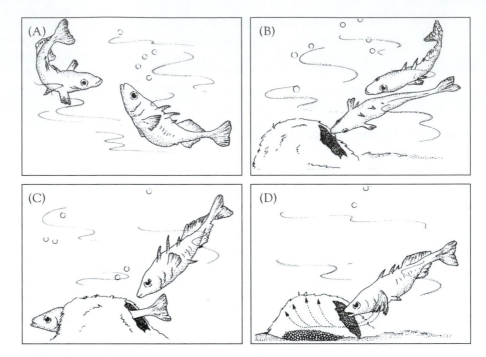

FIGURE 2.2   The sequence of courtship and reproductive behavior in the stickleback.
(A) The male swims towards the female with zigzag motions. (B) The male guides the female to the nest. (C) The female enters the nest and releases her eggs. (D) After fertilizing the eggs, the male fans them to provide sufficient oxygen for development. Adapted from Tinbergen, 1952.

The units of elicited behavior I have been discussing are commonly called **modal action patterns,** or MAPs. The phrase *action pattern* is used instead of *response* because the activities involved are not restricted to a single muscle movement such as the blink of an eye or the flexion of a leg muscle. Elicited responses involved in grooming, foraging, courtship, and parental behavior require a coordinated set of a number of different muscles. The word *modal* is used to signify that most members of the species perform the action pattern in question and do so in a highly similar fashion. An action pattern is a characteristic of the species. For example, infant mammals typically feed by suckling; infant gulls typically feed by gaping and receiving food from a parent; and infant chickens typically feed by pecking small spots on the ground. Because modal action patterns are characteristic of a species, they are examples of **species-typical behavior.**

SIGN STIMULI

Modal action patterns occur in the context of rich and complex arrays of stimulation. Consider, for example, a male quail or male turkey that becomes sexually attracted to a female who comes into view. The female is a source of many visual cues, cues provided by her various body parts (head, neck, torso, legs) and her movements. She may also provide auditory and olfactory stimulation, and if she comes close enough to the male, she provides tactile stimulation. Interestingly, most of these cues are not critical for eliciting male sexual behavior.

To determine which of the various stimuli provided by a female are sufficient to attract a sexually motivated male, experimenters tested males with both live females and taxidermic models of females. In one study (Domjan & Nash, 1988), for example, some of the models consisted of the head and entire body of a female. Other models consisted of just the head and neck of the female or just the body without the head. Figure 2.3 shows the tendency of male quail to approach and remain near these various types of female stimuli.

The male quail responded as vigorously to a complete taxidermic model of a female as they responded to a live female. This result shows that movement cues and auditory and olfactory stimuli provided by a live female are not necessary to elicit the approach response. The birds also responded vigorously to just the visual cues of a female's head and neck. In fact, they ap-

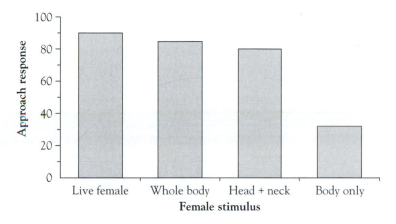

FIGURE 2.3   Approach response of sexually experienced male quail to a live female and to taxidermic models consisting of the whole body of a female, a female's head and neck only, and a female's body without the head and neck. Adapted from Domjan & Nash, 1988.

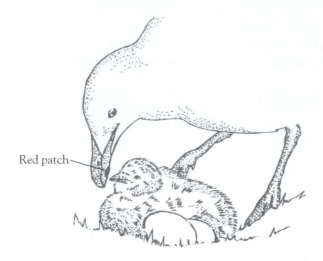

Red patch

FIGURE 2.4   The sign stimulus for the pecking response of gull chicks is a red spot near the tip of the parent's bill.

proached the head-and-neck model almost as much as they responded to a complete female model. This is a remarkable outcome. Evidently male quail can identify a female by means of the visual cues of the female's head and neck alone. The rest of her body, her calls, her smell, her movements—all of these are unnecessary.

The restricted set of stimuli that are required to elicit a modal action pattern is called a **sign stimulus.** As far as male quail and male turkeys are concerned, the female's head and neck are the "sign" that she is a female (Schein & Hale, 1965).

A sign stimulus is often a remarkably small part of the cues that ordinarily precede a modal action pattern. The pecking response of gull chicks, for example, is elicited by a prominent red spot on their mother's or father's bill (see Figure 2.4). The pointed shape of the parent's bill, together with this prominent spot, stimulates the chicks to peck the parent's bill, which then causes the parent to feed the chick by regurgitating food. Other aspects of the parent (the shape of her head, her eyes, how she lands on the edge of the nest, the noises she makes) are not important (Tinbergen & Perdeck, 1950).

The Organization of Elicited Behavior

If each reflex or modal action pattern occurred automatically whenever its eliciting stimulus was encountered, behavior would be somewhat disorganized. Elicited responses do not occur independently of each other. Rather, they are organized in special ways. As we will see in the following chapters, some of this organization is a result of learning and experience. Here I will describe aspects of behavioral organization that are not obviously a product of learning.

MOTIVATIONAL FACTORS

One prominent factor that serves to coordinate modal action patterns is the internal state of the organism. The occurrence of many action patterns depends on the individual's motivational state. In numerous species, for example, courtship and sexual responses occur only during the breeding season, or only in the presence of sufficiently high levels of sex hormones. In fact, the necessary conditions can be even more restrictive. For male sticklebacks to court a female, they not only have to be in the breeding season but they also have to have established a territory and built a nest. These preconditions serve to prime or create the motivation for courtship behavior.

Motivational factors have been identified for a variety of modal action patterns, including aggression, feeding, and various aspects of parental and sexual behavior. The motivational state sets the stage for a modal action pattern, whose actual occurrence is then triggered by a sign stimulus. In a sense, the sign stimulus releases the modal action pattern when the animal is in a particular motivational state. For this reason, a sign stimulus is also sometimes referred to as a **releasing stimulus.**

Ethologists considered the motivational state of the organism to be one of the key factors involved in the organization of behavior (e.g., Lorenz, 1981). Using motivational concepts, they formulated an influential model of how modal action patterns are organized, referred to as the **hydraulic model** of behavior. The hydraulic model assumes that certain factors lead to the buildup of a particular type of motivation or drive. The term *hydraulic* was used by analogy with a hydraulic engine, in which the buildup of pressure causes pistons to move until the pressure is released or dissipated. The hunger drive, for example, is created by the expenditure of energy and the utilization of nutrients. This drive in turn induces selective attention to food-related stimuli and lowers the threshold for activating food-related modal action patterns. Once food is found and eaten, the motivational state of hunger is discharged. Thus, the motivational state facilitates modal action patterns related to eating, and the opportunity to perform those responses in turn reduces the motivational state.

APPETITIVE AND CONSUMMATORY BEHAVIOR

Elicited behavior is also organized sequentially. Certain responses tend to occur before others. Ethologists characterized the response sequence involved in the discharge of a drive state as consisting of two major components. The first of these is **appetitive behavior.** In the case of the feeding system, appetitive behavior consists of responses involved in searching for a patch of food.

Appetitive behavior is quite variable and occurs in response to general spatial cues. For example, in searching for a patch of food, a squirrel will focus on spatial cues that help identify trees and bushes that may contain nuts and fruit. Appetitive behavior tends to occur over a wide area and involves a range of possible activities. During the course of its foraging, the squirrel may run across open grass, scramble over rocks, climb trees, jump from one tree limb to another, and so on.

Once the squirrel encounters an edible nut, its behavior becomes much more stereotyped and restricted. Now the squirrel remains in one place, sits back on its hind legs and tail, takes the nut in its front paws, cracks it open, and chews and swallows the food. These more stereotyped species-typical activities are examples of **consummatory behavior** because they complete or consummate the response sequence. The consummatory modal action patterns end the response sequence because these responses discharge the motivation or drive state.

In the feeding system, consummatory behavior involves the consumption of food, but the apparent similarity in wording in this case is merely a coincidence. In the sexual behavior system, consummatory behavior consists of the copulatory responses that serve to complete a sexual interaction. In the defensive behavior system, consummatory behavior consists of circa strike responses an animal makes when it is not just threatened but physically attacked by a predator (see Chapter 12).

Another way to think about appetitive and consummatory behavior is that appetitive behavior consists of activities that enable an organism to come into contact with the sign stimuli that will elicit the modal action patterns that serve to end the response sequence. For example, the appetitive sexual behavior of the male involves searching for a female. Once the female is encountered, the stimuli provided by her elicit a more restricted range of courtship and copulatory responses. These copulatory responses then discharge the motivation to engage in sexual behavior, thereby consummating or ending the sexual behavior sequence.

BEHAVIOR SYSTEMS

Recent research on the structure of unconditioned behavior has suggested that elicited behavior sequences should be subdivided into more than just two types of behavior, appetitive and consummatory. Timberlake (2001), for example, has characterized the feeding system as consisting of at least three components (see Figure 2.5). According to this more detailed view, the feeding behavior sequence starts with the **general search mode.** In the general search mode, the animal reacts to general features of the environment with responses that enable it to come in contact with a variety of potential sources of food. A honeybee, for example, may fly all around looking for bushes or other plants with flowers.

FIGURE 2.5 **Components of the feeding behavior system.**
The feeding behavior sequence begins with a general search for potential food sites. Once a potential food site has been identified, the animal engages in a focal search of that site. Upon finding the food, the animal engages in food-handling and ingestion responses.

Once an animal has identified a potential source of food, it switches to a more restricted response mode, the **focal search mode.** In the focal search mode, the bee will concentrate on one bush, going from flower to flower. Upon encountering a specific flower, the bee will switch to the *food handling and ingestion mode*. This response mode is similar to what ethologists referred to as consummatory behavior and consists of responses required to extract nectar from the flower and ingest the nectar.

Behavior systems have been described for a variety of different functions that organisms have to accomplish in their lives: caring for young, grooming, defense, and reproduction. Several features of behavior systems are noteworthy:

1. Behavior systems often consist of a sequence of three or more modes of behavior, rather than just appetitive and consummatory behavior. The organism moves from one mode of responding to another (general search to focal search) depending on the environmental events that it encounters.

2. The sequence of response modes is linear. An animal typically moves from one response to the next without skipping a step in the sequence. A squirrel cannot handle food, for example, without first having encountered the food in its focal search mode.

3. Although the response sequence is linear, it is not one-directional. An animal may go either forward or backward in the sequence depending on the circumstances. If the focal search behavior of a squirrel is not successful in locating nuts, the squirrel will move back to its general search mode.

4. Finally, each response mode involves not only characteristic responses but also increased sensitivity or attention to particular kinds of stimuli. In the general search mode, a foraging bee is likely to be looking for flowering bushes as opposed to bushes that don't have flowers. In the focal search mode, it is apt to focus on where the flowers are in the bush it has chosen to search. Finally, in the food-handling mode, it will focus on the part of the flower that contains the nectar. Thus, various modes of behavior differ not

only in terms of the types of response that are involved but also in terms of the types of stimuli that guide the behavior.

Summary

All instances of learning reflect an interaction between the training procedures used and the individual's preexisting behavior. Therefore, understanding how learning occurs requires an appreciation of unconditioned behavioral mechanisms. Unconditioned behavior is not homogeneous and modifiable in any and all directions but has its own determinate structure. The simplest unit of unconditioned behavior is the reflex, which consists of a specific eliciting stimulus and a corresponding elicited response. More complex forms of elicited behavior, studied by ethologists, involve modal action patterns that are elicited by sign stimuli or releasing stimuli. Ethologists identified motivational factors involved in the control of modal action patterns and have pointed out that elicited behavior consists of a predictable sequence of activities that begins with appetitive responses and ends with consummatory behavior. These ideas have been extended in contemporary conceptualizations of behavior systems. A behavior system is a set of response modes that is activated in a coordinated fashion to achieve an important behavioral outcome such as nutrition, defense, or reproduction. Each response mode is characterized by particular responses and increased sensitivity to particular types of stimuli, and the response modes are organized sequentially.

Practice Questions

1. Why is knowledge of unconditioned behavior important for the analysis of learning?

2. What is the reflex arc, and who originated this concept?

3. What is a modal action pattern?

4. What is a sign stimulus?

5. Why is the concept of motivation required to characterize species-typical behavior?

6. In what ways do appetitive and consummatory responses differ?

7. What are the primary characteristics of behavior systems?

Suggested Readings

Baerends, G. P. (1988). Ethology. In R. C. Atkinson, R. J. Herrnstein, G. Lindzey, & R. D. Luce (Eds.), *Stevens' handbook of experimental psychology* (Vol. 1, pp. 765–830). New York: Wiley.

Rachlin, H. (1976). *Behavior and learning* (Chap. 3, pp. 102–154). San Francisco: W. H. Freeman.

Timberlake, W. (2001). Motivational modes in behavior systems. In R. R. Mowrer & S. B. Klein (Eds.), *Handbook of contemporary learning theories* (pp. 155–209). Mahwah, NJ: Erlbaum.

Tinbergen, N. (1951). *The study of instinct*. Oxford: Clarendon Press.

Technical Terms

Appetitive behavior	Hydraulic model
Behavior system	Modal action pattern
Consummatory behavior	Reflex
Elicited behavior	Reflex arc
Ethology	Releasing stimulus
Focal search mode	Sign stimulus
General search mode	Species-typical behavior

CHAPTER THREE

Habituation and Sensitization

DID YOU KNOW THAT:

- Reflexive behavior is not automatic and invariant but can increase or decrease as a result of experience.
- The vigor of elicited behavior is regulated by opposing processes of habituation and sensitization.
- Elicited behavior is determined not only by the eliciting stimulus but also by other recently encountered events.
- Habituation effects are evident in decreased responding; sensitization effects are evident in increased responding.
- Habituation and sensitization effects are both determined by the intensity and frequency of the eliciting stimulus.
- Habituation is more specific to the eliciting stimulus than is sensitization.
- Habituation is an inherent property of all elicited behavior.
- Sensitization reflects a modulatory influence on the mechanisms of elicited behavior.

Having considered the structure of unconditioned behavior in Chapter 2, we are now ready to examine some of the ways in which behavior can be changed or modified by experience. We begin with the phenomena of habituation and sensitization. These are good to start with because habituation and sensitization are two of the simplest and most common forms of behavior change. In addition, habituation and sensitization can occur in all of the more complex learning procedures that are the focus of subsequent chapters.

Habituation and sensitization have been investigated most extensively in reflex systems. A reflex is a fairly simple response that occurs in reaction to a specific eliciting stimulus. Suckling, for example, can be elicited in a newborn infant by placing a soft object in the infant's mouth. As I noted in Chapter 2, the concept of the reflex was originally formulated by Descartes, who assumed that reflexes have two major features. First, Descartes believed, the vigor of the elicited response is directly related to the intensity of the eliciting stimulus. In fact, he thought that the energy required for the reflex response was provided by the eliciting stimulus. Second, he believed, a reflex response will always occur when its eliciting stimulus is presented. For Descartes, reflexes were "automatic" or inevitable reactions to eliciting stimuli.

Descartes was correct in pointing out that certain actions are triggered by eliciting stimuli. But he was wrong in characterizing reflexes as invariant and energized by their eliciting stimuli. Nevertheless, his views continue to dominate how laypersons think about reflexes. People commonly consider reflexes to be automatic and fixed. In fact, the term *reflexive* is sometimes used as a synonym for *automatic*. However, scientists have shown that reflexes do not occur with the same vigor every time. In fact, as we will see in this chapter, elicited behavior can be remarkably flexible. Responses to an eliciting stimulus may increase (showing sensitization) or decrease (showing habituation), depending on the circumstances.

Why should reflexive behavior be modifiable? Why do we need habituation and sensitization? Basically, these processes help us avoid wasting effort on stimuli that are irrelevant and allow us to focus our actions on things that are important. Habituation and sensitization regulate our reflex responses and increase the efficiency of our interactions with the environment. Animals (both human and nonhuman) live in complex environments that provide many forms of stimulation all the time. Even during an activity as seemingly uneventful as sitting quietly in a chair, a person is bombarded by visual, auditory, olfactory, tactile, and internal physiological stimuli. All of these are capable of eliciting responses, but if they all did (as Descartes originally thought), we would be reacting to multitudes of things that are unimportant. Without habituation and sensitization, behavior would be totally enslaved to the vicissitudes of the environment.

Consider, for example, the **orienting response.** We orient and turn toward novel visual and auditory stimuli (someone entering the room, for example). However, if all of the stimuli in our environment were to elicit an orienting response, we would be wasting much of our effort. Many stimuli are not important enough to warrant our attention. While talking to someone in the living room, we need not orient to the sounds of a refrigerator humming in the background or a car going by in the street. Habituation and sensitization serve to regulate our responsivity. They insure that we respond vigorously to some stimuli while ignoring others.

In Chapter 2 I noted that the vigor of elicited behavior is determined by motivational factors and that the sequence of elicited responses is determined by the inherent structure of the behavior system that is activated. I also noted in passing that response systems are sometimes organized by learning and experience. Habituation and sensitization are the first principles of behavioral organization based on experience that we will consider.

General Principles of Regulation

Before turning our attention to specific mechanisms of habituation and sensitization, let us consider in more general terms what it means to "regulate" something. Something is "regulated" if its functions are maintained within acceptable limits or within a defined target range. The temperature in a house, for example, is regulated by a thermostat so that the house remains comfortable. In the winter, the thermostat may be set to turn on the heater whenever the temperature falls below 70° F, and to turn off the heater if the temperature hits 74° F. In this case the target range is 70–74° F. A driver regulates the speed of a car so that the car does not go too much above or below the posted speed limit. A cook regulates the taste of pasta to make sure it is salty enough but not too salty. In all these instances, regulation serves to keep something within acceptable limits—within a target range.

Physiology is replete with examples of regulation, and in physiological systems the target range is typically referred to as the **homeostatic level.** Perhaps the most obvious example of a homeostatic system is temperature regulation in warm-blooded animals, or endotherms. The body temperature of endotherms is regulated so precisely by physiological and behavioral mechanisms that a deviation from the homeostatic level of just one or two degrees is interpreted as a sign of illness. Other familiar homeostatic systems include respiration and blood sugar level. Our respiratory system is designed to limit the accumulation of carbon dioxide in the blood. An increase in serum carbon dioxide above the acceptable level causes drowsiness, coma, and eventual death. Blood sugar levels are also maintained within a target range. A drastic drop in serum glucose level can also result in coma. In contrast, too much serum glucose can cause convulsions.

How is regulation generally achieved? To maintain a system within a desired range, forces that push the system in one direction must be counteracted by forces that return the system to the desired or homeostatic level. Exposure to cold, with a consequent drop in body temperature, elicits shivering, which produces body heat and thereby counteracts the drop in body temperature. A buildup of carbon dioxide in the blood stimulates breathing, which reduces carbon dioxide and increases oxygen intake. A drop in blood sugar triggers the release of stored glucose from the liver and also induces hunger and eating, all of which increase blood sugar level.

In general, regulation is achieved by the activation of **opponent processes,** processes that counteract or oppose each other. Opponent process concepts have been employed in a variety of areas of conditioning and learning. Our first encounter with such processes will be in this chapter. Habituation and sensitization are opposing forces that regulate the vigor of elicited behavior. Habituation causes decrements in reactivity; sensitization causes increments in responding.

Effects of the Repeated Presentation of an Eliciting Stimulus

The relationships that I will describe for habituation and sensitization are general characteristics that may be observed for just about any form of elicited behavior. A common experimental preparation for the study of habituation and sensitization in human infants is illustrated in Figure 3.1. The infant is seated comfortably in front of a screen that is used to present visual stimuli. When a stimulus appears on the screen, the infant looks at the display. The infant's visual attention is measured by noting how long its eyes remain fixated on the stimulus before the infant shifts its gaze elsewhere. How long the infant looks at the stimulus depends on what the stimulus is and how often it has been presented.

Figure 3.2 shows the results of an experiment that was conducted with two groups of 4-month-old babies (Bashinski, Werner, & Rudy, 1985). For each group, a 10-second visual stimulus was presented eight times, with a 10-second interval between trials. The complexity of the visual stimulus differed for the two groups. One group got a 4×4 checkerboard pattern. The other group got a more complex 12×12 checkerboard pattern. Notice that the duration of the visual fixation elicited by each stimulus was not invariant or "automatic." Rather, fixation time changed in different ways depending on the stimulus. With the complex 12×12 pattern, fixation increased from Trial 1 to Trial 2, then declined thereafter. With the simpler 4×4 pattern, visual fixation declined from each trial to the next.

A decrease in the vigor of elicited behavior is called a **habituation effect.** In contrast, an increase in responsivity is called a **sensitization effect.** Habituation was evident throughout the experiment with the 4×4 checkerboard pattern. Habituation was also evident with the 12×12 pattern from Trial 2 to Trial 8, but sensitization occurred from Trial 1 to Trial 2.

Another common experimental preparation for the study of habituation and sensitization involves the **startle response.** The startle response is a sud-

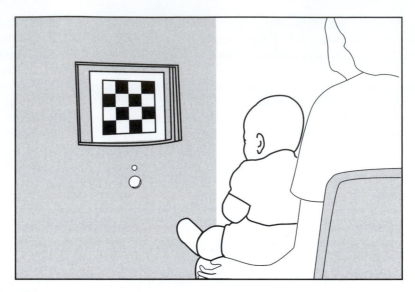

FIGURE 3.1   Experimental setup for the study of visual attention in infants.
The infant is seated in front of a screen that is used to present various visual stimuli. How long the infant looks at the display before diverting its gaze elsewhere is measured on each trial.

---

den movement or flinch caused by a novel stimulus. If someone broke a balloon behind you (making a loud popping sound), you would suddenly hunch your shoulders and pull in your neck. Startle is a common human reaction in a variety of cultures (Simons, 1996). The sudden movement that characterizes the startle reflex can easily be measured, which has encouraged numerous studies of habituation and sensitization of the startle reflex in laboratory rats (e.g., Davis, 1974; Davis, Hitchcock, & Rosen, 1987).

A sudden but soft sound may cause you to startle the first few times it occurs, but you will quickly stop responding to the sound. Similar results are obtained with mild tactile stimuli. When you first put on a comfortable pair of shoes, you feel the gentle pressure of the shoes against your feet. However, this reaction quickly habituates; soon you will be entirely unaware that you are wearing the shoes.

If the tactile stimulus is more intense, it will be more difficult to get used to it, and the pattern of responding may be similar to what we saw in Figure 3.2, in the case of the visual attention of an infant to a 12 × 12 checkerboard pattern. In such cases, responding increases somewhat at first but then declines. Similar results are obtained with the startle reflex if the eliciting stimulus is an intense tone.

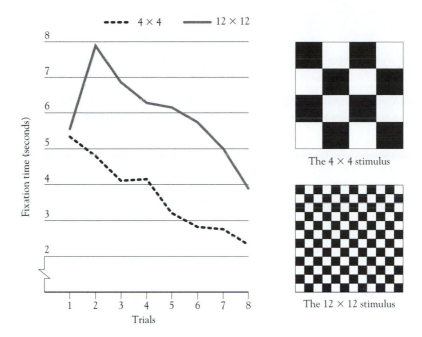

FIGURE 3.2   Visual fixation time for two groups of infants presented with a visual stimulus on eight successive trials.
The stimulus was a 12 × 12 checkerboard pattern for one group and a 4 × 4 checkerboard pattern for the other group. Adapted from Bashinski et al. (1985). Copyright 1985 by Academic Press. Reprinted by permission.

If the eliciting stimulus is very intense, repetitions of the stimulus may result in a sustained increase in responding. If there is a pebble in your shoe creating intense pressure, your irritation will increase with continued exposure to that stimulus, and you may never lose your awareness of the shoe. Similarly, a sustained increase in the startle response may occur if the eliciting stimulus is an intense noise. Soldiers and civilians in a war zone may never get used to the sound of nearby gunfire.

As these examples illustrate, under some circumstances elicited behavior exhibits a monotonic habituation pattern. In other cases, a sensitization effect occurs at first, followed by a decline in responding. Elicited behavior can also show evidence of sustained sensitization.

CHARACTERISTICS OF HABITUATION EFFECTS

Numerous factors have been found to influence the course of habituation and sensitization effects. Here I shall consider some of the major variables.

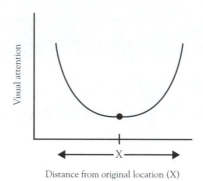

Distance from original location (X)

FIGURE 3.3   **Stimulus specificity of habituation.**
The visual fixation response of infants is initially habituated to a spot of green light presented at a particular location. The location of the light is then varied during a series of test trials. Notice that responding increases as the green light is moved away from its original location. (Note: Data are hypothetical.)

Effects of Stimulus Change.   Perhaps the most important feature of habituation is that it is specific to the particular stimulus that has been repeatedly presented. If a new stimulus is presented, the habituated response will recover, with the degree of recovery determined by how similar the new stimulus is to the habituated one. Stimulus specificity is a defining feature of habituation (Thompson & Spencer, 1966) and has been used profitably to study information processing in infants (e.g., Cohen, 1988; Kaplan, Werner, & Rudy, 1990).

Before they are able to talk, infants cannot tell us in words which stimuli they consider to be similar and which they consider to be different. However, they can provide answers to such questions in their responses to test stimuli following habituation. Consider the following hypothetical experiment involving the visual attention or fixation response of infants. A small, green spot of light is presented repeatedly on the stimulus screen until the infant stops fixating to the light. Then the light is presented again, but in different positions on the screen. Let us assume that all of the test stimuli fall on an imaginary horizontal line, with the original habituated stimulus in the middle. How will the baby respond to the various test stimuli? Which test stimuli will she consider to be different from the habituation training stimulus, and which will she consider to be similar?

The likely outcome is illustrated in Figure 3.3. In this figure, the response to each test stimulus is plotted as a function of how close that test stimulus was to the spot where the light had been presented during habituation training. Notice that the lowest level of responding (most habituation) was obtained with the stimulus presented exactly where it had been during habituation training. However, the baby also does not respond very much to the test stimuli that occurred close to the original training position. Thus, the habituation effect transferred to other nearby locations. This is called **stimulus generalization of habituation.** Test stimuli that were presented at greater distances from the original training position elicited progressively more responding. This illustrates the stimulus specificity of habituation. The habituated response recovers when the test stimulus is sufficiently different from the training stimulus.

The stimulus specificity of habituation helps to rule out an important potential explanation of habituation effects. One might presume that responding declines with repeated stimulations in a habituation procedure because of fatigue. The participant may simply get tired of performing the elicited response. The recovery of responding with a change in the eliciting stimulus rules out fatigue. If habituation were due to fatigue, the participant would not respond to the altered stimulus either.

Tests with novel stimuli are routinely carried out in studies of habituation with infants. Infants can stop looking at a visual stimulus for a variety of reasons. They may become tired or fussy or may fall asleep. To be sure that they are still paying attention and actively participating in the experiment, novel stimuli are introduced. The results of the experiment are considered valid only if the novel stimuli produce recovery of the habituated response.

Effects of Time-Out from Stimulation. Habituation effects are often temporary. They dissipate or are lost as time passes without presentation of the eliciting stimulus. A loss of the habituation effect is evident in a recovery of responding. This is illustrated in Figure 3.4. Because the response recovery is produced by a period without stimulation (a period of rest), the phenomenon is called **spontaneous recovery.**

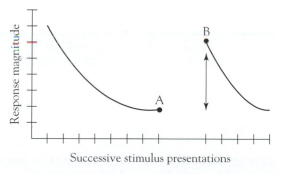

FIGURE 3.4   Spontaneous recovery of a habituated response.
A period of rest without stimulus presentations occurred between points A and B, which caused a recovery of the habituated response. (Note: Data are hypothetical.)

Spontaneous recovery is a common feature of habituation (Thompson & Spencer, 1966). If your roommate turns on the radio while you are studying, you may notice it at first but then come to ignore the sound if it is not too loud. However, if the radio is turned off for a while and then comes back on again, you will again notice that the radio is playing. If your roommate repeatedly turns the radio on and off, you will experience spontaneous recovery over and over again and may become annoyed at having your attention repeatedly commanded by the radio.

The degree of spontaneous recovery is related to the duration of the period of rest. Longer periods without presentation of the eliciting stimulus result in greater recovery of the response. However, in some cases responding does not recover, even with rest periods of several weeks. For example, no spontaneous recovery is evident in habituation of the novelty response to taste.

Animals, including people, are cautious about ingesting a food or drink that has an unfamiliar flavor. This phenomenon is known as **flavor neophobia.** Flavor neophobia probably evolved because things that taste new or unfamiliar may well be poisonous. With repeated exposure to the new taste, the neophobic response becomes attenuated. Coffee, for example, often elicits an aversion response in a child who tastes it for the first time. However, after drinking coffee without ill effect, the child's neophobic response will become diminished or habituated. Furthermore, the habituation is likely to be long-lasting. Having become accustomed to the flavor of coffee, a person is not likely to experience a neophobic response even if he goes a couple of weeks without having any coffee. Studies with laboratory rats have shown no spontaneous recovery of flavor neophobia over periods as long as 17 and 24 days (Domjan, 1976; Siegel, 1974).

Habituation effects have been classified according to whether or not they exhibit spontaneous recovery. Cases in which substantial spontaneous recovery occurs are called **short-term habituation,** while cases in which significant spontaneous recovery does not occur are called **long-term habituation.** Short-term and long-term habituation are not mutually exclusive. Sometimes both effects are observed. Long-term habituation effects are genuine learning effects because they satisfy the criterion of being long-lasting. In contrast, short-term habituation effects do not satisfy this criterion and hence do not constitute learning.

Effects of Stimulus Frequency.   The frequency of a stimulus refers to how often the stimulus is repeated in a given period of time—how often the stimulus occurs per minute, for example. The higher the stimulus frequency, the shorter the period of rest between repetitions of the stimulus. As we saw in the phenomenon of spontaneous recovery, the duration of rest between stimulations can significantly influence responding. Because higher stimulus frequencies permit less spontaneous recovery between trials, responding generally declines more rapidly with more frequent stimulation (Davis, 1970). In

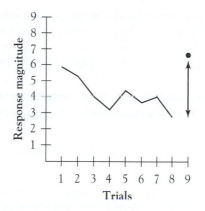

FIGURE 3.5   Dishabituation of a habituated response.
Visual fixation in infants became habituated to a checkerboard stimulus presented in Trials 1–8. Presentation of a tone with the visual stimulus caused dishabituation of the attentional response in Trial 9. Adapted from Kaplan et al., 1990.

contrast, responding does not decline as rapidly if the frequency of stimulation is low.

Effects of Stimulus Intensity.   Habituation is also determined by the intensity of the stimulus. In general, responding declines more slowly if the eliciting stimulus is more intense (Groves, Lee, & Thompson, 1969). For example, laboratory rats are slower to lose their neophobic response to strong flavors than to weak ones (Domjan & Gillan, 1976).

Effects of Exposure to a Second Stimulus.   One of the remarkable features of a habituated response is that it is not determined solely by the eliciting stimulus. The level of responding is also influenced by other stimuli the organism experiences. In particular, exposure to a second stimulus can result in recovery of a previously habituated response. This phenomenon is called **dishabituation** (Thompson & Spencer, 1966).

The results of one experiment on dishabituation are summarized in Figure 3.5. The visual fixation of human infants was measured in response to a 4 × 4 checkerboard pattern (Kaplan et al., 1990). As expected, repetition of the visual stimulus eight times resulted in a decline or habituation of the looking response of the infants. After Trial 8, a tone (1000 Hz, 75 dB) was presented as a dishabituating stimulus along with the checkerboard pattern. Figure 3.5 shows that presentation of the tone caused significant recovery of visual fixation to the 4 × 4 pattern. The response to the original habituated visual stimulus was thus enhanced by presentation of the dishabituating tone.

Unfortunately, the term *dishabituation* is used inconsistently in the research literature. In studies with human infants, *dishabituation* is sometimes used to refer to the recovery of responding that occurs when the original habituated stimulus is replaced by a novel stimulus. In contrast, in research with other species and responses, *dishabituation* is reserved for cases in which the introduction of a new stimulus produces recovery in responding to the original habituated stimulus. I will follow this second convention because it has historical precedence (Thompson & Spencer, 1966).

CHARACTERISTICS OF SENSITIZATION EFFECTS

Sensitization effects are influenced by the same stimulus intensity and time factors that govern habituation phenomena. In general, greater sensitization effects (greater increases in responding) occur with more intense eliciting stimuli (Groves et al., 1969).

Like habituation, sensitization effects can be short-term or long-term (e.g., Davis, 1974; Heiligenberg, 1974). **Short-term sensitization** decays as a result of time without stimulation. Unlike the decay of short-term habituation, which is called "spontaneous recovery," the decay of short-term sensitization has no special name. It is not called "spontaneous recovery," because responding declines (rather than recovers) as sensitization dissipates. In contrast to short-term sensitization, **long-term sensitization** is evident even after appreciable periods without stimulation. As was the case with habituation, long-term sensitization effects satisfy the durability criterion of learning, whereas short-term sensitization effects do not.

One important respect in which sensitization is different from habituation is that sensitization is not as specific to a particular stimulus. As I noted earlier, habituation produced by repeated exposure to one stimulus will not be evident if the stimulus is altered substantially (see Figure 3.3). In contrast, sensitization is not so stimulus-specific. For example, the reactivity of laboratory rats to auditory cues can be increased or sensitized by exposing the animals to painful stimulation applied to the skin (Davis et al., 1987). Once sensitized by pain, the rats show increased reactivity to a wide range of auditory cues. Likewise, the experience of illness increases or sensitizes the reactivity of laboratory rats to taste stimuli, and once taste reactivity has been sensitized, the animals show heightened finickiness to a variety of different taste stimuli (Domjan, 1977).

The Dual-Process Theory of Habituation and Sensitization

So far, I have described the behavioral phenomena of habituation and sensitization. I have not discussed what underlying processes or machinery might produce these behavioral effects. Here we consider a prominent theory of habituation and sensitization, the dual-process theory, which was proposed by

Groves and Thompson (1970). The theory was based on neurophysiological studies of habituation and sensitization, but it can be described as close to the level of a behavioral theory.

The dual-process theory is based on two underlying processes (a habituation process and a sensitization process) whose names are similar to those of the phenomena I described earlier. However, habituation and sensitization *processes* are distinct from habituation and sensitization *phenomena*. To avoid confusing these terms, it is important to keep in mind that habituation and sensitization *phenomena* are performance effects; they are observable changes in behavior. In contrast, habituation and sensitization *processes* refer to the underlying events that are presumed to be responsible for the behavioral habituation and sensitization effects.

THE S-R SYSTEM AND THE STATE SYSTEM

According to the dual-process theory, habituation processes and sensitization processes are presumed to operate in different parts of the nervous system. For the purposes of the dual-process theory, we will conceptualize the nervous system as consisting of two functional components, the S-R system and the state system.

The **S-R system** is the shortest path in the nervous system between an eliciting stimulus and the resulting elicited response. The S-R system corresponds to Descartes's reflex arc. It is the minimal physiological machinery involved in a reflex. Typically, the S-R system consists of three neurons: the **sensory** (or **afferent**) **neuron,** an **interneuron,** and an **efferent** (or **motor**) **neuron.** The eliciting or input stimulus activates the afferent neuron. The afferent neuron in turn activates the interneuron, which then activates the efferent neuron. The efferent neuron forms a synapse with the muscles involved in the elicited response and triggers the behavioral response.

The **state system** consists of all neural processes that are not an integral part of the S-R system but influence the responsivity of the S-R system. Spinal reflexes, for example, consist of an afferent neuron that ends in the spinal cord, an interneuron in the spinal cord, and an efferent neuron that extends from the spinal cord to the relevant muscle (see Figure 2.1). This is the S-R system of a spinal reflex. However, the spinal cord also contains neural pathways that ascend to the brain and ones that descend from the brain. These ascending and descending fibers serve to modulate spinal reflexes and make up the state system for spinal reflexes.

After one understands the categorization of the nervous system into the S-R and state components, the rest of the dual-process theory is fairly simple. As I noted earlier, the dual-process theory presumes the existence of separate habituation and sensitization processes. A critical aspect of the theory concerns the locus of action of these processes. The habituation process is assumed to take place in the S-R system, whereas the sensitization process is assumed to take place in the state system.

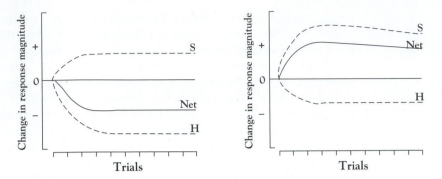

FIGURE 3.6   Mechanisms of the dual-process theory of habituation and sensitization.
The dashed lines indicate the strength of the habituation (H) and sensitization (S) processes across trials. The solid lines indicate the net (or combined) effects of these two processes. In the left panel, the habituation process becomes stronger than the sensitization process, which leads to a progressive decrement in responding. In the right panel, the sensitization process becomes stronger than the habituation process, which leads to a progressive increment in responding.

Habituation and sensitization processes are not directly evident in the behavior of the organism. Rather, observable behavior reflects the net effect of these processes. The habituation and sensitization processes serve as opponent mechanisms regulating reflex responsivity. Whenever the habituation process is stronger than the sensitization process, the net effect is a decline in behavioral output. This is illustrated in the left panel of Figure 3.6. The opposite outcome occurs if the sensitization process is stronger than the habituation process. In that event, the net effect of the two processes is an increase in behavioral output. This is illustrated in the right panel of Figure 3.6.

After being activated, both the habituation process and the sensitization process are assumed to decay with time. This temporal decay assumption is needed in order to explain the short-term nature of some habituation and sensitization effects.

IMPLICATIONS OF THE DUAL-PROCESS THEORY

Like Descartes's reflex arc, the S-R system is the minimal or most primitive mechanism of elicited behavior. Therefore, the S-R system is activated every time an eliciting stimulus is presented. Because the habituation process operates in the S-R system, each activation of the S-R system results in some buildup of the habituation process. This makes habituation a universal feature of elicited behavior. According to the dual-process theory, the habituation process is activated whenever an eliciting stimulus is presented.

The universality of the habituation process does not mean that a habituation effect, or a decrement in responding, will be always observed. Whether a habituation effect is evident will depend on whether the habituation process is counteracted by activation of the sensitization process. Whether a habituation effect is observed will also depend on when the eliciting stimulus is presented relative to its previous occurrence. If two presentations of a stimulus are separated by a long interval of rest, habituation created by the first stimulus will have a chance to decay completely before the stimulus is repeated, and a decrement in responding will not be observed. On the other hand, if the interval between stimulus presentations is too short to permit complete decay of the habituation process, a decrement in responding will occur.

In contrast to the habituation process, the sensitization process is not assumed to be universal. Sensitization occurs in the state system. The state system modulates responsivity of the S-R system, but it is not essential for the occurrence of elicited behavior. Elicited behavior can occur through the S-R system alone. Therefore, sensitization is not a universal property of elicited behavior.

When is the sensitization process activated? An informal way to think about this is that sensitization represents arousal. Sensitization or arousal occurs if the organism encounters a stimulus that is particularly intense or significant. You can become aroused by a loud, unexpected noise or by someone telling you in a soft voice that a close friend was seriously hurt in an accident. The state system and the sensitization process are activated by intense or significant stimuli.

The sensitization process can be activated by the same stimulus that elicits the reflex response of interest. This will be the case if an intense or significant stimulus is used as the eliciting stimulus. The right panel of Figure 3.6 illustrates such a situation. In that example, the eliciting stimulus produced a substantial degree of sensitization, with the result that the net behavioral effect was an increase in responding.

The sensitization process can also be activated by some event other than the eliciting stimulus. Because the state system is separate from the S-R system, the state system can be activated by stimuli that are not registered in the S-R system of the response that is being measured. This is a critical feature of the dual-process theory and another respect in which sensitization is different from habituation. In contrast to habituation, sensitization is not necessarily produced by the eliciting stimulus of interest.

The fact that the sensitization and habituation processes can be activated by different stimuli permits the dual-process theory to explain a number of key phenomena, including dishabituation. As I noted earlier (see Figure 3.5), the presentation of a dishabituating stimulus can result in recovery of a habituated response. In the example summarized in Figure 3.5, the presentation of a tone caused recovery of the habituated visual fixation response to a checkerboard pattern. According to the dual-process theory, this occurred because the tone activated the state system and produced enough sensitization to overcome the previous buildup of habituation to the visual stimulus. In other words, dishabituation is produced by the addition of the sensitization process to a behavioral situation rather than the reversal or weakening of the habituation process. Other evidence also supports this interpretation (see Groves & Thompson, 1970).

The dual-process theory is remarkably successful in characterizing short-term habituation and short-term sensitization effects. However, the theory is inconsistent with occurrences of long-term habituation and long-term sensitization. Explanations of long-term habituation and sensitization typically include mechanisms of associative learning, which I will discuss in Chapters 4–6.

Summary

Reflexive or elicited behavior is commonly considered to be an automatic and invariant consequence of the eliciting stimulus. Contrary to this notion, however, repeated presentations of an eliciting stimulus may result in a monotonic decline in responding (a habituation effect), an increase in responding (a sensitization effect) followed by a decline, or a sustained increase in responding. Thus, far from being invariant, elicited behavior is remarkably sensitive to different forms of prior experience. The magnitude of habituation and sensitization effects depends on the intensity and frequency of the eliciting stimulus. Responding elicited by one stimulus can also be altered by the prior presentation of a different event (as in the phenomenon of dishabituation).

Many of the findings concerning habituation and sensitization may be explained by the dual-process theory, which holds that the processes that produce decreased responding occur in the S-R system, while the processes that produce sensitization occur in the state system. The S-R system is activated every time an eliciting stimulus is presented, making habituation a universal property of elicited behavior. Sensitization, by contrast, occurs only when the organism encounters a stimulus that is sufficiently intense or significant to activate the state system. Through their additive effects, the processes of habituation and sensitization serve to regulate the vigor of elicited behavior.

Practice Questions

1. What are the basic features of habituation and sensitization phenomena?

2. What is the primary purpose of habituation and sensitization phenomena?

3. Which of Descartes's ideas about reflexes are disproved by the phenomena of habituation and sensitization?

4. What is homeostatic regulation and how is it generally achieved?

5. What is the visual attention task that is used in research with infants?

6. What is stimulus generalization of habituation?

7. Why is it important to demonstrate stimulus specificity in studies of habituation?

8. When does spontaneous recovery of a habituated response occur, and how does it help distinguish between short-term and long-term habituation effects?

9. What is dishabituation and how is it different from the stimulus specificity of habituation?

10. What is the effect on sensitization of a period without stimulation?

11. How does the stimulus specificity of habituation compare with the stimulus specificity of sensitization?

12. What are the primary components of the dual-process theory of habituation and sensitization, and how do they help explain various habituation and sensitization phenomena?

13. Why does the dual-process theory characterize habituation but not sensitization as a universal process involving elicited behavior?

Suggested Readings

Groves, P. M., & Thompson, R. F. (1970). Habituation: A dual-process theory. *Psychological Review, 77,* 419–450.

Kaplan, P. S., Werner, J. S., & Rudy, J. W. (1990). Habituation, sensitization, and infant visual attention. In C. Rovee-Collier & L. P. Lipsitt (Eds.), *Advances in infancy research* (Vol. 6, pp. 61–109). Norwood, NJ: Ablex.

Peeke, H. V. S., & Petrinovich, L. (Eds.). (1984). *Habituation, sensitization, and behavior.* New York: Academic Press.

Technical Terms

Afferent neuron   Flavor neophobia
Dishabituation   Habituation effect
Efferent neuron   Homeostatic level

Interneuron
Long-term habituation
Long-term sensitization
Motor neuron
Opponent process
Orienting response
S-R system
Sensitization effect

Sensory neuron
Short-term habituation
Short-term sensitization
Spontaneous recovery
Startle response
State system
Stimulus generalization
  of habituation

CHAPTER FOUR

Pavlovian Conditioning: Basic Concepts

DID YOU KNOW THAT:

- Pavlov viewed classical conditioning as a technique for studying the brain.
- Classical conditioning is not limited to glandular and visceral responses.
- The conditioned response is not always like the unconditioned response.
- Conditioned stimuli become part of the behavior system activated by the unconditioned stimulus.
- Pavlovian conditioning often involves S-S learning rather than S-R learning.
- Which stimulus can serve as a conditioned stimulus in classical conditioning depends on the unconditioned stimulus that is used.
- Associative learning is possible in the random control procedure.
- Pavlovian conditioning is involved in a wide range of behaviors including preferences and aversions, fears and phobias, drug tolerance and addiction, and maternal and sexual behavior.

In Chapter 3, I described ways in which behavior is changed by experience with individual stimuli. Habituation and sensitization may be considered to be instances of single-stimulus learning. We are now ready to consider how organisms learn to put things together—how they learn to associate one event with another. **Associative learning** is different from single-stimulus learning in that the change in behavior that occurs in response to one stimulus depends on when the stimulus previously occurred in relation to another stimulus. Associative learning represents what we learn about combinations of stimuli. The first form of associative learning I will describe is Pavlovian or classical conditioning.

Pavlov's Proverbial Bell

The basic elements of Pavlovian or classical conditioning are familiar to most of us. Accounts usually describe an apocryphal experiment in which Professor Pavlov rang a bell just before giving a bit of food powder to the dogs that he was testing. The dogs were loosely harnessed and hooked up to an apparatus that enabled Pavlov to measure how much they salivated. At first the dogs salivated only when they were given the food powder. However, after several trials with the bell being paired with the food, the dogs also came to salivate when the bell sounded.

The story of Professor Pavlov training his dogs to salivate to a bell is useful for introducing some important technical vocabulary. A stimulus such as food powder that elicits the response of interest without prior training is called an **unconditioned stimulus,** or US. Salivation elicited by the food powder is an example of an **unconditioned response,** or UR. The bell is an example of a **conditioned stimulus,** or CS, and the salivation that develops to the bell is called the **conditioned response,** or CR.

Pavlov's proverbial bell illustrates associative learning, because salivation to the bell depends on presenting the bell in combination with food powder. Ringing the bell each time the dog is about to receive a bit of food presumably results in an association of the bell with food. Once the bell has become associated with food, the dog starts to respond to the bell as if it were food; it starts to salivate when it hears the bell.

Although Pavlov's proverbial bell is familiar and helpful in introducing the technical terms used to describe Pavlovian or classical conditioning, the story is misleading in several ways. Pavlov rarely, if ever, used a bell in his experiments. Initial demonstrations of classical conditioning were conducted with visual conditioned stimuli (the sight of the food that was to be placed in the dog's mouth) rather than auditory cues. The story also suggests that classical conditioning primarily involves the modification of visceral and glandular responses. B. F. Skinner elevated this implication to an axiom. He postulated that classical conditioning can only modify glandular and visceral responses (Skinner, 1938). However, subsequent research has shown this assumption to be unwarranted. Pavlovian conditioning can modify a variety of different responses (Hollis, 1997; Turkkan, 1989), including the skeletal responses involved in approaching a signal for food (see "Appetitive Conditioning" in the next section of this chapter).

Contemporary Pavlovian Conditioning Preparations

Although classical conditioning was discovered in studies of salivary conditioning with dogs, dogs are not used in such experiments any longer, and salivation is rarely the response that is measured. Instead, pigeons, rats, and rabbits commonly serve in the experiments, and several different responses are used to measure learning. In some contemporary Pavlovian conditioning situations, the unconditioned stimulus is a desirable or appetitive stimulus like food. These preparations are used to study **appetitive conditioning.** In other situations, an unpleasant or aversive event is used as the unconditioned stimulus. Such preparations are used to study **aversive conditioning.**

APPETITIVE CONDITIONING

Appetitive conditioning is frequently investigated with pigeons and laboratory rats. Pigeons that serve in appetitive conditioning experiments are mildly hungry and are tested in a small experimental chamber called a **Skinner box** (see Figure 4.1). The conditioned stimulus is a light projected onto a small plastic disk or response key above the food cup. Pecks at the key are automatically detected by an electronic sensing circuit. The conditioning procedure consists of turning on the key light for a few seconds and then presenting a small amount of food.

After a number of pairings of the key light with food, the pigeons come to approach and peck the key as soon as it is lit (Hearst & Jenkins, 1974; Tomie, Brooks, & Zito, 1989). The conditioned approach and pecking behavior develop even if the key light is located some distance from the food cup (Boakes, 1979). The light becomes a signal for food, and the pigeons go where the light is located. Hence, one name for this type of conditioning is **sign tracking.** Because the procedure results in the pigeons pecking the response key without elaborate intervention by the experimenter, the procedure is also called **autoshaping.**

Laboratory rats are also used in Pavlovian conditioning, with food as the unconditioned stimulus. Holland (1977), for example, presented a brief tone paired with pellets of food to laboratory rats. As conditioning proceeded, the tone came to elicit a sudden movement of the head, called a head-jerk response. In another group of rats, a light near the top of the experimental chamber served as the conditioned stimulus. As the light was repeatedly paired with food, the rats came to orient toward the ceiling and get up on their hind legs. These results indicate that rats can learn to associate

FIGURE 4.1   Typical trial for conditioning sign tracking or autoshaping in pigeons.

The CS is illumination of a small circular disk or pecking key for 6 seconds. The US is access to food for 4 seconds. CS-US trials are repeated, with an intertrial interval of about 1 minute.

both tones and lights with food, but different conditioned responses develop with the different conditioned stimuli (Holland, 1984).

AVERSIVE CONDITIONING

Aversive conditioning has been extensively investigated using the eyeblink response. The eyeblink is an early component of the startle reflex. Eyeblink conditioning was first developed with human experimental participants (see Kimble, 1961, pp. 55–59). A mild puff of air to one eye served as the unconditioned stimulus, and a light served as the CS. After a number of pairings of the light with the air puff, the light came to elicit a conditioned eyeblink response. Subsequently, ways of studying eyeblink conditioning were also developed using albino rabbits and rats, to facilitate investigations of the neurophysiology of learning. With these subjects, a mild electrical pulse to the skin near one eye serves as the US, and a brief visual or auditory cue serves as the CS. Pairings of the CS and US result in a conditioned eyeblink response when the CS is presented (Gormezano, Kehoe, & Marshall, 1983).

Another common laboratory technique for studies of aversive conditioning is fear conditioning. This procedure, typically carried out with rats or mice, takes advantage of the fact that animals (including people) tend to become motionless, or freeze, when they are afraid (Bouton & Bolles, 1980). A tone or light serves as the conditioned stimulus, and a brief shock applied

FIGURE 4.2   Rat in a conditioned suppression experiment.
Pressing the response lever occasionally produces a pellet of food. Periodically a
tone is presented, ending in a brief shock through the grid floor. The rat comes to
suppress lever pressing during the tone.

through a grid floor serves as the unconditioned stimulus. After a few pairings of the tone or light with the shock, the CS comes to elicit a freezing response. In the freezing posture, the rat exhibits total lack of movement, except for breathing.

In a variant of fear conditioning known as the **conditioned suppression**
procedure, rats are first trained to press a small bar or response lever to obtain
food (see Figure 4.2). Food is provided only intermittently for lever pressing,
which keeps the rats pressing the lever steadily. After the lever pressing is
well established, aversive conditioning trials are introduced. On each of
these trials, a tone or light CS is presented for a minute, then the rats are
given a brief foot shock. Within a few conditioning trials, presentation of the
CS results in suppression of the food-reinforced lever-press response. The degree of response suppression provides a measure of aversive conditioning of
the CS.

The Nature of the Conditioned Response

In Pavlov's salivary conditioning experiments, the conditioned response
(salivation to a CS) was a glandular visceral response similar in form to the
unconditioned response (salivation to food powder). These were considered
to be universal characteristics of classical conditioning during much of the
twentieth century. Pavlovian conditioning was considered to be primarily a

mechanism for adjusting physiological and glandular responses to the environment through experience (Skinner, 1938), and the conditioned response was assumed to be always similar to the unconditioned response (e.g., Mackintosh, 1974). However, the common contemporary preparations used for the study of Pavlovian conditioning described above show that there is no compelling empirical justification for either of these assumptions.

SKELETAL VERSUS GLANDULAR CONDITIONED RESPONSES

In none of the common contemporary procedures for the study of Pavlovian conditioning is the measured conditioned response a glandular or visceral response. In sign tracking or autoshaping, the conditioned response is approaching and pecking a key light. This response involves skeletal muscles, not the smooth musculature involved in glandular responses. Conditioned eyeblink responses in aversive conditioning and head-jerk and rearing responses observed in appetitive conditioning in rats also involve skeletal rather than smooth musculature. Skeletal responses are likewise involved in the freezing behavior that is the basis for conditioned suppression.

One might argue that the responses measured in contemporary Pavlovian conditioning procedures are only indirect reflections of what is actually being conditioned, and that the "true" conditioned response is in fact a visceral or glandular response. Such an argument may have some validity in the case of conditioned fear or the conditioned suppression procedure. Various physiological manifestations of fear no doubt become conditioned in conditioned suppression. The response suppression that is elicited by the CS may be mediated by these visceral conditioned responses. However, it is less obvious what visceral conditioned responses might give rise to the skeletal responses involved in conditioned sign tracking in pigeons, the conditioned head-jerk and rearing responses of rats, or conditioned eyeblink responding. A more parsimonious characterization of the empirical evidence is that Pavlovian conditioning can result in the modification of skeletal responses.

SIMILARITY OF CONDITIONED AND UNCONDITIONED RESPONSES

What implications do the common contemporary Pavlovian conditioning preparations have for the traditional assumption that the conditioned response is similar in topography to the response elicited by the unconditioned stimulus? Here the evidence is mixed. In some conditioning preparations, the conditioned response does resemble the unconditioned response. This is the case, for example, in eyeblink conditioning, where both the CR and UR involve blinking. In other cases, however, the CR and UR are distinctly different.

In fear conditioning, the unconditioned stimulus is a brief mild shock to the grid floor on which the rat is standing. Because the rat detects the shock through its foot pads, the shock elicits sudden and vigorous jumping. This

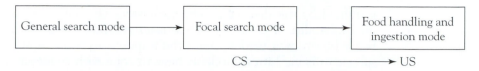

FIGURE 4.3   **Behavior systems and Pavlovian conditioning.**
Conditioning procedures with food as the US involve the feeding system. As a result of pairings of the CS with food, the CS becomes incorporated into the feeding system and comes to elicit food-related responses.

vigorous jumping behavior contrasts dramatically with the lack of movement —freezing—that develops as the conditioned response in this situation.

THE BEHAVIOR SYSTEM APPROACH

If we cannot assume that the conditioned response will always be similar to the unconditioned response, how can we predict what kind of behavior will develop with Pavlovian conditioning? This question remains a major puzzle (e.g., Cunningham, 1997; Stewart & Eikelboom, 1987). Although a definitive answer is not yet available, a promising approach for analyzing the topography of behavioral conditioned responses has been developed in recent years, based on the idea of behavior systems.

I previously introduced the concept of behavior systems in Chapter 2. The concept is relevant to the present discussion because the unconditioned stimulus in a Pavlovian conditioning procedure activates the behavior system relevant to that US. Presentations of food to a hungry animal activate the feeding system; presentations of shock activate the defensive behavior system. The conditioned response that develops depends on how the conditioned stimulus becomes incorporated into the behavior system activated by the US.

The feeding system involves a sequence of response modes starting with general search and then moving on to focal search and ingestive or consummatory behavior (see Figure 4.3). If a CS is presented before the animal receives each portion of food, the CS will become incorporated into one of the response modes of the feeding behavior system, which will in turn determine what type of conditioned response the organism will perform (Timberlake, 2001). If the CS becomes incorporated into the focal search mode, the conditioned response will consist of focal search responses such as approach and sign tracking (Wasserman, Franklin, & Hearst, 1974). In contrast, if the CS becomes incorporated into the ingestive, consummatory response mode, the conditioned response will involve handling and chewing the CS (Boakes, Poli, Lockwood, & Goodall, 1978).

In aversive conditioning, the nature of the conditioned response is determined by the defensive behavior system (Fanselow, 1997). Foot shock used in studies of conditioned fear is an external source of pain, much like being bitten by a predator, and the response to shock is similar to the response to being bitten. Rodents have to cope with snakes and other predators. When a rat is bitten by a snake, it leaps into the air. Similarly, rats jump when they receive brief foot shock.

The rat's defensive response to an impending or possible attack is different from its response to the attack itself. If a rat sees or smells a snake that is about to strike, the rat freezes. In the fear conditioning procedure, the conditioned stimulus signals an impending attack. Therefore, the CS comes to elicit the freezing defensive behavior.

The Contents of Pavlovian Associations

As a result of Pavlovian conditioning, the subject comes to perform a conditioned response when the CS is presented. What learning mechanism is responsible for this conditioned response (CR)? There are two prominent alternatives. According to the first mechanism, the CS comes to elicit the CR directly. This is called **S-R learning** and is the simpler of the two mechanisms. The other possibility is that CS activates a representation of the US, which in turn generates the CR. This second mechanism is called **S-S learning.** Whether Pavlovian conditioning results in an S-S or an S-R association reflects the contents of the learning. Here we shall consider how investigators have distinguished between S-S and S-R learning.

According to the S-S learning mechanism, classical conditioning leads to the formation of an association between the conditioned and unconditioned stimuli. As a result of this association, presentation of the CS activates a neural representation of the unconditioned stimulus (see Figure 4.4).

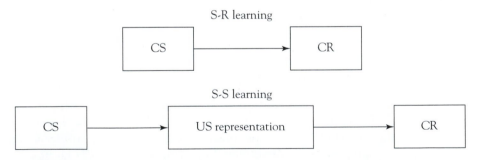

FIGURE 4.4   Distinction between S-R and S-S learning.
In S-R learning, a direct connection or association is established between the CS and the CR. In S-S learning, the CS activates a representation of the US, which in turn leads to the CR.

TABLE 4.1   Design and predictions of US devaluation study

Phase 1	Phase 2	S-R Prediction	S-S Prediction
Experimental Group			
Conditioning	US devaluation	No change in CR	Decline in CR
Control Group			
Conditioning	No devaluation	No change in CR	No change in CR

Expressed informally, this means that upon encountering the CS, the organism will be reminded of the unconditioned stimulus. What it will do when it is stimulated to "think" about the US will depend on its motivation to respond to the US.

EFFECTS OF US DEVALUATION

A powerful technique for differentiating between S-R and S-S mechanisms was popularized by Robert Rescorla (Rescorla, 1973) and is basically a test of performance. The test involves evaluating the vigor of conditioned responding after the individual's motivation to respond to the unconditioned stimulus has been changed. In one type of experiment, motivation to respond to the US is reduced. This manipulation is called **US devaluation.**

Consider, for example, a study of sexual Pavlovian conditioning that was conducted with domesticated male quail (Holloway & Domjan, 1993). Brief exposure to a light CS was paired with access to a female bird once a day. Initially, the visual CS did not elicit any significant behavior. However, because the males were sexually motivated, they always readily copulated with the female that was presented at the end of each conditioning trial. With repeated conditioning trials, the males also started approaching the CS. After 10 conditioning trials, the CS elicited a strong approach response regardless of where the males were at the start of the trial.

According to the S-R learning mechanism, conditioned responding reflects the establishment of a direct connection between the CS and the conditioned response (CR). If such a direct connection has been established, then changing the animal's motivation to perform the unconditioned response should not influence its conditioned responding. An S-R interpretation predicts that once the quail has learned the sexual conditioned approach response, presentation of the CS will elicit the CR even if the birds are no longer sexually motivated.

Holloway and Domjan tested the S-R prediction by reducing the sex drive of one group of birds (see Table 4.1). (This was done by changing the light cycle in the laboratory to mimic winter conditions, when the birds do not breed.) The results of the experiment are summarized in Figure 4.5. Con-

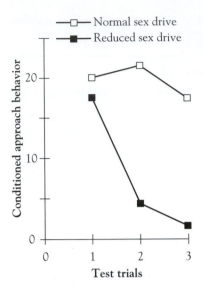

FIGURE 4.5   Effects of US devaluation on sexual-approach conditioned behavior.
Three test sessions were conducted at 1-week intervals after two groups of quail had acquired a conditioned approach response. During the test phase, the sexual motivation of one group of birds was reduced. This US devaluation procedure resulted in a decrease in their conditioned responding. Adapted from Holloway & Domjan (1993).

trary to predictions based on the S-R mechanism, a reduction in sexual motivation reduced conditioned responding to the visual CS.

The results summarized in Figure 4.5 indicate that S-S learning had occurred in the experiment. S-S learning does not involve learning a specific conditioned response. Rather, it involves learning an association between the CS and the US. Once the CS-US association has been established, presentation of the CS activates a representation of the US. That in turn leads to conditioned responding, but only if the participants are motivated to respond to the US. In the quail experiment, the opportunity to copulate with a female was the unconditioned stimulus. After training, the CS elicited conditioned approach behavior, but only if the birds were sexually motivated.

EFFECTS OF US INFLATION

In the example just discussed, motivation to respond to the unconditioned stimulus was reduced as a test for S-S learning. Another approach is to increase motivation to respond to the US. Called **US inflation,** this proce-

TABLE 4.2   Outline of US inflation experiment

Acquisition	US Inflation	S-R Prediction	S-S Prediction
Experimental Group			
Quinine → Salt	Salt deficiency	No effect	Increased quinine intake
No deficiency			
Control Group			
Quinine/Salt unpaired	Salt deficiency	No effect	No effect
No deficiency			

Source: Rescorla & Freberg, 1978.

dure should result in increased conditioned responding according to S-S mechanisms.

In a particularly interesting application of the US inflation method, laboratory rats served as participants and the unconditioned stimulus was the taste of salt (Rescorla & Freberg, 1978, Experiment 3; see also Fudim, 1978). The preference for salt can be greatly increased in animals (including people) by inducing a physiological sodium deficiency. Because creating a sodium deficiency substantially increases unconditioned responses to salt, this is a powerful US inflation procedure. The question addressed by Rescorla and Freberg was whether US inflation would also increase responding to a CS that had become associated with salt (see Table 4.2).

Two groups of laboratory rats were compared. Conditioning was carried out in the absence of sodium deficiency. A weak bitter taste (made by mixing a little quinine in water) served as the CS, and the taste of salt served as the US. For the experimental group, the bitter flavor was paired with the taste of salt (by adding the quinine to a mixture of salt and water). For the control group, the bitter flavor and the taste of salt were presented on alternate days. After these procedures, US inflation was created by inducing sodium deficiency in both groups. The rats were then tested for their response to the bitter flavor presented alone.

During the test, the animals that received the US inflation procedure drank much more of the quinine-flavored water than animals in the control group. This is a remarkable result, because ordinarily rats are averse to drinking quinine. In this study, the taste of quinine was first associated with salt. After conditioning, sodium deficiency increased the value of salt, and this in turn increased the response to the salt-associated quinine flavor.

Stimulus Factors in Classical Conditioning

Early investigators of Pavlovian conditioning assumed that just about any stimulus the organism could detect could be effectively used as a conditioned stimulus. This assumption has turned out to be incorrect. In this section, I will describe two factors that determine the effectiveness of a conditioned stimulus: the novelty of the CS and the nature of the US.

CS NOVELTY AND THE LATENT INHIBITION EFFECT

As I stated in Chapter 3, the novelty of a stimulus is a powerful factor determining its behavioral impact. Repeated exposures to a stimulus may result in a habituation effect, making highly familiar stimuli less effective in eliciting vigorous behavioral reactions than novel stimuli. Habituation can also reduce the effectiveness of a stimulus that is later used as a CS in a Pavlovian conditioning procedure. This phenomenon, extensively examined by Lubow and his colleagues (Lubow, 1989), is called **latent inhibition.**

Studies of the latent inhibition effect are usually conducted in two phases. Subjects are first given repeated presentations of the stimulus that is later to be used as the CS. For example, subjects may be given repeated presentations of a tone that will subsequently be paired with food. During this initial phase of the experiment, the tone is presented by itself, without the food US. Hence this phase of the experiment is called the CS preexposure phase. After the CS preexposure phase, the tone is paired with the food US, using conventional classical conditioning procedures. The typical outcome is that CS preexposure retards the subsequent development of conditioned responding to the tone (Hall, 1991; Lubow, 1989).

The CS preexposure effect has been interpreted as reflecting attentional processes. Repeated presentations of a tone (for example) during the CS preexposure phase are assumed to reduce the subject's attention to the tone, and this in turn is assumed to disrupt subsequent Pavlovian conditioning of the tone. Because of the involvement of attentional processes, the latent inhibition effect has become popular as a technique for studying brain mechanisms and disorders such as schizophrenia that involve deficits in attention (Lubow, 1998; see also Oberling, Gosselin, & Miller, 1997).

CS-US RELEVANCE AND SELECTIVE ASSOCIATIONS

The effectiveness of a stimulus as a CS in Pavlovian conditioning also depends on the US that is employed. As I noted earlier, presentations of a US (e.g., food) serve to activate the behavior system relevant to that US. Thus, the feeding behavior system is activated when food is repeatedly presented to a hungry pigeon. As I previously emphasized, each behavior system is associated with its own distinctive set of responses. Behavior systems are also characterized by enhanced reactivity to a distinctive set of stimuli. Pigeons, for

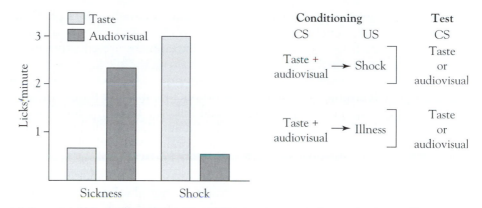

FIGURE 4.6 Procedure and results of the experiment by Garcia and Koelling (1966) demonstrating selective associations in aversion learning.

example, tend to locate food by sight and are therefore especially attentive to visual cues when their feeding system has been activated. This makes visual cues especially effective in Pavlovian conditioning with food.

The first clear evidence that the effectiveness of a conditioned stimulus depends on the unconditioned stimulus that is employed was obtained in studies of aversion conditioning in laboratory rats. The conditioned suppression phenomenon illustrates one type of aversion conditioning. Here a tone or light is paired with shock, with the result that the CS acquires aversive properties. Another type of aversion conditioning is **taste aversion learning.** Here a novel taste is followed by postingestional illness (e.g., a mild case of food poisoning), and the organism learns an aversion to the novel taste as a result.

The conditioned suppression and taste aversion learning phenomena demonstrate that both audiovisual cues and taste cues are highly effective as conditioned stimuli. Interestingly, however, they are effective only in combination with their own particular unconditioned stimulus (see Figure 4.6). Rats do not easily learn an aversion to an auditory or visual cue paired with illness, nor do they easily learn an aversion to a taste cue paired with shock (Domjan & Wilson, 1972; Garcia & Koelling, 1966). Such results illustrate the phenomenon of **CS-US relevance,** or **selective association.** The effectiveness of a conditioned stimulus in a Pavlovian conditioning procedure depends selectively on the unconditioned stimulus that is used (LoLordo & Droungas, 1989).

Like laboratory rats, people also seem to learn aversions to stimuli selectively. People who experience some form of gastrointestinal illness are more likely to learn an aversion to a novel food they ate just before becoming sick than they are to learn an aversion to other types of stimuli they may have encountered. Consistent with selective association, people do not report acquiring a food aversion if they hurt themselves in a physical accident or if they develop an irritating skin rash (Logue, Ophir, & Strauss, 1981; Pelchat & Rozin, 1982). Only illness experiences are effective in inducing a food aversion.

Since the initial demonstrations of selective association in aversion learning, such effects have been found in other forms of learning as well. For example, Shapiro, Jacobs, and LoLordo (1980) found that pigeons are more likely to associate a visual stimulus than an auditory stimulus with food. However, when the birds are conditioned with shock, the auditory cue is more likely to become conditioned than the visual cue.

In identifying selective associations, it is important to keep in mind that instances of selective learning are not absolute. For example, the fact that taste stimuli are more easily associated with gastrointestinal illness than are audiovisual cues does not mean that nontaste cues cannot become associated with illness. Such learning can occur, but it is more difficult to bring about and requires special procedures (e.g., Best, Batson, Meachum, Brown, & Ringer, 1985).

Although selective associations are well established, the reasons why they occur remain open to speculation. One factor that probably contributes to selective association is similarity between the conditioned and unconditioned stimuli. Evidence indicates that similarity between a CS and US facilitates the establishment of associations (Rescorla & Gillan, 1980; Testa, 1974). However, the concept of similarity cannot explain all instances of selective association. It is unclear, for example, how similarity might encourage pigeons to associate auditory cues with shock more readily than they associate visual stimuli with shock. On the face of it, auditory cues do not seem any more like shock than do visual cues.

The Control Problem in Pavlovian Conditioning

The critical feature of Pavlovian conditioning is that it involves the formation of an association between a conditioned stimulus and an unconditioned stimulus. Therefore, before any change in behavior can be attributed to Pavlovian conditioning, one must demonstrate that the effect is not produced by nonassociative factors.

To promote the development of an association, the conditioned and unconditioned stimuli are presented in combination with one another in Pavlovian procedures. It is particularly effective, for example, to present the CS just before the presentation of the US on each conditioning trial. (I will have more to say about this in Chapter 5.) In addition, a number of conditioning trials are usually needed to get a learning effect. Thus, a Pavlovian conditioning procedure involves repeated presentations of the conditioned and unconditioned stimuli. However, as we saw in Chapter 3, repeated presentations of stimuli can also result in habituation and sensitization effects.

It follows that habituation and sensitization effects can occur during the course of Pavlovian conditioning.

Habituation and sensitization effects due to repeated CS and US presentations do not depend on the formation of an association between the CS and US and therefore do not constitute Pavlovian conditioning. Habituation effects are typically of little concern, because habituation results in decreased responding whereas Pavlovian conditioning involves increased responding to the CS. Increased responding to the CS can be due either to sensitization resulting from CS exposures or to dishabituation or sensitization resulting from US presentations. Control procedures must therefore be used to rule out such sensitization effects in studies of Pavlovian conditioning.

A universally applicable and acceptable solution to the control problem in Pavlovian conditioning is not available. Instead, a variety of control procedures have been used, each with its own advantages and disadvantages. In one procedure, CS sensitization effects are evaluated by repeatedly presenting the CS by itself. Such a procedure, called the CS-alone control, is inadequate because it does not take into account the possibility of increased responding to the CS due to dishabituation or sensitization effects of the US. Another control procedure involves repeatedly presenting the US by itself (the US-alone control) to measure US-induced sensitization. This procedure, however, does not consider possible sensitization effects due to repeated CS presentations.

Nearly 40 years ago, Rescorla proposed an ingenious solution, known as the **random control** procedure, that appeared to solve the problems presented by the CS-alone and US-alone controls (Rescorla, 1967). In the random control procedure, the CS and US are both presented repeatedly, but at random times in relation to each other. The random timing of the CS and US presentations is intended to prevent the formation of an association between them without interfering with sensitization processes.

The random control procedure became popular soon after its introduction, but as investigators began to examine it in detail, they discovered some serious difficulties (Papini & Bitterman, 1990). Studies demonstrated that this procedure is not entirely without effect, or neutral, in producing learning. Associative learning can develop in a random control procedure in two different ways. First, random CS and US presentations permit occasional instances in which the CS is presented in conjunction with the US. Random procedures can result in nonrandom patterns in the short run. For example, flipping a coin five times will occasionally yield five heads in a row. If occasional CS-US pairings occur early in training with a random control procedure, conditioned responding may develop (Benedict & Ayres, 1972).

Second, associative learning can also result when the US is presented without the CS in a random control procedure. In such instances the US is being presented along with the background contextual cues of the experimental situation. These cues were ignored throughout much of the early development of Pavlovian conditioning theory. However, more recent research

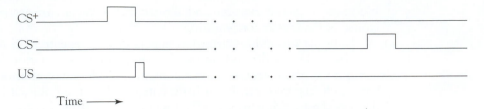

Time ⟶

FIGURE 4.7   Diagram of the discriminative control procedure for Pavlovian conditioning.
Two types of trials occur in random alternation. On some trials, one conditioned stimulus, the CS$^+$, is paired with the US. On the remaining trials, another conditioned stimulus, the CS$^-$, is presented alone. Stronger conditioned responding to CS$^+$ than to CS$^-$ is evidence of associative learning rather than some form of sensitization.

has shown that the repeated presentation of a US in the absence of an explicit CS can result in substantial conditioning of background cues (Balsam & Tomie, 1985; Kremer, 1974).

The conditioning of background cues creates problems for the random control procedure because conditioned contextual cues can provide an active source of interference with the conditioning of explicit conditioned stimuli. Organisms are less likely to associate a conditioned stimulus with food, for example, if the CS occurs in the presence of conditioned background stimuli (Tomie, Murphy, Fath, & Jackson, 1980). To the extent that the random control permits the conditioning of background cues, it does not provide a neutral, nonassociative baseline for demonstrations of Pavlovian conditioning.

Although no entirely satisfactory control procedure for Pavlovian conditioning is available, the **discriminative control** procedure is a reasonable compromise. This procedure is summarized in Figure 4.7. Unlike the random control procedure, discriminative control involves two conditioned stimuli, a CS$^+$ and a CS$^-$. The two CSs may be, for example, a brief tone and a brief light. On half the trials, the CS$^+$ is presented and paired with the US. (The "+" sign indicates that the US is presented with the CS.) On the remaining trials, the CS$^-$ is presented and the US does not occur. (The "−" sign indicates that the US is omitted.) CS$^+$ and CS$^-$ trials are alternated randomly. For half the participants the tone serves as the CS$^+$ and the light serves as the CS$^-$; for the remaining participants these stimulus assignments are reversed.

What would happen if presentations of the US only sensitized responding to the light and tone CSs? Sensitization is not based on an association and thus does not depend on the pairing of a stimulus with the US. Therefore, sensitization is expected to elevate responding to both the CS^+ and the CS^-. If only sensitization occurred in the discriminative control procedure, the participants would respond to the CS^+ and CS^- in a similar fashion.

How about associative learning? In contrast to sensitization, associative learning should be specific to the stimulus that is paired with the US. Therefore, associative learning should elevate responding to the CS^+ more than the CS^-. Greater responding to the CS^+ than to the CS^- in the discriminative control provides evidence of associative learning.

An issue that sometimes arises with the discriminative control is that differential responding to the CS^+ versus the CS^- may occur in different ways. Responding to the CS^+ may be elevated by the training procedure, or responding to the CS^- may be inhibited. (The conditioning of inhibition will be discussed in Chapter 5.) The development of inhibition to the CS^- is not a common outcome, but if it is suspected, additional control procedures are required to reach an unambiguous conclusion.

The discriminative control procedure permits the evaluation of associative effects within a single group of subjects (based on how those subjects respond differently to the CS^+ and the CS^-). Another approach that is frequently employed to evaluate associative effects is the **unpaired control procedure.** In this procedure the CS and US are presented repeatedly, but the stimulus presentations are deliberately scheduled so that the CS and US never occur together or on the same trial. This procedure is administered to a control group, which is compared with an experimental group that receives the CS paired with the US. Greater responding in the paired group as compared to the unpaired group is considered evidence of associative Pavlovian conditioning.

Prevalence of Pavlovian Conditioning

Classical conditioning is typically investigated in laboratory situations. However, we do not have to know a lot about classical conditioning to realize that it is common outside the laboratory as well. Classical conditioning is most likely to develop when one event (the CS) reliably occurs shortly before another (the US). This happens in many areas of life. Stimuli occur in nature in an orderly temporal sequence because of the physical constraints of causation. Some things simply cannot happen before other things have occurred. Social institutions and customs also insure that some things occur in a reliable sequence. Whenever one stimulus reliably precedes another, classical conditioning may take place.

One area of research that has been of particular interest is how people come to judge one event as the cause of another. In studies of human causal judgment, participants are exposed to repeated occurrences of two events (e.g., pictures of a blooming flower and a watering can briefly presented on a computer screen) in various temporal arrangements. In one presentation, for example, the watering can always occurs before the flower; in another it occurs at random times relative to the flower. After observing numerous presentations of both objects, the subjects are asked to indicate their judgment as to the strength of the causal relation between them. Studies of human causal judgment are analogous to studies of Pavlovian conditioning in that both involve repeated experiences with two events and responses based on the extent to which those two events are related to one another. In view of these similarities, one might expect that there is considerable commonality between the outcomes of causal judgment and Pavlovian conditioning experiments. That expectation has been borne out in numerous studies (Miller & Matute, 1996; Shanks & Dickinson, 1987; Wasserman, 1990), suggesting that Pavlovian associative mechanisms may not be limited to Pavlov's dogs but may play a role in the numerous informal judgments of causality we all make in the course of our daily lives.

I described earlier in this chapter how Pavlovian conditioning can result in the acquisition of fear. Conditioned fear responses have been of special interest because they may contribute significantly to anxiety disorders, phobias, and panic disorder (Bouton, 2001; Bouton, Mineka, & Barlow, 2001). Pavlovian conditioning is also involved in drug tolerance and addiction (Baker & Tiffany, 1985; Siegel, 1999; Siegel & Allan, 1998; Siegel & Ramos, 2002). Cues that reliably accompany drug administration can come to elicit drug-related responses through conditioning. In discussing this type of learning on the part of crack addicts, Dr. Scott Lukas of McLean Hospital in Massachusetts described the effects of drug-conditioned stimuli by saying that "these cues turn on crack-related memories, and addicts respond like Pavlov's dogs" (*Newsweek*, February 12, 2001, p. 40).

Pavlovian conditioning is also involved in infant and maternal responses during nursing. Suckling involves mutual stimulation for the infant and mother. To successfully nurse, the mother must hold the baby in a particular position, which provides special tactile stimuli for both the infant and herself. The tactile stimuli experienced by the infant may become conditioned to elicit orientation and suckling responses on the part of the baby (Blass, Ganchrow, & Steiner, 1984). The tactile stimuli experienced by the mother in turn become conditioned to elicit the milk let-down response in anticipation of having the infant suckle. Mothers who nurse their babies frequently may experience the milk let-down reflex when the baby cries or when the usual time for breast-feeding arrives. All these stimuli (special tactile cues, the baby's crying, and the time of normal feedings) reliably precede suckling by the infant.

Pavlovian conditioning is also important in learning about sexual situations. Although clinical observations indicate that human sexual behavior can be shaped by learning experiences, the best experimental evidence of sexual conditioning has been obtained in studies with laboratory animals (Domjan & Holloway, 1998). In these studies, males typically serve as participants, and the unconditioned stimulus is provided either by the sight of a sexually receptive female or by physical access to a female (Domjan, 1998). Subjects come to approach stimuli that signal the availability of a sexual partner (Burns & Domjan, 2000; Hollis, Cadieux, & Colbert, 1989). The presentation of a sexually conditioned stimulus also facilitates various aspects of reproductive behavior. After exposure to a sexual CS, males are quicker to perform copulatory responses (Zamble, Hadad, Mitchell, & Cutmore, 1985), compete more successfully with other males for access to a female (Gutiérrez & Domjan, 1996), show more courtship behavior (Hollis et al., 1989), release greater quantities of sperm (Domjan, Blesbois, & Williams, 1998), show increased levels of testosterone and luteinizing hormone (Graham & Desjardins, 1980), and produce more offspring (Adkins-Regan & MacKillop, 2003; Hollis et al., 1997).

Summary

Although studies of Pavlovian conditioning began with the conditioning of salivation and other glandular responses in dogs, contemporary investigations focus on conditioning skeletal responses in sign tracking, fear conditioning, and eyeblink conditioning. These investigations have shown that different types of conditioned responses can develop, depending on the nature of the conditioned stimulus and the behavior system activated by the unconditioned stimulus.

The vigor of the conditioned response depends not only on the CS but also on the current value of the US. Devaluation of the US causes a decline in the CR, while inflation of the US causes an increase in the CR. These results indicate that Pavlovian conditioning typically results in S-S rather than S-R learning.

Because Pavlovian conditioning involves the learning of an association between a CS and a US, behavioral changes due to mere repetition of the CS and US have to be excluded. The random control procedure is not effective in this regard, because it can result in associative learning. Although an entirely satisfactory control procedure is not available, the discriminative control and unpaired control procedures are reasonably effective. In the discriminative control procedure, one CS is paired with the US and another CS is presented without the US. Differential responding to the two CSs provides evidence of associative learning. In the unpaired control procedure, the CS is presented at times when the US is certain to not occur.

Pavlovian conditioning may occur wherever one event reliably precedes another. Examples include causality judgments, drug tolerance and addiction, suckling and nursing, and learning to predict potential sexual encounters.

Practice Questions

1. What are four common preparations for the study of classical conditioning?

2. What types of responses can be conditioned with Pavlovian procedures?

3. What is the distinction between S-R and S-S learning mechanisms?

4. How do US devaluation and US inflation manipulations help decide between S-R and S-S learning?

5. How does Pavlovian conditioning depend on the type of CS that is used?

6. Why is it necessary to have control procedures for Pavlovian conditioning?

7. How is Pavlovian conditioning involved in nursing and maternal behavior?

Suggested Readings

Bouton, M. E., Mineka, S., & Barlow, D. H. (2001). A modern learning theory perspective on the etiology of panic disorder. *Psychological Review, 108,* 4–32.

Holland, P. C. (1984). Origins of behavior in Pavlovian conditioning. In G. H. Bower (Ed.), *The psychology of learning and motivation* (Vol. 18, pp. 129–174). Orlando, FL: Academic Press.

Hollis, K. L. (1997). Contemporary research in Pavlovian conditioning: A "new" functional analysis. *American Psychologist, 52,* 956–965.

LoLordo, V. M., & Droungas, A. (1989). Selective associations and adaptive specializations: Taste aversions and phobias. In S. B. Klein & R. R. Mowrer (Eds.), *Contemporary learning theories: Instrumental conditioning and the impact of biological constraints on learning* (pp. 145–179). Hillsdale, NJ: Erlbaum.

Papini, M. R., & Bitterman, M. E. (1990). The role of contingency in classical conditioning. *Psychological Review, 97,* 396–403.

Technical Terms

Appetitive conditioning	Conditioned response
Associative learning	Conditioned stimulus
Autoshaping	Conditioned suppression
Aversive conditioning	Discriminative control
CS-US relevance	Latent inhibition

Random control
S-R learning
S-S learning
Selective association
Sign tracking
Skinner box

Taste aversion learning
Unconditioned response
Unconditioned stimulus
Unpaired control procedure
US devaluation
US inflation

CHAPTER FIVE

Stimulus Relations in Pavlovian Conditioning

DID YOU KNOW THAT:

- Delaying the US a bit after presentation of the CS produces stronger evidence of conditioning than presenting the CS and US simultaneously.
- A gap of just half a second between the CS and US can seriously disrupt excitatory fear conditioning.
- Taste aversions can be learned with a delay of several hours between the conditioned and unconditioned stimuli.
- Pavlovian conditioning depends not only on the temporal relation between the CS and US but also on signal relations.
- Different CS/US contingencies produce different levels of conditioned responding because of differences in the conditioning of contextual cues.
- The opposite of conditioned inhibition is facilitation or positive occasion setting—not conditioned excitation.
- In a facilitation procedure, one CS signals that a second CS will be paired with the unconditioned stimulus.

In Chapter 4, I introduced Pavlovian conditioning as a type of learning that involves establishing an association between two stimuli, the conditioned and the unconditioned stimulus. For two stimuli or events to become associated with one another, they have to be related to each other in some way. In the present chapter, I will describe various relations that can exist between a conditioned and unconditioned stimulus. I will also describe how different stimulus relations determine what is learned in Pavlovian conditioning.

Temporal Relation between CS and US

Historically, the most prominent relation in Pavlovian conditioning is the temporal relation between the CS and US—when in time the stimuli occur relative to each other.

SIMULTANEOUS CONDITIONING

Perhaps the simplest temporal arrangement is the presentation of a conditioned and an unconditioned stimulus at the same time. Such a procedure is called **simultaneous conditioning** and involves perfect **temporal contiguity,** or coincidence, between CS and US (see Figure 5.1). Because simultaneous conditioning brings the CS as close as possible to the US, it is reasonable to assume that it would be the most effective temporal relation to produce associative learning. In many cases, however, simultaneous presentation of the CS and US does not yield strong evidence of learning (Bitterman, 1964; Smith, Coleman, & Gormezano, 1969).

DELAYED CONDITIONING

The best evidence for associative learning usually comes from a procedure in which the conditioned stimulus is presented slightly before the unconditioned stimulus on each trial (Schneiderman & Gormezano, 1964). Such a procedure is called **delayed conditioning,** because the unconditioned stimulus is delayed after the presentation of the CS.

An example of a delayed conditioning trial is shown in the middle panel of Figure 5.1. The conditioned stimulus starts first and remains on until the unconditioned stimulus is presented. Notice that there is no gap between the CS and the US.

TRACE CONDITIONING

Introducing a gap between the CS and the US changes a delayed conditioning procedure into **trace conditioning.** A trace conditioning trial is presented in the bottom panel of Figure 5.1 for contrast with the delayed con-

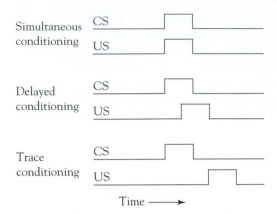

FIGURE 5.1   Procedures for simultaneous, delayed, and trace conditioning. One conditioning trial (involving a presentation of the CS and US) is shown for each procedure. In a typical experiment, the conditioning trial is repeated until evidence of learning develops.

ditioning trial shown in the middle panel. The gap between the conditioned stimulus and the unconditioned stimulus is called the **trace interval.**

Introducing a gap or trace interval between the CS and the US can drastically reduce the degree of conditioned responding that develops. Kamin (1965), for example, compared fear conditioning in two groups of laboratory rats using the conditioned suppression procedure. One group received a delayed conditioning procedure in which a 3-minute tone CS ended in a brief foot shock, with no gap between the tone and shock. For the second group, the tone also started 3 minutes before each presentation of shock but ended half a second before the shock. Thus, the second group received a trace conditioning procedure with just a half-second gap or trace interval. The trace conditioning group exhibited a much lower degree of conditioned suppression than the delayed conditioning group.

Studies with human subjects have shown that in addition to producing a lower degree of conventional conditioned responding, trace conditioning involves a different memory system than delayed conditioning (Clark, Manns, & Squire, 2001). Thus, a short trace interval makes a big difference in how subjects respond to a conditioning procedure.

EFFECTS OF THE CS-US INTERVAL

Another temporal relation that is critical for associative learning is how much time passes between the start of the CS and the presentation of the US. The interval between when the CS begins and when the US is presented is called the **CS-US interval** or the **interstimulus interval.**

As I noted earlier, there is usually no evidence of learning with simultaneous conditioning, where the CS-US interval is zero. More evidence of learning is seen with delayed conditioning procedures, where the CS-US interval is greater than zero. However, the benefits of delaying the US after the start of the CS are rather limited. As the CS-US interval becomes longer and longer, evidence of learning declines. How rapidly responding declines depends on the response system that is being conditioned.

Figure 5.2 illustrates the effects of the CS-US interval in three different conditioning preparations. The left panel represents data from conditioning of the nictitating membrane response of rabbits. The nictitating membrane is a secondary eyelid present in many species. Like closure of the primary eyelid, closure of the nictitating membrane can be elicited unconditionally by a puff of air to the eye. The best results in conditioning the nictitating membrane response are obtained with CS-US intervals of 0.2–0.5 second. If the CS-US interval is shorter, less conditioned responding develops. Moreover, conditioned responding drops off quickly as the CS-US interval is extended past half a second. Little if any learning is evident if the CS-US interval is more than 2 seconds.

Conditioned suppression represents an intermediate case. Here strong learning can occur, with CS-US intervals in the range of 2–3 minutes.

Learning over the longest CS-US intervals is seen in taste-aversion learning. A taste aversion is learned when the ingestion of a novel flavored food (or drink) results in some form of illness or interoceptive distress (Brave-

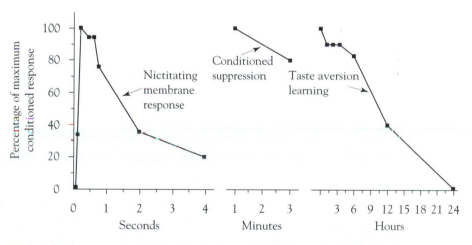

FIGURE 5.2 Strength of conditioned responding as a function of the CS-US interval in conditioning the nictitating membrane response of rabbits (after Schneiderman & Gormezano, 1964; Smith, Coleman, & Gormezano, 1969), conditioned suppression (after Kamin, 1965), and taste aversion learning (after Smith & Roll, 1967).

man & Bronstein, 1985). The novel flavor is the conditioned stimulus, and the unconditioned stimulus is provided by the illness experience.

A taste aversion can be learned even if the illness experience is delayed several hours after ingestion of the novel flavor. This phenomenon was first documented by John Garcia and his associates (e.g., Garcia, Ervin, & Koelling, 1966) and is called **long-delay learning** because it represents learning with CS-US intervals that are a great deal longer than the intervals that will support eyeblink conditioning or conditioned suppression. However, as Figure 5.2 illustrates, even with flavor-aversion learning there is an inverse relation between conditioned responding and the CS-US interval.

TEMPORAL ENCODING OF US OCCURRENCE

The differences in learning that occur between simultaneous, delayed, and trace conditioning and the CS-US interval effects I have just described illustrate that Pavlovian conditioning is highly sensitive to time factors. Recent research by Ralph Miller and his colleagues has provided even more impressive evidence that time is important in Pavlovian conditioning. With the use of complicated and clever experimental designs, Miller has shown that animals learn exactly when the US occurs relative to the CS in a conditioning procedure (e.g., Barnet, Grahame, & Miller, 1993; Cole, Barnet, & Miller, 1995).

Miller's research suggests that Pavlovian conditioning not only produces an association between the CS and US but also teaches organisms when the US will occur. This type of learning is called **temporal coding.** Pavlovian conditioning results in the establishment of a temporal code for when the US occurs in relation to the CS. Once the temporal code has been learned, it is activated whenever the CS is presented, and this enables the organism to predict the precise point in time when the US will occur.

Signal Relation between CS and US

In the previous section, I described some of the ways in which the temporal relation between the CS and US is important in Pavlovian conditioning. Another important factor is the signal relation, or informational relation, between the CS and US. In general, conditioned responding develops more rapidly with procedures in which the CS provides reliable information about the occurrence of the US, that is, the CS serves as a reliable signal for the US.

In the typical delayed conditioning procedure, each conditioning trial consists of the presentation of the CS, followed shortly by the presentation of the US. The US, furthermore, does not occur unless it is preceded by the CS. Thus, occurrences of the US can be predicted perfectly from occurrences of the CS. The CS signals occurrences of the US perfectly, and an association between the CS and US develops quickly.

CS/US CONTIGUITY AND THE BLOCKING EFFECT

How might the signal relation between the CS and US be disrupted? One way is to present the CS with another cue that already predicts the US. In this case the CS will be redundant, and little conditioned responding will develop. If someone has already pointed out to you that your car is about to run out of gas, a similar warning from a second person is redundant and so unlikely to command much of your attention. This idea, first developed experimentally by Kamin, has come to be known as the **blocking effect** (Kamin, 1969).

Kamin studied the blocking effect using the conditioned suppression procedure with laboratory rats, but the phenomenon may be illustrated more effectively by means of a hypothetical example of human taste-aversion learning. Let us assume that you are allergic to shrimp and get slightly ill every time you eat some. Because of these experiences, you acquire an aversion to the flavor of shrimp. However, you continue to eat shrimp on special occasions when you prefer not to offend your host. On one such occasion, you are served shrimp with a steamed vegetable you don't remember eating before. To be polite, you eat some of the vegetable as well as some of the shrimp. The vegetable tastes pretty good, but you end up feeling slightly ill after the meal.

Will you attribute your illness to the shrimp or to the new vegetable you ate? Given your history of bad reactions to shrimp, you are likely to attribute your illness to the shrimp and may not acquire an aversion to the vegetable. In this situation, the presence of the previously conditioned shrimp blocks the conditioning of the novel vegetable flavor even though the novel flavor was just as closely paired with the illness US.

As this example illustrates, the blocking effect shows that what individuals learn about one CS is influenced by the presence of other cues that were previously conditioned with the same US. The conditioned stimuli Kamin used were a light and a tone (see Figure 5.3). For the blocking group, the light CS was first conditioned by pairing it with foot shock a sufficient number of times to produce strong conditioned suppression to the light. In the next phase of the experiment, the tone and light CSs were presented simultaneously, ending in the shock US. A control group received the same pairings of the tone/light compound with shock as the blocking group, but for this group the light had not been conditioned earlier; the light and tone were both novel. The focus of the experiment was on how much fear became conditioned to the novel tone CS. Because of the prior conditioning of the light in the blocking group, a lower degree of conditioned suppression developed to the tone in the blocking group than in the control group.

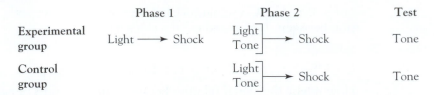

FIGURE 5.3   Diagram of the blocking procedure in a conditioned suppression experiment.

During Phase 1, a light CS is conditioned with foot shock in the experimental group until light produces maximum conditioned suppression. The control group does not receive a conditioning procedure in Phase 1. In Phase 2, both groups receive conditioning trials in which the light CS is presented together with a novel tone CS, and the light/tone compound is paired with shock. Finally, during the test phase, responding to the tone presented alone is measured. Less conditioned suppression develops to the tone in the experimental group than in the control group.

The blocking phenomenon is important because it illustrates that temporal contiguity between a conditioned and an unconditioned stimulus is not sufficient for successful conditioned responding. A strong signal relation is also important. The temporal relation between the novel tone CS and the US was identical for both the blocking and the control groups. Nevertheless, strong conditioned suppression developed only if the tone was not presented with the previously conditioned light CS. The prior conditioning of the light reduced the signal relation between the tone and shock and disrupted fear conditioning.

CS/US CONTINGENCY

Historically, an important approach to characterizing the signal relation between a CS and US has been in terms of the **contingency** between the two stimuli (Rescorla, 1967). The "contingency" between two events refers to the extent to which the presence of one stimulus can serve as a basis for predicting the other. The CS/US contingency is defined in terms of two probabilities (see Figure 5.4). One of these is the probability that the US will occur given that the CS has been presented [p(US/CS)]; the other is the probability that the US will occur given that the CS has not happened [p(US/noCS)].

A situation in which the US always occurs with the CS and never by itself illustrates a perfect positive contingency between the CS and US. Smoke, for example, always indicates that something is burning. Therefore, the presence of the US (fire) can be predicted perfectly from the presence of the CS (smoke). In contrast, a situation in which the US occurs when the

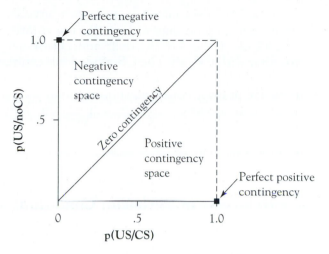

FIGURE 5.4   Contingency between a CS and US.
Contingency between a CS and US is determined by the probability of the US occurring given that the CS has occurred (represented on the horizontal axis) and the probability of the US occurring given that the CS has not occurred (represented on the vertical axis). When the two probabilities are equal (the 45° line), the CS/US contingency is zero.

CS is absent but never occurs on trials with the CS illustrates a perfect negative contingency. In this case, the CS signals the absence of the US. If you use sunblock when you are at the beach in the summertime, you are likely to avoid the sunburn that you would otherwise get from spending a day at the beach. The sunblock signals the absence of aversive stimulation. Finally, if the US occurs equally often with and without the CS, the CS/US contingency is said to be zero. When the contingency between the CS and US is zero, the CS provides no useful information about whether the US will occur or not. This is the case if a dog barks indiscriminately whether or not there is an intruder present. A zero CS/US contingency is also characteristic of the random control procedure I described in Chapter 4.

Originally the contingency between a CS and US was thought to determine the formation of CS-US associations directly. Since then, it has become more common to consider CS/US contingency as a procedural variable that predicts how much conditioned responding will develop. Contemporary analyses of contingency effects have focused on conditioning of the background cues that are present in any situation in which an organism encounters repeated presentations of discrete conditioned and unconditioned stimuli. Procedures involving different CS/US contingencies result in different degrees of context conditioning.

Consider, for example, a procedure involving a zero CS/US contingency. Such a procedure will involve presentations of the US by itself, presentations of the CS by itself, and occasional presentations of the CS together with the US. The US-alone trials can result in conditioning of the background or contextual cues in which the experiment is conducted. The presence of these conditioned background contextual cues may then block future conditioning of the explicit CS on those few occasions when the CS is paired with the US (Tomie, Murphy, Fath, & Jackson, 1980) or disrupt performance of conditioned responding through other means (Miller & Matzel, 1989).

Higher-Order Relations in Pavlovian Conditioning: Conditioned Inhibition

In the examples of Pavlovian conditioning considered thus far, the focus of interest has been on how a CS is directly related to a US. Now let us turn to more complex stimulus relations in Pavlovian conditioning. In higher-order stimulus relations, the focus of interest is not on how a CS signals a US but on how one CS provides information about the relation of a second CS with a US. Thus, the term **higher-order stimulus relations** refers to the signaling or modulation of a simple CS-US pairing. The adjective *higher-order* is used because one of the elements of this relation is a CS-US associative unit. In considering higher-order stimulus relations, I will first discuss conditioned inhibition or negative occasion setting. Then I will move on to facilitation or positive occasion setting.

INHIBITORY CONDITIONING PROCEDURES

Conditioned inhibition was the first higher-order signal relation that was extensively investigated. Concepts of inhibition are prominent in various areas of physiology. Being a physiologist, Pavlov was interested not only in processes that activate behavior but also in those that are responsible for the inhibition of responding. This led him to investigate conditioned inhibition. He considered the conditioning of inhibition to be just as important as the conditioning of excitation (Pavlov, 1927).

In excitatory conditioning procedures, the CS becomes a signal for the impending presentation of the US. In inhibitory conditioning, by contrast, the CS of interest becomes a signal for the absence of the US. However, this only occurs under special circumstances, because ordinarily the absence of something has no particular psychological significance. If I tell you out of the clear blue that I have decided not to give you a million dollars, you are not likely to be upset, because you had no reason to expect that I would ever give you that kind of money. If the absence of something is not meaningful, a CS

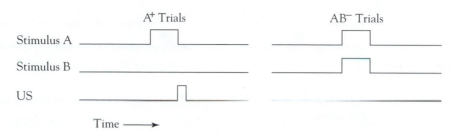

FIGURE 5.5   The standard procedure for conditioned inhibition.
On A⁺ trials, stimulus A is paired with the US. On AB⁻ trials, stimulus B is presented with stimulus A and the US is omitted. The procedure is effective in conditioning inhibition to stimulus B.

---

cannot become a signal for that nonevent. For successful inhibitory conditioning, the absence of the US has to be made a salient event.

I can make you disappointed in not getting a million dollars by having told you previously that you had won a sweepstakes contest with a million-dollar prize. The absence of something is a psychologically powerful event if you have reason to believe that the event will take place. In inhibitory conditioning procedures, the absence of the US is made salient by excitatory conditioning that creates a positive expectation that the US will occur.

The Standard Conditioned Inhibition Procedure.   The standard conditioned inhibition procedure is analogous to a situation in which something is introduced that prevents an outcome that would otherwise occur. A red traffic light at a busy intersection is a signal of potential danger (the US). However, if a police officer indicates that you should cross the intersection despite the red light (perhaps because the traffic lights are malfunctioning), you will probably not have an accident. The red light and the gestures of the officer together are not likely to be followed by danger. The gestures inhibit or block your hesitation to cross the intersection because of the red light.

The standard conditioned inhibition procedure involves two different conditioned stimuli (A and B) and a US (see Figure 5.5). In the example just given, stimulus A was the red traffic light and stimulus B was the police officer's gesture for you to cross the intersection. In laboratory experiments, stimulus A might be a light, stimulus B a tone, and the US a brief shock. On some trials, stimulus A is presented by itself and is paired with the US. These trials are represented as A⁺ (A plus), with the "+" sign indicating the presence of the US. As a result of the A⁺ trials, the organism comes to expect the US when it encounters stimulus A. This sets the stage for inhibitory conditioning.

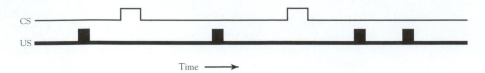

CS

US

Time ⟶

FIGURE 5.6   Negative contingency procedure for producing conditioned inhibition.
The US is presented at random times by itself but not if the CS has occurred recently.

On inhibitory conditioning trials, stimulus B is presented with stimulus A (forming the compound stimulus AB), but the US does not occur. These trials are represented as AB⁻ (AB minus), with the "−" sign indicating the absence of the US. The presence of stimulus A on the AB⁻ trials creates the expectation that the US will occur. This makes the absence of the US psychologically meaningful and serves to condition inhibitory properties to stimulus B.

Typically, A⁺ and AB⁻ trials are presented in an intermixed order in the standard inhibitory conditioning procedure. As training progresses, A gradually acquires conditioned excitatory properties and B becomes a conditioned inhibitor. Given the circumstances required to establish a conditioned inhibitor, as a general rule the excitatory conditioning of A develops faster than the inhibitory conditioning of B.

Negative CS/US Contingency.   The standard inhibitory conditioning procedure (A⁺, AB⁻) is especially effective in making B a conditioned inhibitor, but there are other successful inhibitory conditioning procedures as well. In the negative CS/US contingency procedure, for example, only one explicit conditioned stimulus is used (e.g., a tone), together with a US (see Figure 5.6). The tone and the US occur at irregular times, with the stipulation that the US is not presented if the tone has occurred recently. This stipulation establishes a negative contingency between the tone CS and the US. It insures that p(US/CS) will be less than p(US/noCS) and serves to make the CS a conditioned inhibitor.

Consider a child who periodically gets picked on by his classmates when the teacher is out of the room. This is similar to periodically getting an aversive stimulus or US. When the teacher returns, the child can be sure that he will not be bothered. The teacher thus serves as a CS⁻, signaling a period free from harassment, that is, the absence of the US.

What provides the excitatory context for inhibitory conditioning of the tone CS in the negative contingency procedure? Because the US occurs when the CS is absent, the background contextual cues of the experimental situation become associated with the US. This then enables the conditioning of inhibitory properties to the CS. The absence of the US when the CS occurs in this excitatory context makes the CS a conditioned inhibitor.

BEHAVIORAL MANIFESTATIONS OF CONDITIONED INHIBITION

The behavioral manifestations of excitatory conditioning are fairly obvious. Organisms come to make a new response—the conditioned response—to the CS. What happens in the case of conditioned inhibition? A conditioned inhibitory stimulus has behavioral effects that are the opposite of the behavioral effects of a conditioned excitatory stimulus; that is, a conditioned inhibitory stimulus suppresses or inhibits excitatory conditioned responding. Unfortunately, suppression of responding is evident only under special circumstances.

Consider, for example, the eyeblink response of rabbits. Rabbits blink very infrequently, perhaps once or twice an hour. Presumably a conditioned inhibitory stimulus (CS^-) actively suppresses blinking. But because rabbits rarely blink under ordinary circumstances, how can we tell when a CS^- actively inhibits their blinking?

Inhibition of blinking would be easy to determine if the baseline rate of blinking were elevated. If rabbits blinked 60 times an hour and we presented a conditioned inhibitory stimulus (CS^-), blinking should decline substantially below the 60/hr rate. Thus, the problem of measuring conditioned inhibition can be solved in principle by elevating the baseline rate of responding.

How can the baseline rate of responding be elevated? Perhaps the simplest way is to condition another stimulus as a conditioned excitatory cue (CS^+). Substantial responding should be evident when the CS^+ is presented by itself. Using this as a baseline, then, we can test the effects of a conditioned inhibitory stimulus (CS^-) by presenting the CS^- at the same time as the CS^+. Such a test strategy is called the **summation test** for conditioned inhibition.

Figure 5.7 presents hypothetical results of a summation test. Notice that considerable responding is observed when the CS^+ is presented by itself. Adding a conditioned inhibitory stimulus (CS^-) to the CS^+ results in a great deal less responding than when the CS^+ is presented alone. This is the expected outcome if the CS^- has acquired inhibitory properties. However, presentation of the CS^- might disrupt responding simply by creating a distraction. This possibility is evaluated in the summation test by determining how responding to the CS^+ is affected when a neutral stimulus with no history of either excitatory or inhibitory training is presented. Such a neutral stimulus is represented by CS^0 in Figure 5.7.

In the results depicted in Figure 5.7, CS^0 reduces responding to the CS^+ a small amount. This reflects the distracting effects of adding any stimulus to

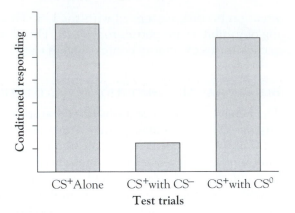

FIGURE 5.7   Procedure and hypothetical results for the summation test of conditioned inhibition.
On some trials a conditioned excitatory stimulus (CS⁺) is presented alone and a high level of conditioned responding is observed. On other trials the CS⁺ is presented with a conditioned inhibitory stimulus (CS⁻) or a neutral stimulus (CS⁰). The fact that CS⁻ disrupts responding to the CS⁺ much more than CS⁰ is evidence of the conditioned inhibitory properties of the CS⁻.

the CS⁺. The reduction in responding is much greater, however, when the CS⁻ is presented with the CS⁺. This outcome shows that the CS⁻ has conditioned inhibitory properties.

Retardation of Acquisition Test.   The summation test is a performance-based test of inhibition. It is based on the assumption that the performance of excitatory conditioned behavior will be suppressed by a conditioned inhibitory stimulus. A second popular approach to the measurement of conditioned inhibition is an acquisition or learning test. This test is based on the assumption that conditioned inhibitory properties will interfere with the acquisition of excitatory properties to that stimulus. Hence this is called the **retardation-of-acquisition test.**

The retardation-of-acquisition test involves comparing the rates of excitatory conditioning for two different groups of participants. The same conditioned stimulus (e.g., a tone) is used in both groups. For the experimental group, the tone is first trained as a conditioned inhibitor. For the comparison group, a control procedure is used that leaves the tone relatively "neutral." (For example, the tone may be presented alone a number of times in a neutral context.) Then for both groups the tone is paired with the US, and the development of excitatory responding to the tone is observed. If inhibitory conditioning was successful in the first stage of the experiment, excitatory conditioned responding should develop more slowly in the experimental group than in the control group during the retardation-of-acquisition test.

Higher-Order Relations in Pavlovian Conditioning: Conditioned Facilitation

A conditioned **facilitation** procedure is similar to the standard inhibitory conditioning procedure in that it involves one unconditioned stimulus and two conditioned stimuli. As in inhibitory conditioning, the stimuli are arranged in such a way that the occasions when one CS (A) is paired with the US are perfectly predicted by a second CS (B). In conditioned inhibition, B signals when A will not be paired with the US. By contrast, in conditioned facilitation, B signals when A will be paired with the US.

The differences between facilitation and inhibition are illustrated in Figure 5.8. In conditioned inhibition, stimulus B occurs on trials when A is not followed by the US (AB → noUS, or AB⁻), and B is absent when A is paired with the US (A → US, or A⁺). This arrangement is reversed in a facilitation procedure. In conditioned facilitation, stimulus B occurs on trials when A is reinforced (AB → US, or AB⁺), and B is absent on trials when A is not reinforced (A → noUS, or A⁻). The result of a facilitation procedure is that the participant responds to A when B is present but does not respond to A when B is absent (Holland, 1992).

Conditional relations such as that represented by the facilitation procedure are not limited to experimental research. Consider the road sign "Slippery When Wet." The sign indicates that ordinarily the road is safe but that it can be dangerous when it is wet. These circumstances exemplify the basic facilitation relation. The correspondence is evident if the roadway stimuli are represented by "A," wetness or rain is represented by "B," and danger is treated as the US. Danger occurs only when cues of the road are encountered in combination with rain (AB → US). No danger is present when cues of the road are encountered without rain (A → noUS).

	Trials with the US	Trials without the US
Conditioned inhibition	A ⟶ US	AB ⟶ no US
Conditioned facilitation	AB ⟶ US	A ⟶ no US

FIGURE 5.8   **Comparison of the types of trials that occur in procedures for conditioned inhibition and conditioned facilitation.**
A and B represent two different conditioned stimuli.

STIMULUS RELATIONS IN CONDITIONED FACILITATION

What kind of associations might produce responding in a facilitation procedure? There are two possibilities, one involving a direct relation of stimulus B with the US, and the other involving an indirect or higher-order relation.

In a facilitation procedure, AB^+ trials are intermixed with A^- trials. The US is only presented on trials when stimulus B occurs. This allows for the acquisition of a direct relation between stimulus B and the US (a B-US association).

A facilitation procedure also contains a higher-order relation. Stimulus B provides perfectly accurate information about the occasions when stimulus A is paired with the US. Stimulus A is paired with the US on trials when stimulus B is present (AB^+) but not on trials when stimulus B is absent (A^-). Therefore, a facilitation procedure may result in the learning of a higher-order relation in which B comes to signal the pairing of stimulus A with the US. This higher-order relation may be represented as B(A-US). Because stimulus B signals the occasions when A is paired with the US, the facilitation procedure is also called **positive occasion setting** (e.g., Holland, 1986).

DISTINGUISHING BETWEEN B-US AND B(A-US) RELATIONS

Types of Conditioned Responses Elicited by Stimuli A and B.   How can we decide whether a facilitation procedure results in the learning of a B-US relation or a B(A-US) relation? One approach has involved conditioned stimuli that elicit different responses, so that the nature of the response that occurs can reveal whether it is elicited by stimulus A or stimulus B. This approach has been used extensively in studies of facilitation in appetitive conditioning (Holland, 1992).

In one experiment (Rescorla, Durlach, & Grau, 1985), pigeons served as participants, a noise resembling static on the radio served as stimulus B, and a key light served as stimulus A. When the noise and key light stimuli were paired with food, they came to elicit different conditioned responses. The key light associated with food elicited conditioned pecking behavior. In contrast, the noise stimulus paired with food elicited increased walking around the experimental chamber but not pecking at the response key. Thus, any key-pecks observed in this experiment could only be interpreted as conditioned behavior elicited by the key light, not as conditioned behavior elicited by the noise CS.

The procedure for the experiment is summarized in Figure 5.9. The key light was paired with food in the presence of the noise stimulus (AB → US). When the noise was absent, the key light did not end in food (A → noUS). The pigeons came to peck the key light when the noise was present but pecked much less when the noise was turned off. This outcome cannot be explained in terms of a direct association between the noise CS and food (a B-US association), because pigeons do not peck a noise stimulus associated with food. It also cannot be explained in terms of a simple association be-

Trials with the US	Trials without the US
Noise present	Noise absent
Light ⟶ Food	Light ⟶ No food

FIGURE 5.9 Outline of the facilitation experiment by Rescorla et al. (1985).

---

tween the key light and food (an A-US association), because such an association would have produced pecking of the key light whether or not the noise was present. The fact that the birds pecked the key light only when the noise was present suggests that they learned a B(A-US) relation, in which the noise set the occasion for responding to the key light.

Effects of Extinction of Stimulus B. An alternative strategy for distinguishing between B-US and B(A-US) relations in a facilitation procedure involves testing the effects of extinguishing stimulus B. Extinction of B involves repeatedly presenting stimulus B by itself (B-noUS). This experience is contrary to a B-US relation and should reduce responding that depends on that relation. However, the repeated presentation of stimulus B by itself is not contrary to a B(A-US) relation. The opposite of B(A-US) is B(A-noUS), not B-noUS. Therefore, extinction of stimulus B should not disrupt responding mediated by a B(A-US) relation. Results consistent with this prediction have been obtained repeatedly (e.g., Holland, 1989; Rescorla, 1985; Ross, 1983). Simple extinction of stimulus B does not weaken the ability of stimulus B to facilitate responding to A following training in a facilitation procedure.

Finally, I should point out that organisms do not invariably learn a B(A-US) relation as a result of a facilitation procedure. Sometimes procedures involving a mixture of AB-US trials and A-noUS trials result in the learning of a B-US relation only; in other cases participants learn both a B-US relation and a higher-order B(A-US) relation. A number of factors beyond the scope of the present discussion determine whether a particular procedure favors the acquisition of a B-US relation or a B(A-US) relation (Holland, 1992; Schmajuk & Holland, 1998).

Summary

Pavlovian conditioning involves the formation of an association or linkage between two events. Typically, the events are individual stimuli, the CS and the US. However, in more complex cases, one of the events is a modulator CS and the other is a CS-US associative unit.

The development of conditioned responding is highly sensitive to the temporal relation between the CS and the US. Delayed conditioning procedures produce the most vigorous responding, but introducing a trace interval of as little as half a second between the CS and US can severely disrupt the development of conditioned behavior. Quantitative aspects of the CS-US interval function vary, depending on the response system that is being conditioned.

Pavlovian conditioning is also highly sensitive to the signal relation between the CS and the US, that is, the extent to which the CS provides information about the US. This is illustrated by the blocking phenomenon and by CS/US contingency effects. Originally, variations in the contingency between CS and US were considered to influence associative processes directly. More recent evidence suggests, however, that different degrees of context conditioning are responsible for CS/US contingency effects.

Higher-order relations in Pavlovian conditioning have been investigated within the context of conditioned inhibition and conditioned facilitation. In conditioned inhibition, a modulator stimulus (stimulus B) indicates when another CS (stimulus A) *is not paired* with the US. The outcome is that B comes to inhibit conditioned responding that normally occurs to stimulus A. In conditioned facilitation, the modulator stimulus B indicates when stimulus A *is paired* with the US. The outcome is that conditioned responding occurs only when stimulus B is present. Information concerning the topography of the conditioned response and the effects of extinguishing stimulus B is used to decide whether the results reflect learning a B(A-US) higher-order relation.

Practice Questions

1. What is the relative effectiveness of simultaneous, delayed, and trace conditioning procedures?

2. What is the effect of the CS-US interval on the acquisition of conditioned responding?

3. Which conditioning procedure produces learning with long delays between CS and US?

4. What is the blocking effect and why is it significant?

5. How do different CS/US contingencies determine what is learned?

6. What procedures produce conditioned inhibition, and how is such learning manifest in behavior?

7. What procedures produce conditioned facilitation, and how is that form of learning different from conditioned excitation?

Suggested Readings

Domjan, M. (1985). Cue-consequence specificity and long-delay learning revisited. *Annals of the New York Academy of Sciences, 443,* 54–66.

Gormezano, I., Kehoe, E. J., & Marshall, B. S. (1983). Twenty years of classical conditioning research with the rabbit. In J. M. Sprague & A. N. Epstein (Eds.), *Progress in psychobiology and physiological psychology* (Vol. 10, pp. 197–275). Orlando, FL: Academic Press.

Holland, P. C. (1992). Occasion setting in Pavlovian conditioning. In G. Bower (Ed.), *The psychology of learning and motivation* (Vol. 28, pp. 69–125). Orlando, FL: Academic Press.

Kamin, L. J. (1965). Temporal and intensity characteristics of the conditioned stimulus. In W. F. Prokasy (Ed.), *Classical conditioning* (pp. 118–147). New York: Appleton-Century-Crofts.

Kamin, L. J. (1969). Predictability, surprise, attention, and conditioning. In B. A. Campbell & R. M. Church (Eds.), *Punishment and aversive behavior* (pp. 279–296). New York: Appleton-Century-Crofts.

Papini, M. R., & Bitterman, M. E. (1990). The role of contingency in classical conditioning. *Psychological Review, 97,* 396–403.

Schmajuk, N. A., & Holland, P. C. (Eds.). (1998). *Occasion setting.* Washington, DC: American Psychological Association.

Technical Terms

Blocking effect
CS-US interval
Conditioned inhibition
Contingency
Delayed conditioning
Facilitation
Higher-order stimulus relation
Interstimulus interval
Long-delay learning

Positive occasion setting
Retardation-of-acquisition test
Simultaneous conditioning
Summation test
Temporal coding
Temporal contiguity
Trace conditioning
Trace interval

CHAPTER SIX

Theories of Associative Learning

DID YOU KNOW THAT:

- According to the Rescorla-Wagner model, learning about one stimulus depends on the associative value of other concurrently present stimuli.

- A CS can lose associative strength even though it is paired with a US.

- Contrary to evidence, the Rescorla-Wagner model predicts that presentations of a conditioned inhibitor by itself will result in loss or extinction of the inhibition.

- Attentional theories assume that what happens on one trial determines how much attention is devoted to the CS on the next trial.

- Many major theories of learning do not consider time in their formulations.

- The duration of the CS is not as important for learning as the ratio between the CS duration and the interval between successive US presentations.

- Conditioned responding depends on the associative value of the CS in comparison to the associative value of other cues that were present at the time the CS was conditioned.

Pavlovian conditioning was originally considered to be a simple form of learning that was produced primarily by pairing or temporal contiguity of the conditioned and unconditioned stimuli. This naive perspective was shattered by the discovery of the blocking effect. As I explained in Chapter 5, the blocking effect shows that a CS paired with a US will not become conditioned if it is redundant with another cue that already signals that US. Thus, temporal contiguity is not sufficient for the development of conditioned responding.

The discovery of the blocking effect stimulated a flurry of theoretical efforts to characterize associative learning. The first and most influential of these theories was the Rescorla-Wagner model. Other theories soon followed. These alternatives sought to explore different ways of characterizing learning and to overcome some of the shortcomings of the Rescorla-Wagner model.

Theories play an important role in science because they help us go beyond merely describing or cataloguing experimental results. To understand a research finding, scientists try to answer several questions. They begin with what happened in a particular experiment. The answer to the *what* question requires a full description of the research results. Once the *what* question has been adequately answered, scientists try to figure out *how* and *why* a particular result was obtained. To answer these questions they examine possible mechanisms that might have produced the results. Theories provide answers to the *how* and *why* questions. They describe the underlying processes or mechanisms that are presumably responsible for the behavioral outcomes that have been observed.

We could characterize the mechanisms of learning in terms of the underlying neurobiological processes that are involved. Alternatively, we could create a model or theory of learning that employs hypothetical constructs or mechanisms. The theories that I will describe in this chapter are of the second type. They are psychological rather than neurobiological theories and are stated in terms of concepts such as "association," "attention," and "surprise." This makes the theories no less rigorous than biological theories. The concept of gravity, for example, is a hypothetical construct. We cannot observe gravity directly; all we see are the consequences of gravity (falling objects). Nevertheless, gravity can be described in precise quantitative terms. The theories I will describe are precise quantitative theories of the same type.

In providing answers to the *how* and *why* questions, theories also help to organize and summarize diverse research findings and to guide future research. The concept of gravity, for example, helps us to characterize the behavior of numerous falling objects in terms of a single equation and allows us to make predictions about the behavior of future moving objects. In an analogous fashion, theories of learning help us to summarize numerous research findings in terms of a few general principles. They also help to guide future research by making precise predictions that require experimental verification.

The Rescorla-Wagner Model

As I mentioned, the discovery of the blocking effect stimulated a flurry of theoretical activity in learning. The basics of the blocking effect are reviewed in Figure 6.1. Subjects first receive one CS (e.g., a light) paired with the US. After conditioned responding to the light is well established, a new CS (e.g., a tone) is added to the light, and the tone/light compound is paired with the US. Blocking is said to occur if the presence of the previously conditioned light blocks the conditioning of the added tone CS.

Why does the presence of the previously conditioned light CS block the acquisition of responding to the added tone CS? Kamin (1969), who originally identified the blocking effect, explained the phenomenon by proposing that a US must be surprising to be effective in producing learning. If the US is signaled by a previously conditioned stimulus, it will not be surprising and therefore will not stimulate the "mental effort" needed for the formation of an association. Expected events are things the organism has already learned about. Hence expected events will not activate processes leading to new learning. In order to be effective, the US must be unexpected or surprising.

The idea that the effectiveness of an unconditioned stimulus is determined by how surprising it is forms the basis of the Rescorla-Wagner model (Rescorla & Wagner, 1972; Wagner & Rescorla, 1972). With the use of this model, the implications of the concept of US surprisingness were extended to a wide variety of conditioning phenomena. The Rescorla-Wagner model dominated research on classical conditioning for about 10 years after its formulation and continues to be employed in a variety of areas of psychology.

What does it mean to say that something is surprising? How might we measure the surprisingness of an unconditioned stimulus? By definition, *an event is surprising if it is different from what is expected.* If you expect a small gift for your birthday and get a car, you will be very surprised. This is analogous to an unexpectedly large US. Likewise, if you expect a car and receive a box of candy, you will also be surprised. This is analogous to an unexpectedly small US. According to the Rescorla-Wagner model, an unexpectedly large US is the basis for excitatory conditioning, or increases in associative value, while an unexpectedly small US is the basis for inhibitory conditioning or decreases in associative value.

Rescorla and Wagner assumed that the surprisingness and hence the effectiveness of a US depends on how different the US is from what the individual expects. Furthermore, they assumed that expectation of the US is related to the conditioned or associative properties of *all* the stimuli that precede the US. Strong conditioned responding indicates strong expectation that the US will occur; weak conditioned responding indicates a low expectation that it will occur.

These ideas can be expressed mathematically by using λ to represent the asymptote of learning possible with the US that is being used and V to rep-

Phase 1	Phase 2	Test
Experimental Group		
A → US	(A + B) → US	B
Control Group		
	(A + B) → US	B

FIGURE 6.1   Review of the design of a blocking experiment. In Phase 1, the experimental group gets stimulus A conditioned to asymptote. Both the experimental and the control group then get stimuli A and B conditioned with the US.

resent the associative value of the stimuli that precede the US. The surprisingness of the US will then be $(\lambda - V)$. According to the Rescorla-Wagner model, the amount of learning on a given trial is assumed to be proportional to $(\lambda - V)$, or US surprisingness. The value of $(\lambda - V)$ is large at the start of learning because V (the associative value of the stimuli preceding the US) is close to zero at this point. Hence, substantial increments in associative strength occur during early conditioning trials. Once the associative value of the cues that precede the US has increased, $(\lambda - V)$ will be small, and little additional learning will occur.

Learning on a given conditioning trial is the change in the associative value of a stimulus. This change can be represented as ΔV. Using these symbols, the idea that learning depends on the surprisingness of the US can be expressed as follows:

$$\Delta V = k(\lambda - V)$$

In this equation, k is a constant related to the salience of the CS and US. This is the fundamental equation of the Rescorla-Wagner model.

APPLICATION TO THE BLOCKING EFFECT

The basic ideas of the Rescorla-Wagner model clearly predict the blocking effect. In applying the model, it is important to keep in mind that expectations of the US are based on all of the cues available to the organism during the conditioning trial. As illustrated in Figure 6.1, the blocking design first involves extensive conditioning of stimulus A so that the subject acquires a perfect expectation that the US will occur whenever it encounters stimulus A. Therefore, at the end of Phase 1, V_A equals the asymptote of learning, or λ ($V_A = \lambda$). In Phase 2, stimulus B is presented together with stimulus A, and the two CSs are followed by the US. According to the Rescorla-Wagner

Phase 1	Phase 2	Test
A → US	(A + B) → US	A, B
B → US		

FIGURE 6.2   Design of overexpectation study.
In Phase 1, subjects receive stimuli A and B, each paired individually with the US (one food pellet). Phase 1 is continued until stimuli A and B are each conditioned to asymptote. In Phase 2, stimuli A and B are presented together, creating an overexpectation of the one pellet US. As a consequence, the associative values of A and B decrease in Phase 2.

model, no conditioning of stimulus B will occur in Phase 2 because the US is now perfectly predicted by the presence of stimulus A: $(\lambda - V_{A+B}) = 0$.

The control group receives the identical training in Phase 2, but for them the presence of stimulus A does not lead to an expectation of the US. Therefore, the US is surprising for the control group and produces new learning.

LOSS OF ASSOCIATIVE VALUE DESPITE PAIRINGS WITH THE US

The Rescorla-Wagner model is consistent with such fundamental facts of classical conditioning as acquisition and the blocking effect. However, much of the importance of the model has come from its unusual predictions. One such prediction is that under certain circumstances the conditioned properties of stimuli will decline despite continued pairings with the US. How might this happen? Stimuli are predicted to lose associative value if they are presented together on a conditioning trial after having been trained separately. Such an experiment is outlined in Figure 6.2.

Figure 6.2 shows a two-phase experiment. In Phase 1, stimuli A and B are paired with the same US (e.g., one pellet of food) on separate trials. This continues until both A and B have been conditioned completely—until both stimuli predict perfectly the one food pellet US, or $V_A = V_B = \lambda$. Phase 2 is then initiated. In Phase 2, stimuli A and B are presented simultaneously for the first time, and this stimulus compound is followed by the same US—one food pellet. The question is, what happens to the conditioned properties of stimuli A and B as a result of the Phase 2 training?

Note that the same US that was used in Phase 1 continues to be presented in Phase 2. Given that there is no change in the US, informal reflection suggests that the conditioned properties of stimuli A and B should also remain unchanged during Phase 2. Contrary to this commonsense prediction, the Rescorla-Wagner model instead predicts that the conditioned properties of the individual stimuli A and B will decrease in Phase 2.

As a result of training in Phase 1, stimuli A and B both come to predict the one food pellet US ($V_A = \lambda; V_B = \lambda$). When stimuli A and B are presented simultaneously for the first time, in Phase 2, the expectations based on the individual stimuli are assumed to add together, with the result that two food pellets are predicted as the US ($V_{A+B} = V_A + V_B = 2\lambda$). This is an overexpectation, because the US remains only one food pellet. Thus, there is a discrepancy between what is expected (two pellets) and what occurs (one pellet). At the start of Phase 2, the participants find the US surprisingly small. To bring their expectations of the US in line with what actually occurs in Phase 2, the participants have to decrease their expectancy of the US based on stimuli A and B. Thus, stimuli A and B are predicted to lose associative value despite continued presentations of the same US. The loss of associative value is predicted to continue until the sum of the expectancies based on A and B equals one food pellet. The predicted loss of conditioned response to the individual stimuli A and B in this type of procedure is highly counterintuitive but has been verified experimentally (see Khallad & Moore, 1996; Kremer, 1978; Lattal & Nakajima, 1998; Rescorla, 1999).

CONDITIONED INHIBITION

How does the Rescorla-Wagner model explain the development of conditioned inhibition? Consider, for example, the standard inhibitory conditioning procedure (see Figure 5.5). This procedure involves two kinds of trials: trials on which the US is presented (reinforced trials) and trials on which the US is omitted (nonreinforced trials). On reinforced trials, a conditioned excitatory stimulus (CS^+) is presented. On nonreinforced trials, the CS^+ is presented together with the conditioned inhibitory stimulus, CS^-.

In order to apply the Rescorla-Wagner model to the conditioned inhibition procedure, reinforced and nonreinforced trials must be considered separately. To accurately anticipate the US on reinforced trials, the CS^+ has to gain excitatory properties. The development of such conditioned excitation is illustrated in the left panel of Figure 6.3. Excitatory conditioning involves the acquisition of positive associative value and ceases once the organism predicts the US perfectly on each reinforced trial.

What happens on nonreinforced trials? On these trials, both the CS^+ and CS^- occur. Once the CS^+ has acquired some degree of conditioned excitation (because of its presentation on reinforced trials), the organism will expect the US whenever the CS^+ occurs, even on nonreinforced trials. However, the US does not happen on nonreinforced trials. Therefore, this is a case of overexpectation, similar to the example illustrated in Figure 6.2. To accurately predict the absence of the US on nonreinforced trials, the associative value of the CS^+ and the value of the CS^- have to sum to zero (the value represented by no US). How can this be achieved? Given the positive associative value of the CS^+, the only way to achieve a net zero expectation of the US on nonreinforced trials is to make the associative value of the CS^-

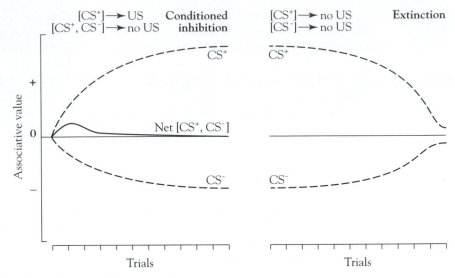

FIGURE 6.3   Predicted associative values of CS⁺ and CS⁻ during the course of conditioned inhibition training (left) and extinction (right).
During conditioned inhibition training, when the CS⁺ is presented alone, it is followed by the US; in contrast, when the CS⁺ is presented with the CS⁻, the US is omitted. The net associative value of CS⁺ and CS⁻ is the sum of the associative values of the individual stimuli. During extinction, the conditioned stimuli are presented alone, and the US never occurs.

---

negative. Hence, the Rescorla-Wagner model explains conditioned inhibition by assuming that the CS⁻ acquires negative associative value (see the left panel of Figure 6.3).

EXTINCTION OF EXCITATION AND INHIBITION

In an extinction procedure, the conditioned stimulus is presented repeatedly without the US. (I will have a lot more to say about extinction in Chapter 10.) Let us consider predictions of the Rescorla-Wagner model for extinction. These predictions are illustrated in the right panel of Figure 6.3. When the CS⁺ is first presented without the US in extinction, there will be an overexpectation of the US. With continued presentation of the CS⁺ by itself, the expectation elicited by the CS⁺ will gradually be brought in line with the absence of the US, by gradual reduction of the associative value of the CS⁺ to zero.

The Rescorla-Wagner model predicts an analogous scenario for extinction of conditioned inhibition. At the start of extinction, the CS⁻ has negative associative value. This may be thought of as creating an underprediction of the US: the organism predicts less than the zero US that occurs on extinction trials. To bring expectations in line with the absence of the US, the negative associative value of the CS$^-$ is gradually lost, and the CS$^-$ ends up with zero associative strength.

PROBLEMS WITH THE RESCORLA-WAGNER MODEL

The Rescorla-Wagner model has stimulated a great deal of research and led to the discovery of many new and important phenomena in classical conditioning (Siegel & Allan, 1996). Not unexpectedly, however, the model has also encountered some difficulties since it was proposed in 1972 (see Miller, Barnet, & Grahame, 1995).

One of the difficulties with the model that became evident early on is that its analysis of the extinction of conditioned inhibition is incorrect. As I pointed out in the previous section (see Figure 6.3), the model predicts that repeated presentations of a conditioned inhibitor (CS$^-$) by itself will lead to loss of conditioned inhibition. This, however, does not occur (Witcher & Ayres, 1984; Zimmer-Hart & Rescorla, 1974). In fact, some investigators have found that repeated nonreinforcement of a CS$^-$ can enhance its conditioned inhibitory properties (see, e.g., DeVito & Fowler, 1987; Hallam, Grahame, Harris, & Miller, 1992). Curiously, an effective procedure for reducing the conditioned inhibitory properties of a CS$^-$ does not involve presenting the CS$^-$ at all. Rather, it involves extinguishing the excitatory properties of the CS$^+$ with which the CS$^-$ was presented during inhibitory training (Best, Dunn, Batson, Meachum, & Nash, 1985b; Lysle & Fowler, 1985).

Another difficulty is that the Rescorla-Wagner model views extinction as the reverse of acquisition, or the return of the associative value of a CS to zero. However, as I will discuss in Chapter 10, a growing body of evidence indicates that extinction should not be viewed as simply the reverse of acquisition. Rather, extinction appears to involve the learning of a new relationship between the CS and US (namely, that the US no longer follows the CS).

Another puzzling finding that has been difficult to incorporate into the Rescorla-Wagner model is that under certain conditions the same CS may have both excitatory and inhibitory properties (Barnet & Miller, 1996; Matzel, Gladstein, & Miller, 1988; McNish, Betts, Brandon, & Wagner, 1997; Robbins, 1990; Tait & Saladin, 1986; Williams & Overmier, 1988). The Rescorla-Wagner model allows for conditioned stimuli to have only one associative value. This value may be excitatory or inhibitory, but not both.

Other Models of Classical Conditioning

Devising a comprehensive theory of classical conditioning is a formidable challenge. Given that classical conditioning has been studied for about a century, a comprehensive theory must account for many diverse findings. No theory available today has been entirely successful in accomplishing that goal. Nevertheless, interesting new ideas about classical conditioning continue to be proposed and examined. Some of these proposals supplement the Rescorla-Wagner model. Others are incompatible with the model and move the theoretical debate in some startling new directions.

ATTENTIONAL MODELS OF CONDITIONING

According to the Rescorla-Wagner model, how much is learned on a conditioning trial depends on the effectiveness of the unconditioned stimulus. North American psychologists have favored theories of learning that focus on changes in US effectiveness. In contrast, British psychologists have approached phenomena such as the blocking effect by postulating changes in how well the CS commands the subject's attention. The general assumption is that for conditioning to occur, subjects must pay close attention to the CS. Procedures that disrupt attention to the CS are expected to disrupt learning as well (Mackintosh, 1975; McLaren & Mackintosh, 2000; Pearce & Hall, 1980).

How noticeable a stimulus is, or how much attention it commands, is called the **salience** of the stimulus. Attentional theories differ in their assumptions about what determines the salience of a CS on a given trial. Pearce and Hall (1980), for example, assumed that how much attention an animal devotes to the CS on a given trial is determined by how surprising the US was on the preceding trial (see also Hall, Kaye, & Pearce, 1985; McLaren & Mackintosh, 2000). Animals have a lot to learn if the US was surprising to them on the preceding trial. Therefore, under such conditions they will pay closer attention to the CS on the next trial; CS salience will increase. In contrast, if a CS was followed by an expected US, the subject will pay less attention to that CS on the next trial. An expected US is assumed to decrease the amount of attention commanded by the CS.

An important feature of attentional theories is that they assume that the surprisingness of the US on a given trial alters the degree of attention commanded by the CS on future trials. For example, if Trial 10 ends in a surprising US, the salience of the CS on Trial 11 will increase. Thus, US surprisingness is assumed to have only a *prospective* or *proactive* influence on attention and conditioning. This is an important difference from US-reduction models such as the Rescorla-Wagner model, in which the surprisingness of the US on a given trial determines what is learned on that same trial.

The assumption that the US on a given trial influences only what is learned on the next trial has permitted attentional models to explain certain findings (e.g., Mackintosh, Bygrave, & Picton, 1977). However, this same assumption has made it difficult for the models to explain other results. In particular, the models cannot explain blocking that occurs on the first trial of Phase 2 of the blocking experiment (see, for example, Azorlosa & Cicala, 1986; Balaz, Kasprow, & Miller, 1982; Dickinson, Nicholas, & Mackintosh,

1983; Gillan & Domjan, 1977). According to attentional models, blocking occurs because in Phase 2 of the blocking experiment the lack of surprisingness of the US reduces attention to the added CS. However, such a reduction in salience can occur only after the first Phase 2 trial. Therefore, attentional models cannot explain the blocking that occurs on the first trial of Phase 2 of the blocking experiment.

TEMPORAL FACTORS AND CONDITIONED RESPONDING

Neither the Rescorla-Wagner model nor CS modification models were designed to explain the effects of time in conditioning. However, time is obviously a critical factor. One important temporal variable is the CS-US interval. As I noted in Chapter 5, conditioned responding is generally inversely related to the CS-US interval or CS duration. Beyond an optimal point, procedures with longer CS-US intervals produce less responding (see Figure 5.2). This relation appears to be primarily a characteristic of responses closely related to the US (such as focal search). If behaviors that are ordinarily farther removed from the US are measured (such as general search), responding is greater with procedures that involve longer CS-US intervals. Both findings illustrate that the duration of the CS is an important factor in conditioning.

Another important temporal variable is the interval between successive trials. Generally, more conditioned responding is observed with procedures in which trials are spaced farther apart. Of greater interest, however, is the fact that the intertrial interval and the CS duration act in combination to determine responding. Numerous studies have shown that the critical factor is the relative duration of these two temporal variables rather than the absolute value of either one by itself (Gallistel & Gibbon, 2000; Gibbon & Balsam, 1981; but see Domjan, 2003).

Consider, for example, an experiment by Holland (2000). The experiment was conducted with laboratory rats, and food presented periodically in a cup was the US. Presentations of the food were signaled by a CS that was white noise. Initially the rats went to the food cup only when the food was delivered. However, as conditioning proceeded, they started going to the food cup as soon as they heard the noise CS. Thus, nosing of the food cup (a form of focal search) served as the anticipatory conditioned response. Each group was conditioned with one of two CS durations, either 10 seconds or 20 seconds, and one of six intertrial intervals (ranging from 15 seconds to 960 seconds). Each procedure could be characterized in terms of the ratio (I/T) between the intertrial interval (I) and the CS duration, which Holland called the trial duration (T).

The results of the experiment are summarized in Figure 6.4. Time spent nosing the food cup during the CS is shown as a function of the relative value of the intertrial interval (I) and the trial duration (T) for each group of subjects. Notice that conditioned responding was directly related to the I/T ra-

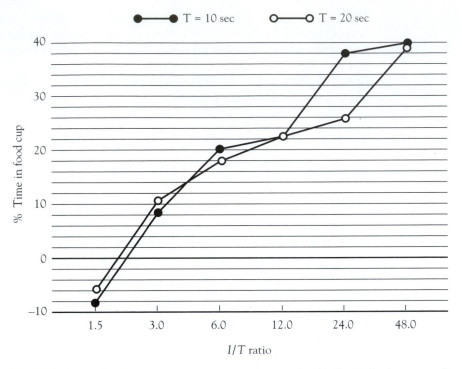

FIGURE 6.4   **Percent time rats spent nosing the food cup during an auditory CS in conditioning with either a 10-second or a 20-second trial duration (T) and various intertrial intervals (I) that created I/T ratios ranging from 1.5 to 48.0.**
Data are shown in relation to responding during baseline periods when the CS was absent. Adapted from Figure 2, p. 125, P. C. Holland, in *Animal Learning & Behavior*, Vol. 28. Copyright © 2000 Psychonomic Society, Inc. Reprinted with permission.

tio. At each *I/T* ratio, the groups that received the 10-second CS responded similarly to those that received the 20-second CS.

Various interpretations have been offered for why conditioned responding is so strongly determined by the *I/T* ratio. An early explanation was the **relative-waiting-time hypothesis** (Jenkins, Barnes, & Barrera, 1981; see also scalar expectancy theory, Gibbon & Balsam, 1981). This hypothesis focused on how long one has to wait for the US under two different conditions: (1) when the CS is present (CS waiting time), and (2) in the experimental situation irrespective of the US (context waiting time). Jenkins et al. assumed that the CS is informative about the occurrence of the US only if the CS waiting time is substantially less than the context waiting time. With a low *I/T* ratio, the CS waiting time is similar to the context waiting time. In this case, the CS provides little new information about when the US will occur, and not much conditioned responding will develop. In contrast, with a high *I/T* ratio, the CS waiting time is much shorter than the context waiting time. This makes the CS highly informative about when the US will occur, and conditioned responding will be more vigorous.

More recently, these ideas have been elaborated within the context of a comprehensive theory of temporal factors and conditioning called rate expectancy theory (Gallistel & Gibbon, 2000). This theory assumes that organisms perceive and remember temporal aspects of a conditioning procedure (such as the intertrial interval and CS duration) and that conditioned responding depends on decision processes that involve comparing these temporal variables. Originally, these temporal variables were considered to be performance factors that only influenced the behavioral manifestations of learning. However, it is now clear that these temporal variables are directly involved in the basic learning processes themselves (Holland, 2000; Lattal, 1999).

THE COMPARATOR HYPOTHESIS

The relative-waiting-time hypothesis and related theories were developed to explain certain temporal features of excitatory conditioning and manipulations of CS/US contingency. One of the important contributions of these theories was to emphasize that conditioned responding depends not only on what happens during the CS but also on what happens in the experimental situation in general. The idea that both of these factors influence many learning phenomena has been developed in greater detail by R. Miller and his collaborators in the **comparator hypothesis** (Denniston, Savastano, & Miller, 2001; Miller & Matzel, 1988, 1989).

The comparator hypothesis is similar to the relative-waiting-time hypothesis in assuming that conditioned responding depends on the relationship between the target CS and the US, as well as on the relationship between contextual cues and the US. The associative strength of other cues present during training with the target CS is especially important. Another constraint of the comparator hypothesis is that it only allows for the formation of excitatory associations with the US. Whether conditioned responding reflects excitation or inhibition is assumed to be determined by the relative strengths of excitation conditioned to the target CS as compared to the excitatory value of the contextual cues that were present with the target CS during training.

The comparator process is represented by the balance in Figure 6.5. In this figure, a comparison is made between the excitatory value of the target CS and the excitatory value of the other cues that are present during the training of the CS. If CS excitation exceeds the excitatory value of the con-

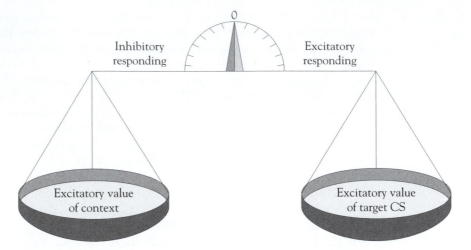

FIGURE 6.5   Illustration of the comparator hypothesis.
Responding to the target CS is represented by the reading on the balance. If the excitatory value of the target CS exceeds the excitatory value of the other cues present during training of the target CS, the balance tips in favor of excitatory responding to the CS. As the associative value of the contextual cues increases, the comparison becomes less favorable for excitatory responding and may tip in favor of inhibitory responding.

textual cues, the balance of the comparison will be tipped in favor of excitatory responding to the target CS. As the excitatory value of the other cues becomes stronger, the balance of the comparison will become less favorable for excitatory responding. In fact, if the excitatory value of the contextual cues becomes sufficiently strong, the balance may eventually be tipped in favor of inhibitory responding to the target CS.

Unlike the relative-waiting-time hypothesis, the comparator hypothesis emphasizes associations rather than time. It assumes that organisms learn three associations during the course of conditioning. These are illustrated in Figure 6.6. The first association (Link 1 in Figure 6.6) is between the target CS (X) and the US. The second association (Link 2) is between the target CS (X) and the comparator contextual cues. Finally, there is an association between the comparator stimuli and the US (Link 3). With all of these links in place, once the CS is presented it activates the US representation directly (through Link 1) and indirectly (through Links 2 and 3). A comparison between the direct and indirect activations determines the degree of excitatory or inhibitory responding that occurs.

It is important to note that the comparator hypothesis makes no assumptions about how associations become established. Rather, it describes

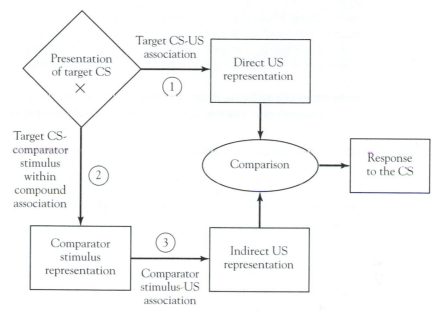

FIGURE 6.6   The associative structure of the comparator hypothesis.
The target CS is represented as X. Excitatory associations result in activation of
the US representation, either directly by the target (Link 1) or indirectly (through
Links 2 and 3). (From Friedman, Blaisdell, Escobar, & Miller, 1998.)

how CS-US and context-US associations determine responding to the target CS. Thus, unlike US-modification and attentional models, the comparator hypothesis is a theory of *performance*, not a theory of learning.

An important corollary to the comparator hypothesis is that the comparison between CS-US and context-US associations is made at the time of
testing for conditioned responding. As a consequence of this assumption,
the comparator hypothesis makes the unusual prediction that extinction of
context-US associations following training of a target CS will enhance responding to that target CS. This prediction has been confirmed repeatedly
(e.g., Blaisdell, Gunther, & Miller, 1999). US-modification and attentional
theories of learning cannot explain such results.

The comparator hypothesis has also been tested in studies of conditioned
inhibition. The hypothesis attributes inhibitory responding to situations in
which the association of the target CS with the US is weaker than the association of contextual cues with the US. The contextual cues in this case are
the stimuli that provide the excitatory context for inhibitory conditioning.
Interestingly, the hypothesis predicts that extinction of these conditioned
excitatory stimuli following inhibitory conditioning will reduce inhibitory

responding. Thus, the comparator hypothesis is unique in predicting that extinction of conditioned inhibition is best accomplished not by presenting the CS^- alone but by extinguishing the CS^+ cues that provided the excitatory context for inhibitory conditioning. As I noted earlier in my discussion of the extinction of conditioned inhibition, this unusual prediction has been confirmed (Best, Dunn et al., 1985b).

Although the comparator hypothesis accurately predicts the effects of extinction of contextual and other comparator cues after training, efforts to obtain the opposite effect have been less successful. The model predicts that increasing the excitatory value of contextual cues after training (Link 3 in Figure 6.6) will reduce conditioned responding to the target CS. A number of experiments have failed to verify this outcome (e.g., Robbins, 1988), but this failure is not universal. Furthermore, the negative findings are not entirely unexpected, because increasing the excitatory value of the contextual cues may weaken the association between the target stimulus and the comparator (Link 2 in Figure 6.6) (see Denniston et al., 2001).

On balance the comparator hypothesis has identified some important contextual constraints on conditioned responding. One of its major contributions has been to emphasize that differences in conditioned responding may reflect differences in performance rather than in learning. In fact, it views even a robust phenomenon such as the blocking effect as a failure of performance rather than of learning. It predicts, for example, that postconditioning extinction of a blocking stimulus will elevate conditioned responding to the blocked CS. Recent studies have verified this unusual prediction (Blaisdell et al., 1999). Given these successes, other theories of learning will have to address such postconditioning modulations of responding more successfully. Rate estimation theory, for one (see Gallistel & Gibbon, 2001) has risen to the challenge.

Overview of Theoretical Alternatives

Each of the new models I have described emphasizes a different aspect of classical conditioning. The relative-waiting-time hypothesis addresses a fairly small range of phenomena involving the temporal distribution of conditioned and unconditioned stimuli, although its successor (rate expectancy theory) is much more far-reaching. The comparator hypothesis is also ambitious, but as a theory of performance rather than learning, it does not provide an explanation of how associations are acquired. Attentional models attempt to address the same wide range of phenomena as the Rescorla-Wagner model, but they also have some of the same difficulties as that model. All of these models have been important in directing our attention to previously ignored aspects of classical conditioning. None of them, however, has come to dominate the study of classical conditioning in the same way as the Rescorla-Wagner model did in the 1970s.

Practice Questions

1. What is a theory and what are its advantages?

2. Describe the basic idea of the Rescorla-Wagner model. What aspect of the model allows it to explain the blocking effect and make some unusual predictions?

3. How does the Rescorla-Wagner model explain conditioned inhibition?

4. In what respects are attentional theories of learning different from other theories?

5. What is the primary difficulty that attentional theories have in explaining the blocking effect?

6. What is the relative-waiting-time hypothesis, and what aspects of a conditioning procedure does it focus on?

7. What are the basic tenets of the comparator hypothesis, and how does this model explain the blocking effect?

8. Compare and contrast predictions of the Rescorla-Wagner model and the comparator hypothesis for extinction of conditioned inhibition.

Suggested Readings

Gallistel, C. R., & Gibbon, J. (2000). Time, rate, and conditioning. *Psychological Review, 107,* 289–344.

Mackintosh, N. J. (1975). A theory of attention: Variations in the associability of stimuli with reinforcement. *Psychological Review, 82,* 276–298.

McLaren, I. P. L., & Mackintosh, N. J. (2000). An elemental model of associative learning: I. Latent inhibition and perceptual learning. *Animal Learning & Behavior, 28,* 211–246.

Miller, R. R., & Matzel, L. D. (1988). The comparator hypothesis: A response rule for the expression of associations. In G. H. Bower (Ed.), *The psychology of learning and motivation* (pp. 51–92). Orlando, FL: Academic Press.

Miller, R. R., Barnet, R. C., & Grahame, N. J. (1995). Assessment of the Rescorla-Wagner model. *Psychological Bulletin, 117,* 363–386.

Pearce, J. M., & Hall, G. (1980). A model for Pavlovian learning: Variations in the effectiveness of conditioned but not of unconditioned stimuli. *Psychological Review, 87,* 532–552.

Rescorla, R. A., & Wagner, A. R. (1972). A theory of Pavlovian conditioning: Variations in the effectiveness of reinforcement and nonreinforcement. In A. H. Black & W. F. Prokasy (Eds.), *Classical conditioning II:*

Current research and theory (pp. 64–99). New York: Appleton-Century-Crofts.

Technical Terms

Comparator hypothesis	Relative-waiting-time hypothesis
I/T ratio	Salience

CHAPTER SEVEN

Instrumental or Operant Conditioning

DID YOU KNOW THAT:

- Learning a new instrumental response often involves putting familiar response components into new combinations.

- Variability in behavior is a great advantage in learning new responses.

- The deleterious effects of reinforcement delay can be overcome by presenting a marking stimulus immediately after the instrumental response.

- Thorndike's Law of Effect does not involve an association between the instrumental response and the reinforcer.

- Instrumental conditioning can result in the learning of three binary associations and one higher-order association.

- The various associations that develop in instrumental conditioning are difficult to isolate from each other, which creates major problems for studying the neurophysiology of instrumental learning.

- Pavlovian associations acquired in instrumental conditioning procedures can disrupt performance of instrumental responses.

The various procedures that I have described so far (habituation, sensitization, and Pavlovian conditioning) all involve presentations of different types of stimuli according to various arrangements. The procedures produce changes in behavior—increases and decreases in responding—as a result of these stimulus presentations. Although they differ in significant ways, an important common feature of habituation, sensitization, and Pavlovian conditioning is that they are defined independently of the actions of the organism. What the participants do as a result of the procedures does not influence the stimuli they receive.

In a sense, studies of habituation, sensitization, and Pavlovian conditioning represent how organisms learn about events that are beyond their control. Adjustments to uncontrollable events are important because many aspects of the environment are beyond our control. What day a class is scheduled, how long it takes to boil an egg, how far it is between city blocks, and when the local post office is open are all beyond our control. However, while learning about uncontrollable events is important, not all learning is of this sort. Another important category of learning involves situations in which the presentation of an unconditioned stimulus depends on the individual's actions. Such cases involve **instrumental** or **operant conditioning.**

In instrumental conditioning procedures, whether or not a significant stimulus or event occurs depends on the behavior of the organism. Common examples of instrumental behavior include pulling up the covers to get warm in bed, putting ingredients together to make lemonade, changing the TV channel to find a particular show, and saying "Hello" to someone to get a greeting in return. In all of these cases, a particular response is required to obtain a specific stimulus or consequent outcome. Because the response is instrumental in producing the outcome, the response is referred to as **instrumental behavior.** The consequent outcome (the warmth, the tasty lemonade, the TV show, the reciprocal greeting) is referred to as the **reinforcer.**

If an instrumental behavior is defined in terms of a particular operation or manipulation of the environment, it is called **operant behavior.** For example, we may define turning a doorknob far enough to open a door as an operant response. In this case, it does not matter what muscle movements are used to turn the doorknob, provided it gets turned far enough to release the door. The knob could be turned with a person's right hand, left hand, or fingertips or with a full grip of the knob. Such variations in response topography are ignored in studies of operant behavior.

A common example of operant behavior in animal research involves a laboratory rat pressing a response lever in a small experimental chamber (see Figure 7.1). (We previously encountered this example in discussions of conditioned suppression in Chapter 4.) Whether or not a lever-press response has occurred can be determined by placing a microswitch under the lever. In a typical experiment, presses of the lever with enough force to activate the microswitch are counted as operant responses, using a computer interface system. Lever presses that are too weak to activate the switch are ignored by

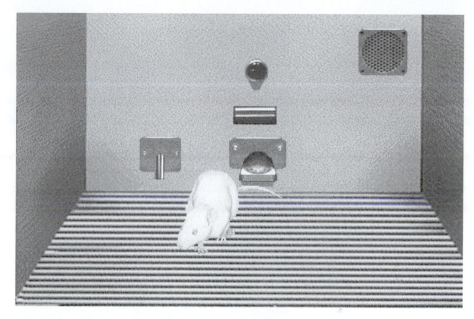

FIGURE 7.1.   A common laboratory preparation for the study of operant behavior.

Photo shows a rat in a lever-press chamber. The lever is behind the rat on the wall above a cup into which a food pellet is delivered if the rat presses the lever.

---

the system. In this case the lever-press response "operates" on the environment by activating the microswitch.

Another common example of operant behavior in animal research is a pigeon pecking a circular disk or response key on a wall (see Figure 4.1). A microswitch behind the response key is used to detect instances of the key-peck response.

The Traditions of Thorndike and Skinner

The intellectual traditions of classical conditioning were established by one dominant figure, Ivan Pavlov. In contrast, the intellectual traditions of instrumental or operant conditioning have their roots in the work of two American giants of twentieth-century psychology, Edward L. Thorndike and B. F. Skinner. The empirical methods as well as the theoretical perspectives of these two scientists were strikingly different, but the traditions founded by each of them have endured to this day. I will first consider the distinctive experimental methods used by Thorndike and Skinner and then note some differences in their theoretical perspectives.

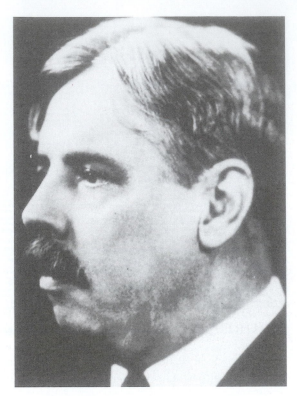

FIGURE 7.2.   Edward L. Thorndike (1874–1949).
Archives of the History of American Psychology.

METHODOLOGICAL CONSIDERATIONS

Thorndike was interested in studying animal "intelligence." To do this, he designed a number of escape tasks for young cats in a project that became his Ph.D. dissertation at Harvard University (Thorndike, 1898). Each task involved a **puzzle box** of some kind. A different type of response was required in order to get released from each box. The puzzle was to figure out how to get out of the box.

Thorndike would put a kitten into a puzzle box on successive trials and measure how long the kitten took to escape and obtain a piece of fish. In some puzzle boxes, the kittens had to make just one type of response to get out (e.g., turning a latch). In others, several actions were required, and these had to be performed in a particular order. Thorndike found that with repeated trials in a particular box, the kittens got quicker and quicker at escaping. Their escape latencies decreased.

The discrete-trial method.   Thorndike's experiments illustrate the **discrete-trial method** used in the study of instrumental behavior. In the discrete-trial

FIGURE 7.3.   B. F. Skinner (1904–1990).
Bettmann/CORBIS.

---

method, the participant has the opportunity to perform the instrumental response only at certain times (during discrete trials) as determined by the experimenter. In the case of Thorndike's experiments, the kittens could only perform the instrumental-escape response when they were placed in a puzzle box. When they made the required response, they were released from the box. The next trial did not begin until Thorndike decided to put them back in.

The discrete-trial method was subsequently adopted by investigators who used mazes of various sorts to study instrumental conditioning. Mazes are most commonly used with laboratory rats and were introduced into the investigative artillery available to scientists by Willard Small, who built a maze in an effort to mimic the tunnel-like structures of the underground burrows in which rats live (Small, 1899, 1900).

A common type of maze is the **straight-alley runway** (see Figure 7.4). In a straight-alley runway, an animal is first placed in the start box. The start-box door is then lifted to allow the animal to go to the goal box at the other end of the runway. Upon reaching the goal box, the animal is given a small piece of food and then removed until it is time to run the next trial. The

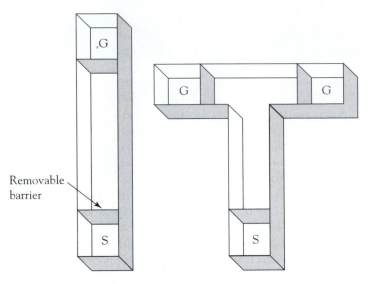

FIGURE 7.4.   Top view of a runway and a T-maze.
S is the start box; G is the goal box.

speed of running from the start box to the goal box is measured on each trial. Learning results in increased speeds of running.

Another common apparatus is the **T-maze.** This also has a start box. After the subject is released from the start box, it is permitted to go to a choice point, where it has to select one or the other arm of the T to enter next. The T-maze, therefore, is particularly suited for measuring choice behavior.

The discrete-trial method requires numerous manipulations. The experimenter has to pick up the rat, place it in the start box, wait for it to reach the goal box, remove it from the goal box, and then put it in a holding area for the intertrial interval. Another distinctive characteristic of the discrete-trial method is that how long the participant has to wait between trials is determined by the experimenter.

The free-operant method.   The major alternative to the discrete-trial method for the study of instrumental behavior is the **free-operant method.** The free-operant method was developed by B. F. Skinner (Skinner, 1938). Skinner made numerous contributions, both methodological and conceptual, to the study of behavior, and these two types of contributions were often interrelated. The free-operant method is a case in point.

Skinner's development of the free-operant method began with an interest in designing an automated maze for rats—a maze in which the rats would automatically return to the start box after each trial. Such an apparatus would have the obvious advantage that the rat would be handled only at the start and the end of a training session, freeing up the experimenter to do other things in the interim. An automated maze would also permit the rat rather than the experimenter to decide when to start its next trial. This would permit the investigation of not only how rapidly the rat completed an instrumental response but how frequently it engaged in the instrumental behavior. Thus, an automated maze promised to provide new information that could not be obtained with the discrete-trial method.

Skinner tried several different approaches to automating the discrete-trial maze procedure. Each approach incorporated some improvements on the previous design, but as the work progressed the apparatus became less and less like a maze (Skinner, 1956). The end result was what has come to be known as the Skinner box.

We have already encountered the Skinner box, while discussing the definition of an operant response. For rats, the Skinner box is a small, rectangular chamber. One wall has a lever that the rat can press over and over again; there is a food cup nearby, into which small pieces of food can be dropped by a pellet dispenser. Each lever-press response is electronically detected by the closure of a microswitch, and the apparatus can be programmed so that a piece of food is delivered each time the rat presses the lever.

In the Skinner box, the response of interest is defined in terms of the closure of a microswitch. The computer interface ignores whether the rat presses the lever with one paw or the other or with its tail. Another important feature of the Skinner box is that the operant response can occur at any time. The interval between successive responses is determined by the participant rather than by the experimenter. Because the operant response can be made at any time, the method is called the "free-operant" method.

The primary conceptual advantage of the free-operant method is that it allows the participant to repeatedly initiate the instrumental response. Skinner focused on this aspect of behavior. How often a rat initiates the operant response can be quantified in terms of the frequency of the response in a given period of time, or the **rate of responding.** Rate of responding has come to serve as the primary measure of behavior in experiments using the free-operant method.

The Establishment of an Instrumental or Operant Response

People often think about instrumental or operant conditioning as a technique for training new responses. In what sense are the responses new? Does instrumental conditioning always establish entirely new responses, does it combine familiar responses in new ways, or does it establish a familiar response in a new situation?

LEARNING WHERE AND WHAT TO RUN FOR

Consider, for example, a hungry rat learning to run from one end of a runway to the other for a piece of food. An experimentally naive rat is slow to run the length of the runway at first. This is not, however, because it enters the experiment without the motor skill of running. Rats do not have to be taught to run, just as children don't have to be taught to walk. What they have to be taught is *where* to run and what to run *for*. In the straight-alley runway, the instrumental conditioning procedure provides the stimulus control and the motivation for the running response. It does not establish the running response in the participant's repertoire.

CONSTRUCTING NEW RESPONSES FROM FAMILIAR COMPONENTS

The instrumental response of pressing a lever is a bit different from running. An experimentally naive rat has probably never encountered a lever before and never performed a lever-press response. Unlike running, lever pressing has to be learned in the experimental situation. But does it have to be learned from scratch? Hardly.

An untrained rat is not as naive about pressing a lever as one might think. Lever pressing consists of a number of components: balancing on the hind legs, raising one or both front paws, extending a paw forward over the lever, and then bringing the paw down with sufficient force to press the lever and activate the microswitch. Rats perform responses much like these at various times while exploring their cages, exploring each other, or handling pellets of food. What they have to learn in the operant conditioning situation is how to put the various response components together to create a lever-press response.

Pressing a lever is a new response only in the sense that it involves a new combination of response components that already exist in the participant's repertoire. In this case, instrumental conditioning involves the construction or synthesis of a new behavioral unit from preexisting response components (Schwartz, 1981).

SHAPING NEW RESPONSES

Can instrumental conditioning also be used to condition entirely new responses, responses that an individual would never perform without instrumental conditioning? Most certainly. Instrumental conditioning is used to shape remarkable feats of performance in sports, ice skating, ballet, and musical performance—feats that almost defy nature. A police dog can be trained to climb a 12-foot vertical barrier, a sprinter can learn to run a mile in 4 minutes, and a golf pro can learn to drive a ball 200 yards in one stroke. Such responses are remarkable because they are unlike anything the participants are likely to do without special training.

In an instrumental conditioning procedure, the individual has to perform the required response before the outcome or reinforcer is delivered. Given this restriction, how can instrumental procedures be used to condition responses that never occur on their own? The learning of entirely new responses is possible because of the variability of behavior. Variability is perhaps the most obvious feature of behavior. Organisms rarely do the same thing twice in exactly the same fashion. Response variability is usually considered a curse, because it makes predicting and controlling behavior difficult. However, for learning new responses, variability is a blessing.

The delivery of a reinforcer does not result in repetition of the same exact response that produced the reinforcer the first time. If a rat, for example, is reinforced for pressing a lever with a force of 2 grams, it will not press the lever with exactly that force thereafter. Sometimes it will respond with less pressure, other times with more.

The first panel in Figure 7.5 shows what the distribution of responses might look like in an experiment where lever pressing is reinforced only if a force greater than 2 grams is used. Notice that many, but not all, of the responses exceed the 2-gram criterion. A few of the responses exceed a force of 3 grams, but none exceeds 4 grams.

Because the variability in behavior includes responses as forceful as 3 grams, we can change the response criterion so that reinforcement is now only provided if the rat presses the lever with a force exceeding 3 grams. After several sessions with this new force requirement, the distribution of lever presses will look something like what is shown in the second panel of Figure 7.5.

Responding remains variable after the shift in the response requirement. Increasing the force requirement shifts the force distribution to the right so that the majority of the lever presses now exceed 3 grams. One consequence of this shift is that the rat occasionally presses the lever with a force of 4 grams or more. Notice that these responses are entirely new. They did not occur originally.

Since we now have responses exceeding 4 grams, we can increase the response requirement again. We can change the procedure so that now the reinforcer is given only for responses that have a force of at least 4 grams. This will result in a further shift of the force distribution to yet higher values, as shown in the third panel of Figure 7.5. Now most of the responses exceed 4 grams, and sometimes the rat presses the lever with a force greater than 5 grams. Responses with such force are very different from what the rat started out doing.

The procedure I just described is called **shaping.** Shaping is used when the goal is to condition instrumental responses that are not in the participant's existing behavioral repertoire. New behavior is shaped by imposing a series of response criteria. The response criteria gradually take the participant from its starting behavioral repertoire to the desired target response (e.g., Deich, Allan, & Zeigler, 1988; Galbicka, 1988; Pear & Legris, 1987).

In setting up a shaping procedure, the desired final performance must be clearly defined. This sets the goal or end point of the shaping procedure. Next, the existing behavioral repertoire of the participant has to be documented so that the starting point is well understood. Finally, a sequence of training steps have to be designed to take the participant from its starting

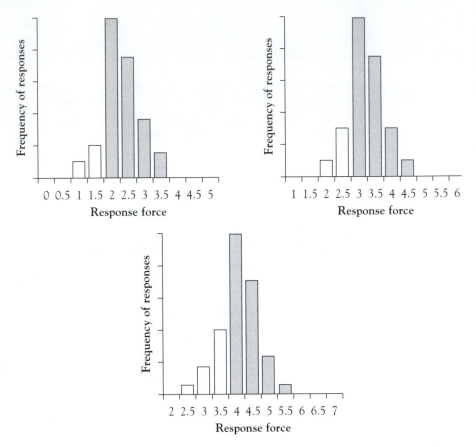

FIGURE 7.5. **Frequency of lever-press responses involving various degrees of force.**
In the first panel, only responses greater than 2 grams in force resulted in delivery of the reinforcer. In the second panel, only responses greater than 3 grams in force were reinforced. In the third panel, only responses greater than 4 grams in force were reinforced. (Data are hypothetical.)

behavior to the final target response. The sequence of training steps involves successive approximations to the final response. Therefore, shaping is typically defined as "the reinforcement of successive approximations."

Shaping is useful not only in training entirely new responses but also in training new combinations of existing response components. Riding a bicycle, for example, involves three major response components: steering, pedaling, and maintaining balance. Children learning to ride usually start by learning to pedal. Pedaling is a new response. It is unlike anything a child is likely to have done before getting on a bicycle. To enable the child to learn to pedal without having to balance, parents start by giving a child a tricycle or a bicycle with training wheels. While learning to pedal, the child is not likely to pay much attention to steering and will need help to make sure she does not drive into a bush or off the sidewalk.

Once the child has learned to pedal, she is ready to combine this with steering. Only after the child has learned to combine pedaling with steering is she ready to add the balance component. Adding the balance component is the hardest part of the task. This is why parents often wait until a child is proficient in riding a bicycle with training wheels before letting her ride without them.

The Importance of Immediate Reinforcement

Instrumental conditioning is basically a response selection process. The response (or unique combination of response components) that results in the delivery of the reinforcer is selected from the diversity of actions the organism performs in the situation. It is critical to this response selection process that the reinforcer be delivered immediately after the desired or target response. If the reinforcer is delayed, other activities are bound to occur between the target response and the reinforcer, and one of these other activities may be reinforced instead of the target response (see Figure 7.6).

Delivering a primary reinforcer immediately after the target response is not always practical. For example, the opportunity to go to a playground serves as an effective reinforcer for children in elementary school. However, it would be disruptive to allow a child to go outside each time he finished a math problem. A more practical approach is to give the child a coin or token for each problem completed, and then allow these tokens to be exchanged for the opportunity to go to the playground. With such a procedure, the primary reinforcer (access to the playground) is delayed after the instrumental response. But, the instrumental response is immediately followed by a stimulus (the token) that is associated with the primary reinforcer.

$$R_1 \; R_2 \; R_3 \; R_4 \; R_X \; O \qquad\qquad R_1 \; R_2 \; R_X \; R_3 \; R_4 \; O$$

Immediate reinforcement   Delayed reinforcement

FIGURE 7.6. **Diagram of immediate and delayed reinforcement of the target response R_X.**
R_1, R_2, R_3, etc. represent different activities of the organism. O represents delivery of the reinforcer. Notice that when reinforcement is delayed after R_X, other responses occur closer to the reinforcer.

A stimulus that is associated with a primary reinforcer is called a **conditioned** (or **secondary**) **reinforcer.** The delivery of a conditioned reinforcer immediately after the instrumental response overcomes the ineffectiveness of delayed reinforcement in instrumental conditioning (e.g., Winter & Perkins, 1982).

The ineffectiveness of delayed reinforcement can also be overcome by presenting a **marking stimulus** immediately after the target response. A marking stimulus is not a conditioned reinforcer and does not provide information about a future opportunity to obtain primary reinforcement. Rather, it is a brief visual or auditory cue that distinguishes the target response from the other activities the participant is likely to perform during a delay interval. In this way the marking stimulus makes the instrumental response more memorable and helps overcome the deleterious effect of the reinforcer delay (Lieberman, McIntosh, & Thomas, 1979; Thomas & Lieberman, 1990).

Event Relations in Instrumental Conditioning

Methodologically, the most obvious events in instrumental conditioning are the instrumental response and the reinforcer. The response may be represented by R and the reinforcer or response outcome by O. The relation between the response and the reinforcer may be characterized as the **R-O association.** Beginning with the earliest theoretical efforts, however, investigators were aware that there is more to an instrumental conditioning situation than merely the response and its reinforcing outcome.

Thorndike pointed out that organisms experience a unique set of stimuli when performing an instrumental response. In Thorndike's experiments these stimuli were provided by the puzzle box in which the participants were placed at the start of a training trial and the particular latch they had to manipulate in order to get out.

We don't know whether Thorndike's animals focused on the visual features of the puzzle box or the tactile cues of the latch they had to manipulate. But that has no bearing on the theoretical analysis. Regardless of which particular stimuli the participant paid attention to, once it was assigned to a puzzle box it experienced a unique set of cues whenever it performed the required escape response. The stimuli an organism experiences whenever it performs a required instrumental response may be represented by S.

These considerations suggest that an instrumental conditioning situation is made up of not only the response R and the reinforcer outcome O but also the set of stimuli S in the presence of which the instrumental response occurs. The three components—S, R, and O—allow for the establishment of several event relations in addition to the R-O relation. None of these is solely responsible for instrumental behavior, but each contributes in some way.

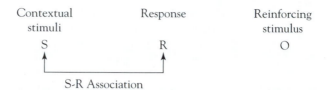

FIGURE 7.7.   **Diagram of the S-R association in instrumental conditioning.**

THE S-R ASSOCIATION: THORNDIKE'S LAW OF EFFECT

Thorndike proposed that during the course of instrumental conditioning an association comes to be established between the response R and the environmental stimuli S (see Figure 7.7). In fact, Thorndike believed that this **S-R association** was the only thing learned in instrumental conditioning. He summarized his thinking in the **Law of Effect.** The Law of Effect states that instrumental learning involves the formation of an association between the instrumental response R and the stimuli S in the presence of which the response is performed. The reinforcer delivered after the response serves to strengthen or "stamp in" the S-R association, but the reinforcer is not one of the elements of that association.

According to the Law of Effect, instrumental learning does not involve learning to associate the response with the reinforcer. It does not involve the establishment of an R-O association or learning about the reinforcer. Rather, instrumental conditioning results only in the establishment of an S-R association. The reinforcer outcome O is significant merely as a catalyst for the learning of the S-R association.

It may seem counterintuitive to assume that organisms do not learn about the reinforcer in instrumental conditioning. However, the Law of Effect was consistent with other theorizing early in the twentieth century. The Law of Effect is an adaptation of the concept of elicited behavior to instrumental learning. Elicited behavior is a response to a particular stimulus. In an analogous fashion, the Law of Effect considers the instrumental response R to be a response to the stimulus context S. The Law of Effect thus provided a fairly straightforward causal account of instrumental behavior. However, research conducted toward the end of the twentieth century has shown that this account is grossly incomplete.

S-O AND S(R-O) RELATIONS

Another event relation in instrumental conditioning that has received considerable theoretical and empirical attention is the relation between the antecedent stimuli S and the reinforcer outcome O (see Figure 7.8). Because

FIGURE 7.8.   Diagram of the S-O association in instrumental conditioning.

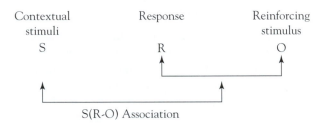

FIGURE 7.9.   Diagram of the S(R-O) association in instrumental conditioning.

the instrumental response R results in delivery of the reinforcer O in the presence of the contextual cues S, S is paired with O. This is assumed to result in the learning of the **S-O association** (Hull, 1930, 1931). The S-O association is much like a Pavlovian CS-US association and has some of the same behavioral consequences. For example, the establishment of the S-O association presumably results in Pavlovian conditioned responses being elicited by S.

The three event relations we have considered thus far—R-O, S-R, and S-O—are binary or direct associations between pairs of elements of the instrumental conditioning situation. Another way in which S, R, and O may become related in instrumental conditioning is through a higher-order relation that may be referred to as the **S(R-O) association** (see Figure 7.9). One of the first theoreticians to recognize the S(R-O) relation was B. F. Skinner (1938).

Skinner emphasized that in instrumental conditioning the presentation of reinforcer O is contingent on the prior occurrence of the response R, not on the prior occurrence of S. The R-O contingency, however, is in effect only in the presence of S. Therefore, he suggested, a higher-order relation becomes established in which S signals the existence of the R-O contingency or sets the occasion for the R-O association. Skinner referred to this as a "three-term contingency." The three-term contingency may be represented as S(R-O). The S(R-O) relation in instrumental conditioning is analogous to the higher-order B(A-US) relation in Pavlovian conditioning, which was described in Chapter 5.

Experimental investigations of the associative structure of instrumental conditioning have provided evidence for all four of the types of association I have described: R-O, S-R, S-O, and S(R-O). Thorndike was the first to identify and emphasize the importance of the S-R association in instrumental conditioning. This association and the mechanisms of the Law of Effect were subsequently employed in more elaborate neobehaviorist theories (e.g., Amsel, 1958; Hull, 1930, 1931; Spence, 1956). These theories, as well as the subsequent so-called two-process theories of learning (see Rescorla & Solomon, 1967), also emphasized the importance of the S-O association in instrumental conditioning. More recently, investigators have turned their attention to the importance of the R-O and S(R-O) relations as critical components of instrumental learning (e.g., Colwill & Rescorla, 1986, 1990).

IMPLICATIONS FOR NEURAL MECHANISMS

The complexity of the associative structure of instrumental learning that has been documented at the behavioral level presents serious challenges for scientists trying to discover the neural mechanisms or neural circuitry underlying instrumental behavior. This is unlike the situation for Pavlovian conditioning. As we saw in Chapters 4 and 5, there are both simple and more complex forms of Pavlovian conditioning. Simple forms of Pavlovian excitatory conditioning are mediated by just an S-S association. More complex forms involve higher-order relations, B(A-US). Unfortunately, such simple and complex associations cannot be isolated in instrumental conditioning.

Instrumental learning involves binary associations (S-R, S-O, and R-O), as well as the higher-order S(R-O) relation. However, one cannot design an instrumental conditioning procedure that involves one of these factors to the exclusion of the others. For example, one cannot design an instrumental procedure that permits S-O associations without allowing R-O associations, because the delivery of O contingent on R is an inherent feature of instrumental conditioning. Therefore, investigators of the neural mechanisms of instrumental conditioning cannot isolate one associative component to the exclusion of others, which makes their job very difficult. Studies of the neural mechanisms of instrumental conditioning must consider multiple associative mechanisms (and their interactions) all at the same time.

IMPLICATIONS FOR CONSTRAINTS ON INSTRUMENTAL CONDITIONING

Understanding the associative structure of instrumental conditioning also provides insight into some enduring puzzles in instrumental learning. Thorndike, for example, tested animals in a variety of different puzzle boxes (Thorndike, 1911). His young cats had to do different things in different boxes. In some boxes, the cats had to yawn or scratch themselves to be let out. Learning proceeded slowly in these boxes. Even after extensive training, the cats did not make vigorous and bona fide yawning responses; rather, they performed rapid abortive yawns. Thorndike obtained similar results with the scratch response: the cats made rapid, halfhearted attempts to scratch themselves. These two examples illustrate the general finding that self-care and grooming responses are difficult to condition with food reinforcement.

Another category of instrumental behavior that is difficult to condition with food reinforcement is the release of a coin or token. Two of Skinner's graduate students, Keller and Marion Breland, became fascinated with the possibilities of animal training and set up a business that supplied trained animals for viewing in amusement parks, department store windows, and zoos. As a part of their business, the Brelands trained numerous species of animals to do various entertaining things (Breland & Breland, 1961).

For one display, they tried to get a pig to pick up a coin and drop it into a piggy bank to obtain food. Although the pig did what it was supposed to a few times, as training progressed it became reluctant to release the coin and rooted it along the ground instead. This rooting behavior came to predominate, and the project had to be abandoned. The Brelands referred to this as "misbehavior" because it was contrary to the outcome that should have occurred based on instrumental conditioning principles. Others subsequently referred to examples of such behavior as "biological constraints on learning." Several different factors are probably responsible for the **constraints on learning** that have been encountered in conditioning grooming and coin-release behavior (Shettleworth, 1975). One of the most important factors seems to be the development of S-O associations in instrumental conditioning (Timberlake, Wahl, & King, 1982). In the coin-release task, the coin becomes associated with the food reinforcer and serves as stimulus S in the S-O association. In instrumental reinforcement of grooming, stimulus S is provided by the contextual cues of the conditioning situation.

Because S-O associations are much like Pavlovian associations between a CS and US, Pavlovian conditioned responses related to the reinforcer come to be elicited by S. Pavlovian responses conditioned with food consist of approaching and manipulating the conditioned stimulus. These food-anticipatory responses are incompatible with self-care and grooming. They are also incompatible with releasing and thereby withdrawing from a coin that has come to signal the availability of food.

Analyses of the associative structures of instrumental conditioning indicate that Pavlovian associations develop during the course of instrumental conditioning. These Pavlovian associations can yield conditioned responses that are incompatible with the required instrumental response and prevent increases in certain instrumental responses, such as grooming and coin-release responses.

Summary

In instrumental conditioning, the delivery of a biologically significant event or reinforcer depends on the prior occurrence of a specified instrumental or operant response. The instrumental behavior may be a preexisting response that the organism has to perform in a new situation, a set of familiar response components that the organism has to put together in an unfamiliar combination, or an activity that is entirely novel to the organism. Successful learning in each case requires delivering the reinforcer immediately after the instrumental response or providing a conditioned reinforcer or marking stimulus immediately after the response.

Instrumental conditioning was first examined by Thorndike, who developed discrete-trial procedures that enabled him to measure how the latency of an instrumental response changes with training. Skinner's efforts to automate a discrete-trial procedure led him to develop the free-operant method, which allows measurement of the probability or rate of an instrumental behavior. Both discrete-trial and free-operant procedures consist of three components: contextual stimuli S, the instrumental response R, and the reinforcer outcome O. Reinforcement of R in the presence of S allows for the establishment of four different types of associations: S-R, S-O, R-O, and S(R-O) associations. Because these associations cannot be isolated from one another, investigating the neurophysiology of instrumental learning is much more difficult than studying the neurophysiology of Pavlovian conditioning. Moreover, the S-O association can create serious response constraints on instrumental conditioning.

Practice Questions

1. What are the differences between the discrete-trial and free-operant methods?

2. Why is response variability critical to the shaping of new responses?

3. Why is a delay in reinforcement detrimental to instrumental conditioning? How can a delay in reinforcement be "bridged"?

4. What types of associations may be formed in instrumental conditioning? Which of these was the basis for Thorndike's Law of Effect?

5. What are the implications of the associative structure of instrumental conditioning for the neurobiology of instrumental learning?

Suggested Readings

Colwill, R. M. (1994). Associative representations of instrumental contingencies. In D. L. Medin (Ed.), *The psychology of learning and motivation* (Vol. 31, pp. 1–72). San Diego: Academic Press.

Colwill, R. M., & Rescorla, R. A. (1986). Associative structures in instrumental learning. In G. H. Bower (Ed.), *The psychology of learning and motivation* (Vol. 20, pp. 55–104). San Diego: Academic Press.

Rescorla, R. A., & Solomon, R. L. (1967). Two-process learning theory: Relationships between Pavlovian conditioning and instrumental learning. *Psychological Review, 74,* 151–182.

Timberlake, W., & Lucas, G. A. (1989). Behavior systems and learning: From misbehavior to general principles. In S. B. Klein & R. R. Mowrer (Eds.), *Contemporary learning theories: Instrumental conditioning and the impact of biological constraints on learning* (pp. 237–275). Hillsdale, NJ: Erlbaum.

Technical Terms

Conditioned reinforcer
Constraints on learning
Discrete-trial method
Free-operant method
Instrumental behavior
Instrumental conditioning
Law of Effect
Marking stimulus
Operant behavior
Operant conditioning
Puzzle box

R-O association
Rate of responding
Reinforcer
S-O association
S-R association
S(R-O) association
Secondary reinforcer
Shaping
Straight-alley runway
T-maze

CHAPTER EIGHT

Schedules of Reinforcement

DID YOU KNOW THAT:

- Schedules of reinforcement determine rates and patterns of responding.
- Ratio schedules produce higher rates of responding than interval schedules.
- Interval schedules do not provide the reinforcer automatically after the passage of a particular time interval.
- Schedule effects are related to the feedback function that characterizes each schedule of reinforcement.
- Training of a response chain does not have to begin with the last component of the chain.
- Reinforcement can be simultaneously available for two or more response alternatives.
- The Matching Law describes choice behavior.
- According to the Matching Law, relative rates of responding equal relative rates of reinforcement.

Examples of instrumental conditioning were described in Chapter 7 with the implication that the reinforcing outcome is delivered each time the required instrumental response occurs. Situations in nature in which there is a direct causal link between an instrumental response and a reinforcer come close to this ideal. Nearly every time you turn on the faucet, you get running water; nearly every time you pick up the phone, you hear a dial tone; and most of the time you buy an attractive piece of pastry, you end up with something good to eat. However, even in these cases, the relation between responding and the reinforcer is not perfect. The water main to your house may break, the phone may malfunction, and the pastry may be stale. In many instrumental conditioning situations, not every occurrence of the instrumental response is successful in producing the reinforcer.

Whether a particular occurrence of the instrumental response results in the reinforcer can depend on a variety of factors. Sometimes, the response has to be repeated a number of times before the reinforcer is delivered. In other situations, the response is only reinforced after a certain amount of time has passed. In yet other cases, both response repetition and the passage of time are critical. The rule that specifies which occurrence of the instrumental response is reinforced is called a **schedule of reinforcement.**

Schedules of reinforcement have been of great interest because they determine many aspects of instrumental behavior. The rate and pattern of responding, as well as persistence in extinction, are all determined by the schedule of reinforcement. Seemingly trivial changes in a reinforcement schedule can produce profound changes in how frequently an organism responds and when it engages in one activity rather than another. Schedules of reinforcement also determine the persistence of instrumental behavior in extinction, when reinforcement is no longer available.

The Cumulative Record

The rate and pattern of responding produced by various schedules of reinforcement are typically investigated by means of free-operant procedures. Computers are programmed to record occurrences of the operant response (e.g., lever pressing in rats) as well as to determine which response is reinforced. Training sessions last about an hour each day, and typically numerous sessions are provided. After extensive experience with a particular schedule of reinforcement, the rate and pattern of responding stabilizes. The results are conveniently represented in terms of a **cumulative record.**

A cumulative record is a special kind of graph in which the horizontal axis represents the passage of time and the vertical axis represents the total or cumulative number of responses that have occurred up to a particular point in time (see Figure 8.1). If the participant does not respond for a while, its total or cumulative number of responses stays the same, and the resultant

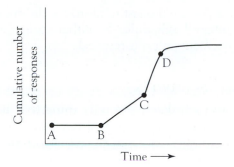

FIGURE 8.1   **An example of a cumulative record used to represent patterns of responding across time in free-operant studies of schedules of reinforcement.**
The section from Point A to Point B represents no responding. The section from Point B to Point C represents a low rate of responding. The section from Point C to Point D represents a high response rate. After Point D, the rate of responding declined to zero.

curve on the cumulative record is a flat horizontal line, as between Points A and B in Figure 8.1. Each response that is made is added to the previous total. Thus, each time the participant responds, the cumulative record goes up a bit. Because responses cannot be taken away, the cumulative record never goes down.

The slope of the cumulative record represents the participant's rate of responding. Slope is calculated by dividing the vertical displacement between two points on a graph by the horizontal displacement between those two points. Vertical displacement on a cumulative record represents a particular number of responses, and horizontal displacement represents time. Thus, the slope of a cumulative record represents responses per unit of time, or the rate of responding. Low rates of responding produce a shallow slope on the cumulative record (e.g., from Point B to Point C in Figure 8.1). Higher response rates result in a steeper slope (e.g., from Point C to Point D in Figure 8.1).

Simple Schedules of Reinforcement

For simple schedules of reinforcement, which occurrence of the response is reinforced depends either on the number of responses that have been performed since the last reinforcer or on how much time has passed since the last reinforcer. If the frequency of response is the critical factor determining reinforcement, the procedure is called a **ratio schedule.** If the timing of the response since the last reinforcer is the critical factor, the procedure is called an **interval schedule.** In either case, the participant cannot obtain reinforcement unless it responds.

RATIO SCHEDULES

In ratio schedules, the only thing that determines whether a response is reinforced is the number of responses the participant has performed since the last reinforcer. How much time it took to make those responses does not matter.

Fixed-Ratio Schedule of Reinforcement.   There are two major types of ratio schedules, fixed and variable. In a **fixed-ratio schedule,** the participant must perform a fixed number of responses for each delivery of the reinforcer. For example, each work sheet in a third-grade math class may have four problems on it, and students may receive a star for each work sheet they complete. This would be a fixed-ratio-4 schedule of reinforcement, abbreviated as FR 4.

Fixed-ratio schedules occur in situations where there is always a fixed amount of effort required to complete a job or obtain the reinforcer. Checking attendance in a class by reading the roll requires reading the same number of names each time. Completing a newspaper delivery route requires going to the same number of houses each time. Walking up a flight of stairs requires going up the same number of stairs each time. All of these are examples of fixed-ratio schedules.

Figure 8.2 illustrates the stable pattern of responding that results from ratio schedules of reinforcement. The hatch marks in the records represent the delivery of the reinforcer. The typical result of reinforcing behavior on a fixed-ratio schedule is shown in the left side of the figure. Two features of this pattern are noteworthy. First, notice that after each hatch mark or reinforcer, the response rate is zero. The participant stops responding. This is called the **postreinforcement pause.** After the postreinforcement pause, a steady and high rate of responding occurs until the next delivery of the reinforcer. This is called the **ratio run.**

As illustrated in Figure 8.2, fixed-ratio schedules produce a break-run pattern of responding. Either the participant does not respond at all (in the postreinforcement pause) or it responds at a steady and high rate (in the ratio run). The duration of the postreinforcement pause is determined by the ratio requirement. Higher ratio requirements result in longer durations for the postreinforcement pause (Felton & Lyon, 1966).

Variable-Ratio Schedule of Reinforcement.   A **variable-ratio schedule** is similar to a fixed-ratio schedule in that the only factor determining which repetition of the instrumental response is reinforced is the number of responses that have been performed. The difference between fixed- and

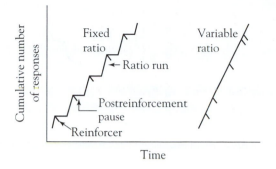

FIGURE 8.2 **Typical results of training on a fixed-ratio and variable-ratio schedule of reinforcement.**
The data were obtained with pigeons pecking a response key on an FR 120 and VR 360 schedule of food reinforcement. The hatch marks indicate when the reinforcer was delivered. Adapted from Ferster & Skinner (1957).

---

variable-ratio schedules is that in a variable-ratio schedule, the number of responses required varies from one reinforcer delivery to the next.

When putting in golf, for example, reinforcement is provided by the ball going into the cup. On occasion, you may get the ball into the cup on the first try. More often, you will have to hit the ball several times before you succeed. Whether or not the ball goes into the cup depends only on your hitting the ball with the putter. How long you take between swings is irrelevant. This, then, is a ratio schedule. But the number of putting responses varies from one putting green to another, making it a variable-ratio schedule.

A variable-ratio schedule is abbreviated as VR. If on average you need to hit the ball three times to get it into the cup, you would be on a VR 3 schedule of reinforcement. The typical result of a variable-ratio schedule is illustrated in the right panel of Figure 8.2. Unlike fixed-ratio schedules, variable-ratio schedules produce a steady and high rate of responding, with no predictable pauses.

INTERVAL SCHEDULES

In ratio schedules, the passage of time is irrelevant; in interval schedules, by contrast, time is a critical factor. Specifically, in interval schedules, whether a response is reinforced depends on when the response occurs after the start of the interval cycle. As with ratio schedules, there are two prominent types of interval schedules, fixed and variable.

Fixed-Interval Schedule of Reinforcement. In a **fixed-interval schedule,** a fixed amount of time has to pass before a response can be reinforced. Fixed-interval schedules occur in situations in which it takes a certain amount of

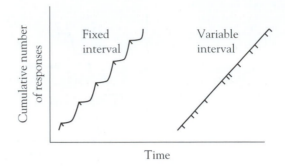

FIGURE 8.3   Typical results of training on a fixed-interval and variable-interval schedule of reinforcement.
The data were obtained with pigeons pecking a response key on an FI 4-min and VI 2-min schedule of food reinforcement. The hatch marks indicate when the reinforcer was delivered. Adapted from Ferster & Skinner (1957).

time for the reinforcer to be prepared or set up. Consider, for example, making a gelatin dessert (Jello, for example). After the ingredients are mixed, the Jello has to be cooled in the refrigerator for a certain amount of time (let's say an hour) before it is ready to eat. In this example, the reinforced response is taking the Jello out of the refrigerator to eat. If you take the Jello out too early, it will be watery and your response will not be reinforced. Attempts to eat the Jello before the hour is up will not be reinforced. Another important feature of this example (and of interval schedules generally) is that once the reinforcer is ready, it remains available until the individual responds to obtain it. When the Jello is done, you don't have to eat it right away. It will be there for you even if you wait to eat it the next day.

In a fixed-interval schedule of reinforcement, a fixed amount of time has to pass before the reinforcer becomes available. However, the reinforcer is not provided automatically at the end of the fixed interval. To obtain the reinforcer, the specified instrumental response has to be made. Early responses have no consequence. They do not produce the reinforcer early, nor do they result in a penalty. Finally, the reinforcer can be obtained at any time after it has been set up. In a simple interval schedule, the participant does not have to respond within a set period once the reinforcer has become available.

Fixed-interval schedules are abbreviated FI, followed by a number indicating the duration of the fixed interval during which responding is not reinforced. Figure 8.3 shows data obtained from a pigeon pecking a response key on a free-operant FI 4-min schedule of food reinforcement. On this schedule, delivery of the reinforcer at the end of one fixed interval starts the next cycle. Four minutes after the start of the cycle, the reinforcer becomes available again and is delivered if the pigeon pecks the response key.

The pattern of responding on a fixed-interval schedule is similar to that which occurs on a fixed-ratio schedule. There is little or no responding at the beginning of the fixed interval. Because the interval begins just after delivery of the previous reinforcer, the lack of responding here is called a post-reinforcement pause. Responding increases as the end of the interval gets closer, with the participant responding at a high rate just as the fixed interval ends. The entire response pattern is called an FI scallop, because it resembles the ridges on the shell of a scallop.

Variable-Interval Schedule of Reinforcement.   **Variable-interval schedules** are similar to fixed-interval schedules except that the amount of time it takes to set up the reinforcer varies from trial to trial. The response of checking to see if a teacher has finished grading your paper is reinforced on a variable-interval schedule. It takes some time to grade a paper, but how long it takes varies from one occasion to the next. Checking to see if your paper has been graded is reinforced only after some time has passed since the start of the schedule cycle. Early responses (responses that occur before the paper has been graded) are not reinforced. In contrast, you can get your grade any time after the paper has been graded.

Variable-interval schedules are abbreviated VI, followed by a number indicating the average duration of the intervals during which responding is not reinforced. Figure 8.3 shows data obtained from a pigeon pecking a response key on a free-operant VI 2-min schedule of food reinforcement. On this schedule, the reinforcer became available on average 2 minutes after the start of each schedule cycle.

Responding on variable-interval schedules is similar to responding on VR schedules of reinforcement. In both cases, a steady rate of behavior occurs, with no predictable pauses or changes in rate. However, interval schedules tend to produce lower rates of responding than ratio schedules.

In simple interval schedules, once the reinforcer has become available it remains there until the organism responds and obtains the reinforcer. The cycle then starts over again. Picking up your letters from a mailbox, for example, is on a variable-interval schedule. Checking the mail before it is delivered doesn't speed up delivery of the mail; but once the letters have been placed in your mailbox, you don't have to pick them up right away. They will remain there even if you don't get them until the next day.

Simple interval schedules can be modified so that once the reinforcer has been set up, it remains available only for a limited period of time. This limited interval is formally called a *limited hold*. For example, it takes a certain amount of time to bake a pan of cookies. Once the required time has passed, however, if you don't take the cookies out of the oven, they will burn. This is an interval schedule with a limited hold. The reinforcer is "held" for a limited period of time after it becomes available, and the response must occur during this hold period to be reinforced. Adding a limited hold to an interval schedule increases the rate of responding, provided the hold is not so short that the participant frequently misses the reinforcer altogether.

Mechanisms of Schedule Performance

A key concept involved in analyses of the mechanisms of schedule effects is the feedback function that characterizes the schedule. Delivery of a reinforcer in an instrumental procedure can be viewed as feedback for the instrumental response. Schedules of reinforcement determine how this feedback is arranged. One way to describe the arrangement is to show how the rate of reinforcement obtained is related to the rate of responding. This relationship is the **feedback function.**

FEEDBACK FUNCTIONS FOR RATIO SCHEDULES

Feedback functions for ratio schedules are perhaps the easiest to understand. In a ratio schedule, how soon (and how often) the organism gets reinforced is determined only by how rapidly the required number of responses is performed. The faster the organism responds, the faster it obtains the reinforcer.

Figure 8.4 shows examples of feedback functions for several ratio schedules. On an FR 1 or continuous-reinforcement schedule, the participant is reinforced for each occurrence of the instrumental response. Therefore, the

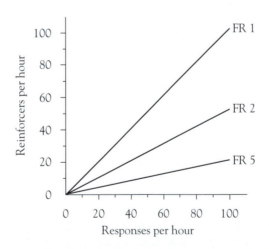

FIGURE 8.4   Feedback functions for ratio schedules of reinforcement. Notice that each feedback function is a straight line. Because of that, every increase in the response rate results in a corresponding increase in the rate of reinforcement.

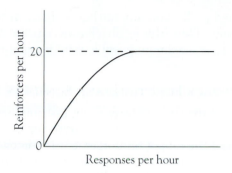

FIGURE 8.5   Feedback function for a variable-interval 3-min schedule of reinforcement.
Responding is assumed to be distributed randomly in time. Notice that no matter how rapidly the organism responds, its maximum reinforcement rate is 20 per hour.

rate of reinforcement is equal to the rate of responding. This results in a feedback function with a slope of 1.0.

If more than one response is required for reinforcement, the rate of reinforcement will be less than the rate of responding, and the slope of the feedback function will be less than 1.0. For example, on an FR 5 schedule of reinforcement, the participant receives one reinforcer for every fifth response. Under these circumstances, the rate of reinforcement is one-fifth the rate of responding, and the slope of the feedback function is 0.2.

Regardless of its slope, the feedback function for a ratio schedule is always a straight line. For this reason, an increase in the rate of responding always yields an increase in the rate of reinforcement. This is true for both fixed- and variable-ratio schedules.

FEEDBACK FUNCTIONS FOR INTERVAL SCHEDULES

Interval schedules have feedback functions that differ markedly from those of ratio schedules. Figure 8.5 shows the feedback function for a VI 3-min schedule of reinforcement. On such a schedule, the reinforcer becomes available on average 3 minutes after the last time it was delivered. Therefore, no matter how often or how rapidly the organism responds, the maximum number of reinforcers it can obtain is limited to 20 per hour.

As with ratio schedules, if the participant does not make any responses on an interval schedule, it will not obtain any reinforcers. Increases in the rate of responding above zero will increase its chances of getting whatever reinforcers become available. Up to a point, therefore, increased responding is accompanied by higher rates of reinforcement. However, once the participant responds often enough to get all of the 20 reinforcers that can be obtained each hour, any further increase in response rate will have no further benefit. Thus, the feedback function for an interval schedule becomes flat once the maximum possible reinforcement rate has been achieved.

FEEDBACK FUNCTIONS AND SCHEDULE PERFORMANCE

One of the striking facts about instrumental behavior is that ratio schedules produce considerably higher rates of responding than interval schedules, even if the rate of reinforcement is comparable in the two cases (McDowell & Wixted, 1988; Peele, Casey, & Silberberg, 1984; Reynolds, 1975). Why ratio schedules produce higher response rates than interval schedules is related to differences in their respective feedback functions. Because the feedback function for an interval schedule reaches a maximum with a particular rate of responding, increases in the response rate beyond that point provide no additional benefit. Thus, increases in response rate are not differentially reinforced beyond a particular point on interval schedules. In contrast, no such limit exists with ratio schedules. On ratio schedules, increases in response rate always result in higher rates of reinforcement. There is no limit to the differential reinforcement of higher rates of responding. Thus, ratio schedules may produce higher rates of responding, because such schedules differentially reinforce high response rates without limit.

While feedback functions have played an important role in efforts to explain schedule performance, they have some conceptual limitations. One serious problem is that feedback functions are sometimes difficult to characterize. This is particularly true for interval-based schedules. In interval schedules, reinforcement depends not only on the rate of responding but also on how the responses are distributed in time. The feedback function for a VI 3-min schedule presented in Figure 8.5 assumes that responses are distributed randomly in time. Other assumptions may alter the initial increasing portion of the feedback function. In spite of such complications, however, many investigators believe that the nature of schedule performance is ultimately determined by how schedules of reinforcement provide feedback for instrumental behavior.

Chained Schedules of Reinforcement

In simple schedules of reinforcement, only one operant response is involved. The participant is allowed to repeat that response in the same situation, with the schedule determining which occurrence of the response is reinforced. However, many instrumental-response situations involve a sequence of responses. Consider, for example, something as simple as getting into a car. One has to unlock the car door, open the door, put one leg into the car, bend over and ease into the seat, put the other leg into the car, and then close the car door. Such behavior sequences involve **chained schedules** of reinforcement. Chained schedules are of particular interest in rehabilitation training, special education, and working with developmentally challenged individuals.

A chained schedule involves a sequence of responses. Each response constitutes a component of the chained schedule, and each response component has its own associated stimulus. The primary reinforcer is not provided until the participant has completed all of the components of the chain and has done so in the correct order.

HETEROGENEOUS CHAINS

The most familiar type of chained schedule involves a sequence of different responses, each of which is performed in the presence of a different stimulus. Consider, for example, putting on a pullover sweater. The goal or reinforcer is warmth or perhaps the enjoyment of having the sweater on your body. To get to that point, you must first put each of your arms into the arms of the sweater. Then you must lift the sweater above your head and pull it over your head and neck. Finally, you must pull the bottom of the sweater down around your waist.

Notice that putting on the sweater involves a series of different responses. In addition, each response occurs in the presence of a different stimulus. You start with the sweater in front of you. This is the stimulus for putting your arms into the sweater. Having the sweater on your arms is the stimulus for pulling the sweater over your head. Having the sweater around your neck is the stimulus for pulling the bottom of it down around your waist. The reinforcer is the enjoyment of wearing the sweater, and it is available only at the end of the chain of responses. No satisfaction or reinforcement is experienced if the response sequence is interrupted partway—while the sweater is covering your head, for example.

Many activities can be analyzed as response chains: opening a can, doing your homework, or mowing the lawn. All of these activities involve a sequence of different responses, each response occurring in the presence of a different stimulus. If the response chain is made up of a sequence of different responses, it is called a **heterogeneous chain.**

HOMOGENEOUS CHAINS

Another type of chained schedule is called a **homogeneous chain.** In a homogeneous chain, the various components all involve the same response, but each component occurs in the presence of a different stimulus and involves a different schedule requirement. The example presented in Figure 8.6 involves two response components, FR 15 and FI 3-min, each with its associated stimulus, S_1 and S_2. During S_1 (which might be a red light), the participant has to respond 15 times to satisfy the FR 15 requirement. After the fifteenth response, S_2 (e.g., a green light) is presented, and the FI 3-min re-

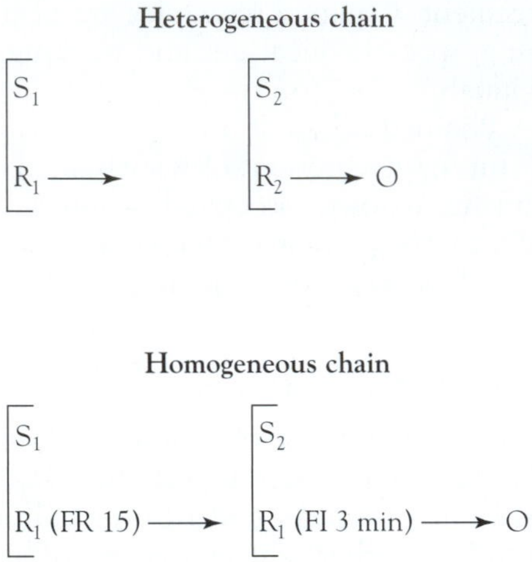

Heterogeneous chain

$$\begin{bmatrix} S_1 \\ \\ R_1 \longrightarrow \end{bmatrix} \qquad \begin{bmatrix} S_2 \\ \\ R_2 \longrightarrow O \end{bmatrix}$$

Homogeneous chain

$$\begin{bmatrix} S_1 \\ \\ R_1 \ (FR \ 15) \longrightarrow \end{bmatrix} \qquad \begin{bmatrix} S_2 \\ \\ R_1 \ (FI \ 3 \ min) \longrightarrow O \end{bmatrix}$$

FIGURE 8.6   Difference between heterogeneous and homogeneous chains.

In a heterogeneous chain, the organism has to perform a sequence of different responses (R_1 followed by R_2) to obtain the reinforcer outcome O. In a homogeneous chain, the organism has to perform the same response (R_1) on one reinforcement schedule (FR 15) followed by another (FI 3-min) to obtain the reinforcer O. In both cases, each response component has its own associated stimulus.

quirement comes into effect. On the FI 3-min schedule, the primary reinforcer is delivered for the first response that occurs after S_2 has been on for 3 minutes.

With a homogeneous chain, each component of the schedule produces a pattern of responding that is characteristic of the simple schedule in effect in that component. On an FR 15/FI 3-min chained schedule, the participants would pause and then respond at a steady and high rate in the FR 15 component. They would then pause and show a scalloped pattern of pecking in the FI 3-min component.

Homogeneous-chain schedules are in effect when a person has to perform the same response under different contingencies during different parts of a task. Consider, for example, using screws to install two hinges and a latch on the lid of a storage chest. Each hinge requires four screws and the latch two screws. The job is a homogeneous-chain schedule with three components, one for each of the hinges and the third for the latch. Completing each component requires putting in a certain number of screws. Thus, each component involves a fixed-ratio schedule in which putting in one screw constitutes a response. The sequence can be represented as $S_1(FR \ 4) \rightarrow S_2(FR \ 4) \rightarrow S_3(FR \rightarrow 2)$, where S_1 and S_2 represent the hinges and S_3 represents the latch.

TRAINING RESPONSE CHAINS

Techniques for the establishment of response chains are of great interest for teachers, especially if their students require extensive instruction. Some years ago, the conventional wisdom was that response chains are learned most readily with a backward-chaining procedure (Ferster & Perrott, 1968). In backward chaining, the last response or response component of the chain is taught first because it is closest to the delivery of the reinforcer. Earlier response components are then added once the participant has mastered the end of the chain.

In the case of putting on a sweater, for example, the last response is pulling the sweater around the waist. To train this response, the teacher would place the sweater around the child's head and shoulders and encourage her to pull the sweater down. Once the child masters the last response, the response just before the last one would be added. In our case, the sweater would be held above the child and she would be encouraged to pull it over her head and then over her body. Gradually, the earlier steps would be added until the child is able to perform all of the responses in the sequence.

The backward-chaining method is intended to take advantage of the primary reinforcer to condition the terminal response of the chain. Through such training, the stimulus that signals the terminal component is presumed to become a conditioned or secondary reinforcer. Once this stimulus has acquired conditioned-reinforcing properties, it can reinforce the response that occurs in the previous component, thereby enabling the previous stimulus to acquire conditioned-reinforcing properties. This method of reinforcement of responses and conditioning of secondary reinforcers gradually works its way back to the beginning of the response chain, until the entire chain has been learned.

Backward chaining is an effective approach to training response sequences. However, response chains can also be taught effectively by starting from the beginning and initially reinforcing the first response in the chain. Once the first response has been learned, the second one can be added, and then the third, fourth, and so on. Such a forward-chaining procedure can be as effective as backward chaining (see Sulzer-Azaroff & Mayer, 1991). However, when a forward-training sequence is used, each component of the chain must be reinforced with the primary reinforcer at first.

Concurrent Schedules

In each of the schedules of reinforcement considered so far, the organism can either perform the specified instrumental response or not do so. These procedures are usually considered not to involve a choice, but in fact all instrumental conditioning situations involve a choice. With simple and chained schedules, the choice is to perform the response specified by the reinforcement schedule or to do something else.

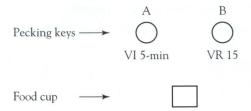

FIGURE 8.7   Diagram of a concurrent schedule of reinforcement.
Pecking the response key on the left is reinforced on a VI 5-min schedule of reinforcement. Pecking the response key on the right is reinforced on a VR 15 schedule of reinforcement.

Investigators have become convinced that a complete understanding of instrumental behavior requires an understanding of why organisms choose to engage in one response rather than another. Unfortunately, simple and chained schedules of reinforcement are not good for analyzing how choices are made. In simple and chained schedules, the alternative to the instrumental response, the "something else" the individual might do, is poorly specified and not measured. These shortcomings are remedied in concurrent schedules. Concurrent schedules of reinforcement provide clearly defined and measured alternative responses and thereby permit studying more directly how organisms elect to engage in one activity rather than another.

As you might suspect, whether you do one thing or another depends on the benefits you derive from each activity. In the terminology of conditioning, how often you engage in activity A as compared to activity B will depend on the schedule of reinforcement in effect for response A as compared to the schedule of reinforcement in effect for response B. On a playground, Joe could play with Peter, who likes to play vigorous physical games, or Joe could play with Matt, who prefers to play quietly in the sandbox. If Joe is not getting much enjoyment from playing with Peter, he can go play with Matt. Concurrent schedules are used to model this kind of a situation in the laboratory.

A concurrent schedule provides at least two response alternatives, A and B (see Figure 8.7). Responding on alternative A is reinforced on one schedule of reinforcement (e.g., VI 5-min), and responding on B is reinforced on a different schedule (e.g., VR 15). Both response alternatives (and their corresponding reinforcement schedules) are available at the same time, and the participant can switch from one activity to the other at any time. Because the two choices are available at the same time, the procedure is called a **concurrent schedule.**

Numerous factors determine how organisms distribute their behavior between two response alternatives. These include the nature of each type of response, the effort and time involved in switching from one response to the other, the attractiveness of the reinforcer provided for each response, and the schedule of reinforcement in effect for each response. Experiments have to be designed carefully so that the effects of each of these factors can be observed without being confounded with other features of the choice situation.

Investigators of operant conditioning have been most interested in how choice is determined by the schedule of reinforcement in effect for each response alternative. In an effort to focus on this variable, they have designed procedures that minimize the contribution of other factors. Studies of concurrent schedules are often carried out with pigeons. One wall of the experimental chamber has two response keys positioned at about the height of the bird's head. A feeder through which the bird can obtain grain is centered below the two keys. This arrangement has the advantage that the two responses require the same effort. Although pecks on the right and left keys are reinforced on different schedules, the reinforcer in each case is the same type of food. Another advantage is that the pigeon can easily switch from one response to the other because the left and right keys are located near each other.

If similar effort is required for the response alternatives, if the same reinforcer is used for both responses, and if switching from one side to the other is fairly easy, the distribution of responses between the two alternatives will depend only on the schedule of reinforcement in effect for each response. The results of numerous experiments fit the **matching law** (Herrnstein, 1970). According to the matching law, *the relative rate of responding on a response alternative is equal to the relative rate of reinforcement obtained with that response alternative*. For example, 70% of the responses will be made on the left side of a two-key chamber if 70% of all reinforcers are earned on the left side.

In a concurrent choice situation, organisms tend to match relative rates of responding to relative rates of reinforcement. Departures from matching occur if the response alternatives require different degrees of effort, if different reinforcers are used for each response alternative, or if switching from one response to the other is made more difficult (Davison & McCarthy, 1988; Williams, 1994).

Summary

Schedules of reinforcement are of interest because in many cases responding does not produce a reinforcer every time. A response may be reinforced after a fixed or variable number of responses have occurred (FR and VR schedules) or after a fixed or variable amount of time has passed since the last reinforcer (FI and VI schedules). Fixed but not variable schedules produce rapid responding just before delivery of the reinforcer and a pause just after reinforcement. In general, ratio schedules produce higher rates of responding than interval schedules; this difference is related to the contrasting feedback functions for ratio and interval schedules.

Reinforcement may be also scheduled for a chain of responses or a choice between two or more activities. Response chains may consist of a series of components that involve the same type of activity (homogeneous chains) or a series of different activities (heterogeneous chains). A concurrent schedule is said to be in effect if reinforcement is available for two (or more) different activities at the same time. Responding on concurrent schedules tends to follow the Matching Law.

Practice Questions

1. What does the slope of a cumulative record represent?

2. How are ratio schedules different from interval schedules of reinforcement?

3. What is a feedback function?

4. How do feedback functions differ for interval schedules and ratio schedules?

5. What is a chained schedule of reinforcement, and how can subjects be trained to respond on such a schedule?

6. What is a concurrent schedule, and what rule governs behavior on concurrent schedules?

7. What is the Matching Law?

Suggested Readings

Cole, M. R. (1999). Molar and molecular control in variable-interval and variable-ratio schedules. *Journal of the Experimental Analysis of Behavior, 71,* 319–328.

Ferster, C. B., & Skinner, B. F. (1957). *Schedules of reinforcement.* New York: Appleton-Century-Crofts.

Williams, B. A. (1994). Reinforcement and choice. In N. J. Mackintosh (Ed.), *Animal learning and cognition* (pp. 81–108). San Diego: Academic Press.

Technical Terms

Chained schedule	Feedback function
Concurrent schedule	Fixed-interval schedule
Cumulative record	Fixed-ratio schedule

Heterogeneous chain
Homogeneous chain
Interval schedule
Matching law
Postreinforcement pause

Ratio run
Ratio schedule
Schedule of reinforcement
Variable-interval schedule
Variable-ratio schedule

CHAPTER NINE

Theories of Reinforcement

DID YOU KNOW THAT:

- Reinforcers need not reduce a biological drive or need.
- Responses, as well as stimuli, can serve as reinforcers.
- According to contemporary perspectives, reinforcement does not "strengthen" the instrumental response.
- Instrumental conditioning procedures not only increase the rate of the instrumental response; they also decrease the rate of the reinforcer response.
- Instrumental conditioning procedures restrict how an organism distributes its behavior among its response alternatives.
- Reinforcement effects are a by-product of the new response choices an organism is forced to make when its activities are constrained by an instrumental conditioning procedure.
- The effect of an instrumental conditioning procedure depends on all of the activities of a participant and how these activities are organized. An important factor is the availability of substitutes for the reinforcer activity.

In Chapter 8, I discussed various types of instrumental conditioning procedures and their behavioral outcomes. There is no doubt that reinforcement procedures can produce dramatic changes in behavior. The issue I turn to next is how reinforcement causes these effects. That question is addressed by theories of reinforcement.

All good theories have to be consistent with the findings they are intended to explain. In addition, good theories should stimulate new research that serves to evaluate and increase the precision of the theory. Good theories also provide new insights and new ways of thinking about familiar phenomena.

The story of the development of theories of reinforcement is a marvelous example of creativity in science. The story is peppered with examples of small refinements in thinking that brought a particular theory in line with new data. The story also includes dramatic new departures and new ways of thinking about reinforcement. And there are interesting cases in which incremental changes in thinking culminated in major new perspectives on the problem.

A theory of reinforcement must answer two questions about instrumental conditioning. The first question concerns the identity of reinforcers: What makes something a reinforcer or how can we predict whether something will be an effective reinforcer? The second question concerns the mechanism of reinforcement effects: How does a reinforcer produce its effects, or how does a reinforcer produce an increase in the probability of the reinforced response?

Thorndike and the Law of Effect

The first systematic theory of reinforcement was provided by Thorndike, soon after his discovery of instrumental conditioning (Bower & Hilgard, 1981). According to Thorndike, a positive reinforcer is a stimulus that produces a "satisfying state of affairs." However, Thorndike did not go on to tell us why something was "satisfying." Therefore, his answer to our first question, "What makes something effective as a reinforcer?" was not very illuminating.

One can determine whether a stimulus, such as a pat on the head for a dog, is a "satisfier" by seeing whether the dog increases a response that results in getting petted. However, such evidence does not reveal why a pat on the head is a reinforcer. By calling reinforcers "satisfiers," Thorndike provided a label for reinforcers, but he did not give us an explanation for what makes something effective as a reinforcer.

Thorndike was somewhat more forthcoming on the second question, "How does a reinforcer produce an increase in the probability of the reinforced response?" His answer was provided in the **Law of Effect.** As I noted in Chapter 7, according to the Law of Effect a reinforcer establishes an association or connection between the instrumental response R and the stimuli

FIGURE 9.1   Diagram of Thorndike's Law of Effect.
The reinforcer O acts retroactively to strengthen the S-R association.

S in the presence of which the response is performed. The reinforcer produces an S-R association (see Figure 9.1).

The Law of Effect explains how reinforcement increases the future probability of the instrumental response. Because of the S-R association that is established by reinforcement, stimulus S comes to produce the instrumental response R, in much the same way that an elicited response is produced by its eliciting stimulus. The basic mechanism of the Law of Effect was considered a reasonable explanation for increased instrumental responding and accepted by major behavioral theorists during the next 50 years. However, in hindsight, widespread acceptance of the Law of Effect is rather remarkable.

Although the Law of Effect predicts increased instrumental responding in the training environment, it does so through a bit of magic rather than a well-established process. Thorndike did not say very much about how a reinforcer after an instrumental response can act retroactively to strengthen an association between the response and the stimuli in the presence of which the response was made. That part of the Law of Effect had to be taken on faith. Furthermore, despite the widespread acceptance of the Law of Effect during the next 50 years, no one has filled the gap left by Thorndike. The mechanism whereby a reinforcer acts backward in time to strengthen an S-R association remains to be specified.

In summary, Thorndike provided little more than a name in answer to the question, What makes something effective as a reinforcer? His answer to the question, How does a reinforcer produce an increase in the probability of the reinforced response? was successful in that it accurately predicted the behavioral effects of reinforcement. But the answer was superficial, because it simply stated that an S-R association was formed without specifying exactly how this came about.

Hull and Drive Reduction Theory

The next major theorist we will consider is Clark Hull. (For a review of Hullian theory, see Amsel & Rashotte, 1984.) Hull accepted the S-R mechanism of the Law of Effect, and concentrated instead on the question that Thorndike had pretty much ignored, What makes something effective as a reinforcer? To answer this question, Hull made use of the concept of **homeo-**

stasis, which had been developed to explain the operation of physiological systems. (I introduced the concept of homeostasis previously in connection with habituation and sensitization in Chapter 3.)

According to the homeostatic model, organisms defend a stable state with respect to certain biologically critical factors. Consider, for example, food intake (see Figure 9.2). In order to survive, organisms must maintain a stable or optimal supply of nutrients. Food deprivation creates a challenge to the nutritional state of the organism. It creates a need for food. The psychological consequence of this is the motivational or **drive state** of hunger, which can be reduced by the ingestion of food. According to Hull, food is an effective reinforcer because it reduces the hunger drive. More generally, Hull proposed that what makes a stimulus reinforcing is its effectiveness in reducing a drive state. Hence, his theory is called the **drive reduction theory** of reinforcement.

PRIMARY REINFORCERS

Common laboratory examples of instrumental reinforcement are consistent with Hull's drive reduction theory. Mild food deprivation is routinely used to make food an effective instrumental reinforcer for rats and pigeons in laboratory situations. Similarly, mild water deprivation makes water an effective reinforcer. Rats will respond to obtain heat when they are in a cold environment and to obtain cold air in a hot environment. Deprivation procedures and other circumstances that challenge a biological homeostatic system create drive states, and stimuli that reduce these drive states are effective reinforcers for instrumental behavior.

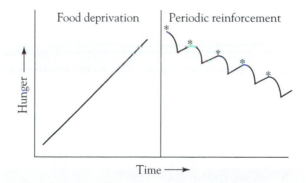

FIGURE 9.2   **Illustration of the mechanisms of drive reduction reinforcement using hunger as an example.**
Deliveries of the food reinforcer are indicated by asterisks.

Hull's drive reduction theory provides a successful account of reinforcers such as food and water. Stimuli that are effective in reducing a biological need without prior training are called **primary reinforcers.** However, if Hull's theory could only characterize reinforcers that reduce primary biological drives, it would be rather limited. Many effective reinforcers do not satisfy a biological drive or need. You may find the smell of Italian food reinforcing, but the smell of food does not reduce hunger. Likewise, a $20 bill does not reduce a biological drive or need, but it is a highly effective reinforcer.

SECONDARY REINFORCERS AND ACQUIRED DRIVES

Hull's theory has been successfully extended to stimuli such as the smell of food by adding the principle of Pavlovian conditioning. As one repeatedly eats spoonfuls of a particular food, the smell of that food becomes associated with the reduction of hunger through Pavlovian conditioning. This makes the food's aroma a **conditioned** or **secondary reinforcer.** The concept of conditioned reinforcer extended Hull's theory to stimuli that do not reduce a drive state directly but gain their reinforcing properties through association with a primary reinforcer.

Another way in which Hull's theory has been extended beyond events that involve primary biological drives is through the concept of a conditioned drive state. Stimuli that become associated with a primary drive state are assumed to elicit a **conditioned** or **acquired drive.** Reduction of a conditioned or acquired drive is assumed to be reinforcing in the same manner as the reduction of a primary or biological drive state.

The concept of conditioned or acquired drive has been used most extensively in the analysis of aversively motivated behavior. You can lose your balance and fall on a moving escalator. If the fall is severe enough, you may become afraid of escalators. Such conditioned fear is an example of a conditioned or acquired drive. According to Hull's drive reduction theory, a reduction in the intensity of the acquired drive will be reinforcing. Therefore, any response that enables you to escape from the conditioned fear of escalators will be reinforced. Walking away from the escalator and using an elevator will be reinforced by reduction of the conditioned fear elicited by the escalator. (I will have more to say about these mechanisms when I discuss avoidance behavior in Chapter 12.)

SENSORY REINFORCEMENT

Although Hull's theory was successfully extended to situations that do not involve primary biological drives, the theory has not been able to explain all instances of reinforcement. For example, investigators have found that rats kept in the dark will press a response lever to turn on a light, and rats kept in an illuminated chamber will press a response lever to produce periods of darkness. Chimpanzees will perform instrumental responses that are rein-forced by nothing more than the opportunity to watch an electric toy train move around a track. These are all examples of **sensory reinforcement.** In many situations, sensory stimulation with no apparent relation to a biologi-cal need or drive state can serve as an effective reinforcer (see Berlyne, 1969). Music, beautiful paintings, and other works of art are examples of sen-sory reinforcers for human beings.

The growing weight of evidence for sensory reinforcement, along with the success of alternative conceptualizations of reinforcement, led to the abandonment of Hull's drive reduction theory. As we shall see, the theories that emerged were highly creative, involving radical new ways of thinking about the issues of instrumental reinforcement.

Reinforcers as Responses

The modern era in reinforcement theory was ushered in by the work of David Premack, who approached reinforcement from an entirely different perspec-tive. Like Hull, Premack considered situations such as a rat pressing a re-sponse lever for food. However, instead of thinking of the reinforcer as a pellet of food, he thought of the reinforcer as the act of eating the food. For Premack, the question was not what made food a reinforcing stimulus, but what made eating a reinforcing response. Premack framed the issues of re-inforcement in terms of responses, not in terms of stimuli (Premack, 1965).

THE PREMACK PRINCIPLE

What makes eating different from pressing a response lever in a standard Skinner box? Many answers are possible. The rat has to learn to press the lever, but it does not have to learn to eat. Eating can occur not just in the Skinner box but anywhere the rat finds food. Eating involves a special set of muscles and activates digestive processes. Another difference between eating and pressing a lever is that a food-deprived rat in a Skinner box is much more likely to eat than to press the lever if it is given free access to both activities. Premack focused on this last difference and elevated it to a general principle.

According to Premack, the critical precondition for reinforcement is not a drive state. Rather, it is the existence of two responses that differ in their likelihood of occurrence when the organism is given free access to both ac-tivities. Given two such responses, Premack proposed that *the opportunity to perform the higher probability response will serve as a reinforcer for the lower prob-ability response.* This general claim is known as the **Premack principle.** A more descriptive name for it is the **differential probability principle.**

According to the differential probability principle, the specific nature of the instrumental and reinforcer responses does not matter. Neither of them has to involve eating or drinking, and the organism need not be hungry or thirsty. The only requirement is that one response be more likely than the other. Given such a differential response probability, the more likely response can serve as a reinforcer for the less likely response.

The Premack Revolution

The Premack principle took the scientific community by storm. It was a radical departure from previous ways of thinking about reinforcers. For the first time, scientists started thinking seriously about reinforcers as responses rather than as special stimuli. And, for the first time, the distinction between conditioned and unconditioned reinforcers became irrelevant. Whether a reinforcer reduced a drive state or only provided sensory stimulation was also irrelevant. Premack was unconcerned with how one response might have come to be more likely than another. For him, the only thing that mattered was that the reinforcer response be more likely than the instrumental response.

For Hull, all reinforcers were ultimately related to unconditioned biological needs or drives. Secondary or conditioned reinforcers were effective only through association with primary reinforcers. The Premack principle was important because it liberated psychologists from the grip of stimulus views of reinforcement and views of reinforcement rooted in biological needs and drives. Moreover, the Premack principle provided a convenient tool for the application of instrumental conditioning procedures in a variety of educational settings, including homes, classrooms, psychiatric hospitals, mental retardation centers, and correctional institutions.

Applications of the Premack Principle

In all educational settings, students are encouraged to learn and perform new responses. The goal is to get the students to do things that they did not do before and things they would not do without special encouragement. In other words, the goal is to increase the likelihood of low-probability responses. Instrumental conditioning procedures are ideally suited to accomplish this task. But the teacher first has to find an effective reinforcer. Withholding a student's lunch so that food may be used as a reinforcer is not socially acceptable and would create a great deal of resentment. Candy and other food treats are effective reinforcers for young children without food deprivation but are not good for them nutritionally.

The Premack principle provides a way out of this dilemma (Homme, de-Baca, Devine, Steinhorst, & Rickert, 1963). According to Premack, a reinforcer is any activity the participant is more likely to engage in than the instrumental response. Some students may like to watch TV a lot; others may enjoy some time on the playground; still others may enjoy helping the teacher. Whatever the high-probability response may be, the Premack principle suggests that one can take advantage of it in encouraging the student to engage in a less likely behavior. All one must do is provide access to the high-probability response only if the student first performs the lower-probability behavior (Charlop, Kurtz, & Casey, 1990).

Consider, for example, a mentally retarded student who enjoys playing on swings but refuses to attend classes for learning to read. The goal is to teach this student to attend classes regularly. The Premack principle suggests that an effective instrumental conditioning procedure could be set up in which attending class is reinforced by the opportunity to play on a swing after each class session.

The Premack principle facilitated the application of instrumental conditioning to a variety of educational settings. It enabled teachers to employ a variety of activities rather than food items as reinforcers, and it encouraged them to take advantage of each student's unique set of preferred activities. In this way, training procedures could be tailor-made to fit a student's particular likes and dislikes.

THEORETICAL PROBLEMS

The Premack principle continues to be used in educational settings. However, it has been superseded by other concepts in theoretical analyses of reinforcement. The differential response probability principle has two major shortcomings. The first shortcoming involves the measurement or calculation of response probabilities. We all have an intuitive sense of what it means to say that one response is more likely than another, but assigning a precise numerical value to the probability of a response can be difficult. Furthermore, the likelihood of a given response may change unexpectedly. A youngster may enjoy swimming one morning but then not enjoy swimming later that day.

There is no straightforward solution to the theoretical problems posed by the difficulty in measuring response probabilities and the fact that they fluctuate. However, there are ways to get around these problems in practical applications of the Premack principle. For example, a system can be set up in which students are given points for performing the target instrumental response correctly. The students could then be permitted to exchange their points for various response opportunities (watching TV, reading a comic book, going out to the playground, getting some crayons and paper, and so forth), depending on what they wanted to do at the moment. Such systems are called token economies and have been instituted in a variety of behavioral settings (Kazdin, 1985). If a wide-enough range of reinforcer activities is provided, one need not obtain precise measurements of the probability of each reinforcer response or worry about fluctuations in reinforcer preferences.

The second major shortcoming of the Premack principle is that it is merely a formula or rule for identifying reinforcers. It does not tell us how reinforcers work. It answers the question, What makes something effective as a reinforcer? but it does not answer the question, How does a reinforcer produce an increase in the probability of the reinforced response?

The Response Deprivation Hypothesis

The next major development in theories of reinforcement was the **response deprivation hypothesis,** proposed by Timberlake and Allison (1974). The response deprivation hypothesis was designed to solve some of the theoretical problems that were left unresolved by the Premack principle.

Timberlake and Allison followed in Premack's footsteps in thinking of reinforcers as responses rather than as stimuli. Their starting point, like Premack's, was to think about the difference between an instrumental response and a reinforcer response. However, their consideration of this question led them down a different path. Timberlake and Allison suggested that the critical difference between instrumental and reinforcer responses is that the participant has free access to the instrumental response but is restricted in performing the reinforcer response.

In a typical Skinner box, for example, the rat can press the response lever at any time, but it is not at liberty to eat pellets of food at any time. Eating can occur only after the rat has pressed the lever, and even then the rat can only eat the small portion of food that is provided. Timberlake and Allison suggested that these restrictions on the reinforcer response are what makes eating an effective reinforcer. In their view, instrumental conditioning situations deprive the participant of free access to the reinforcer response. For this reason the Timberlake-Allison proposal is called the response deprivation hypothesis.

RESPONSE DEPRIVATION AND THE LAW OF EFFECT

The response deprivation hypothesis captures an important idea. The idea is obvious if one considers what would happen if there were no restrictions on eating for a rat in a Skinner box. Imagine a situation in which the rat receives a week's supply of food each time it presses the response lever. According to Thorndike's Law of Effect, a week's worth of food should be a highly satisfying state of affairs and therefore should result in a strong S-R bond and a large increase in lever pressing. But this hardly makes sense from the rat's point of view. A more sensible prediction is that if the rat receives a week's supply of food for each lever press, it will press the response lever about once a week, when its food supply is depleted.

According to the response deprivation hypothesis, what makes food an effective reinforcer is not that food satisfies hunger or that eating is a high-probability response. Rather, the critical factor is that an instrumental conditioning procedure places a restriction on eating. It is this response deprivation that makes eating reinforcing. If the response deprivation is removed (by providing a week's supply of food), instrumental responding will not increase; the instrumental response will not be reinforced.

RESPONSE DEPRIVATION AND RESPONSE PROBABILITY

Notice that the response deprivation hypothesis does not require the computation of response probabilities. Thus, the response deprivation hypothesis avoids the first shortcoming of the Premack principle. To apply response deprivation, one merely has to determine the rate of a response during a baseline period in the absence of any restrictions and then limit access to the reinforcer response to below the baseline level.

An interesting prediction of the response deprivation hypothesis is that even a low-probability response can be made into a reinforcing event. According to the response deprivation hypothesis, the opportunity to perform a low-probability response can be used to reinforce a higher-probability behavior if access to the low-probability response is restricted below its already low baseline rate. Such a prediction is contrary to the Premack principle but has been confirmed by experimental evidence (Allison & Timberlake, 1974; Eisenberger, Karpman, & Trattner, 1967).

RESPONSE DEPRIVATION AND THE LOCUS OF REINFORCEMENT EFFECTS

In addition to avoiding the problems involved in computing response probabilities, the response deprivation hypothesis shifted the locus of the explanation of reinforcement. In earlier theories, reinforcement was explained in terms of factors that were outside the instrumental conditioning procedure itself. With drive-reduction theory, the external factor involved procedures that established a drive state. With the Premack principle, the external factor involved the differential baseline probabilities of the reinforcer and instrumental responses. In contrast, with the response deprivation hypothesis, the locus of reinforcement rests with how the instrumental conditioning procedure constrains the organism's activities. This was a new idea. Never before had someone suggested that reinforcement effects are determined by the response restrictions that are inherently involved in all instrumental conditioning procedures.

The response deprivation hypothesis moved our understanding of reinforcement forward in that it avoided some of the problems of the Premack principle. However, just like the Premack principle, the response deprivation hypothesis only provided an answer to the question, What makes something effective as a reinforcer? The answer to the other major question, How does a reinforcer produce an increase in the probability of the reinforced response? had to await the development of the behavioral regulation approach.

The Behavioral Regulation Approach

In many ways the **behavioral regulation** approach is similar to the response deprivation hypothesis. Like its predecessor, the behavioral regulation approach rejects the assumption that reinforcers are special kinds of stimuli or special kinds of responses. In addition, the behavioral regulation approach accepts that reinforcement effects are determined by how an instrumental conditioning procedure restricts an organism's activities. In fact, the behavioral regulation approach builds on this idea in order to answer the second question about reinforcement, How does a reinforcer produce an increase in the probability of the reinforced response? (Allison, 1989; Timberlake, 1980, 1984).

The behavioral regulation approach borrowed the concept of homeostasis from physiology and drive reduction theory and extended it to response choice. Behavioral homeostasis is analogous to physiological homeostasis in that both involve defending the optimal or preferred level of a system. Physiological homeostatic mechanisms exist to maintain physiological parameters (e.g., blood levels of oxygen and glucose) close to an optimal or ideal level. The homeostatic level is "defended" in the sense that deviations from the target blood levels of oxygen or glucose trigger compensatory physiological mechanisms that return the systems to their respective homeostatic levels.

THE BEHAVIORAL BLISS POINT

In behavioral regulation, what is defended is the organism's preferred distribution of activities, its **behavioral bliss point.** This term refers to how an organism distributes its activities among available response options in the absence of procedural restrictions. The bliss point is the participant's preferred response choices before an instrumental conditioning procedure is imposed.

Consider, for example, a teenager named Kim. Left to her own devices, during the course of a 24-hour day, Kim might spend 3 hours a day talking to friends on the telephone, 1.5 hours eating, 4 hours driving around, 10 hours sleeping, 2 hours watching TV, 3 hours listening to music, and half an hour doing schoolwork. This distribution of activities would constitute the behavioral bliss point for Kim. Notice that at the bliss point, Kim devotes only half an hour each day to doing schoolwork.

IMPOSING AN INSTRUMENTAL CONTINGENCY

Kim's parents may want to introduce an instrumental conditioning procedure in order to increase the amount of time Kim devotes to schoolwork. They could do this by restricting her access to music. For example, they could require that Kim spend a minute doing schoolwork for every minute that she gets to listen to music.

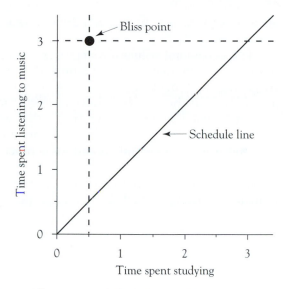

FIGURE 9.3   Illustration of the behavioral regulation approach to instrumental conditioning.
The bliss point represents how much time a person spends studying and listening to music in the absence of an instrumental conditioning procedure or schedule constraint. The schedule line represents how much time the person can devote to each activity when she is required to spend 1 minute studying for each minute spent listening to music.

Before the instrumental contingency, listening to music and doing homework were independent activities for Kim. How much time she spent on one activity had little to do with how much time she spent on the other. This characterized the bliss point. The behavioral bliss point for listening to music and studying is illustrated in the upper left quadrant of Figure 9.3.

Requiring Kim to spend a minute on homework for every minute of music listening ties the two activities together in a special way. Now time spent on homework must equal time spent on music. This relationship is illustrated by the 45° line in Figure 9.3, also called the **schedule line.** With the instrumental conditioning procedure in effect, studying is no longer independent of listening to music. The two activities are tied together and restricted to the schedule line.

The contingency between studying and listening to music illustrated by the schedule line in Figure 9.3 restricts Kim's behavior so that she can no longer distribute her responses as she did at the behavioral bliss point. The schedule line does not go through the behavioral bliss point. Therefore, the instrumental contingency is a challenge to the behavioral bliss point, analogous to the way in which a drive state is a challenge to physiological homeostasis.

The behavioral regulation approach is similar to physiological homeostatic models in that deviations from the preferred level are assumed to trigger mechanisms of adjustment that move the system back toward the preferred level. In the case of behavioral regulation, these mechanisms of adjustment involve moving the participant's response choices or her distribution of activities back toward the behavioral bliss point.

Once the instrumental conditioning procedure has been put into effect for Kim (1 minute of music listening for 1 minute of schoolwork), she can never get all the way back to her preferred response allocation. Every possible route for returning to the behavioral bliss point involves some cost or disadvantage. If Kim elects to listen to music for as long as she would like (ideally 3 hours a day), she would have to do much more schoolwork than she likes. On the other hand, if she spent as little time doing schoolwork as she prefers (half an hour per day), she would have to settle for much less music than she likes.

Instrumental conditioning procedures constrain response options. They disrupt the free flow of behavior and interfere with how an organism selects among its available response alternatives. Furthermore, most cases are like Kim's in that the instrumental conditioning procedure does not allow the participant to return to the behavioral bliss point. The most that can be achieved is to approach the bliss point under the constraints of the instrumental conditioning procedure.

RESPONDING TO SCHEDULE CONSTRAINTS

How an organism goes about moving back toward its behavioral bliss point after an instrumental contingency has been imposed depends on the costs and benefits of various strategies. If doing schoolwork is much more unpleasant for Kim than the potential loss of music-listening time, then she will not increase her schoolwork very much but will give up time spent listening to music. In contrast, if the potential loss of music time is much more aversive for Kim than increased effort devoted to schoolwork, she will adjust to the constraint imposed by the instrumental conditioning procedure by substantially increasing her time doing schoolwork.

A particularly important factor determining how an individual responds to schedule constraints is the availability of substitutes for the reinforcer activity (Green & Freed, 1993). Instrumental conditioning procedures are powerful only if no substitutes are available for the reinforcer activity. But if the participant has something it can substitute for the reinforcer, restricting access to the reinforcer will not increase instrumental responding.

If Kim loves music and cannot derive the same satisfaction from any other type of activity (if Kim has no substitute for music), then music will be a very powerful reinforcer. In this case, she will adjust to the instrumental procedure with a large increase in schoolwork. Quite a different outcome will occur if Kim does not like music any more than watching TV. If watching TV is a good substitute for listening to music, the instrumental contingency will have little effect on how much schoolwork Kim does. In this case, she will respond to the schedule constraint by substituting TV watching for listening to music, without any increase in time spent on schoolwork.

As this example illustrates, one must be very careful to assess the availability of substitutes in designing a practical application of instrumental conditioning principles. Unfortunately, these substitutes may not be clearly evident before an instrumental contingency is imposed. Kim's parents, for example, may not have been aware that Kim considers watching TV a substitute for listening to music. In fact, Kim may not have been aware of this herself before the instrumental contingency linked studying with listening to music. For this reason, it is important to monitor the full range of activities of the individual when an instrumental conditioning procedure is imposed to produce a desired change in behavior.

CONTRIBUTIONS OF BEHAVIORAL REGULATION

The behavioral regulation approach has advanced our understanding of instrumental behavior because it has encouraged thinking about instrumental conditioning and reinforcement within the context of the participant's entire behavioral repertoire. Behavioral regulation focuses attention on the fact that instrumental conditioning procedures do not operate in a behavioral vacuum. Rather, instrumental conditioning procedures disrupt the free flow of behavior; they interfere with how the participant allocates its behavior among available response options. Behavioral regulation also focuses attention on the fact that constraints on response choices may have effects not only on the instrumental and reinforcer responses. Schedule constraints may also result in changes to related or substitutable responses that are not directly part of the instrumental procedure.

The behavioral regulation approach encourages us to think about instrumental behavior from a broader perspective than previous conceptualizations. It encourages us to consider all of the activities of a participant—how they are organized and how that organization determines the effects of schedule constraints. This approach is a far cry from the more limited stimulus-response perspective that dominated earlier theories of reinforcement. However, it brings along with it challenges of its own. It is difficult to predict a reinforcement effect unless we know all of the features of an individual's behavioral organization that influence his or her responses to a schedule constraint.

Summary

A theory of reinforcement has to tell us (1) what makes something a reinforcer and (2) how a reinforcer produces its effects. Early theories assumed that reinforcers were special types of stimuli. According to the most influential of these theories, a stimulus will be reinforcing if it is effective in reducing a drive state. Drive reduction theory was dominant for several decades but ran into some difficulties (e.g., it could not explain sensory reinforcement) and was supplanted by response theories of reinforcement. Among the most prominent of these was Premack's differential response probability principle, according to which a reinforcer is not a drive-reducing stimulus but rather the opportunity to make a response whose baseline probability is higher than the baseline probability of the instrumental response.

The Premack principle formed the basis of numerous applications of reinforcement in clinical and educational settings. However, difficulties with measuring response probabilities stimulated the next theoretical development, the response deprivation hypothesis. According to this hypothesis, the opportunity to perform a response will be an effective reinforcer if the instrumental conditioning procedure restricts access to that activity below its baseline rate. The response deprivation hypothesis shifted the focus of attention from reinforcers as special stimuli or responses to how an instrumental conditioning procedure constrains the organism's activities. This idea was developed further in the behavioral regulation approach.

According to the behavioral regulation approach, organisms have a preferred or optimal distribution of activities in any given situation. The introduction of an instrumental conditioning procedure disrupts this optimal response distribution, known as the behavioral bliss point. Typically, adjustment to the disruption is made by increasing the rate of the instrumental response while decreasing the rate of the reinforcer response. The extent of this response reallocation is governed by the schedule of reinforcement imposed and the availability of substitutes for the reinforcer response.

Practice Questions

1. What are the two fundamental questions a theory of reinforcement must answer?

2. What is the Law of Effect, and what are its shortcomings as a theory of reinforcement?

3. What is the drive reduction theory of reinforcement, and why has it been supplanted by other approaches?

4. What is the Premack principle, and what are its advantages and disadvantages?

5. What advantage does the response deprivation hypothesis have over the Premack principle?

6. How did the response deprivation hypothesis shift the locus of the explanation of reinforcement?

7. What advantages does behavioral regulation theory have over earlier theories of reinforcement?

8. How does the availability of substitutes affect behavioral regulation predictions of reinforcement?

Suggested Readings

Allison, J. (1983). *Behavioral economics*. New York: Praeger.

Premack, D. (1965). Reinforcement theory. In D. Levine (Ed.), *Nebraska symposium on motivation* (Vol. 13, pp. 123–180). Lincoln: University of Nebraska Press.

Tierney, K. J. (1995). Molar regulatory theory and behavior therapy. In W. O'Donohue & L. Krasner (Eds.), *Theories of behavior therapy* (pp. 97–128). Washington, DC: American Psychological Association.

Timberlake, W., & Farmer-Dougan, V. A. (1991). Reinforcement in applied settings: Figuring out ahead of time what will work. *Psychological Bulletin, 110*, 379–391.

Technical Terms

Acquired drive	Homeostasis
Behavioral bliss point	Law of Effect
Behavioral regulation	Premack principle
Conditioned drive	Primary reinforcer
Conditioned reinforcer	Response deprivation hypothesis
Differential probability principle	Schedule line
Drive reduction theory	Secondary reinforcer
Drive state	Sensory reinforcement

CHAPTER TEN

Extinction of Conditioned Behavior

DID YOU KNOW THAT:

- Extinction results in increased response variability and decreased responding.
- Extinction is not the opposite of acquisition.
- Extinction leaves much of the associative structure of instrumental conditioning intact.
- Extinction performance is much more context specific than acquisition.
- The unexpected absence of reinforcement produces frustration.
- The schedule of reinforcement that was in effect during acquisition determines how rapidly responding declines in extinction.
- Behavior does not become more resistant to the effects of extinction if excessive reinforcement training is used (overtraining) or if a large reinforcer is used, especially with continuous reinforcement.

So far, our discussion of classical and instrumental conditioning has centered on various aspects of the acquisition and maintenance of conditioned behavior. Learning is important because it provides needed flexibility in how individuals interact with their environment. But if learned behavior is an adaptation to a changing environment, then the loss of conditioned behavior should be just as prevalent as its acquisition. Not many reinforcement schedules remain in effect throughout an organism's lifetime. Responses that are successful at one stage may cease to be effective as circumstances change. Children, for example, are praised for drawing crude representations of people and objects in nursery school, but the same type of drawing is not considered good if made in high school.

Acquisition of conditioned behavior involves procedures in which a reinforcing outcome is presented. **Extinction** involves omitting the reinforcer or unconditioned stimulus. In classical conditioning, extinction involves repeated presentations of the conditioned stimulus without the US. In instrumental conditioning, extinction involves no longer presenting the reinforcer as a consequence of the instrumental response. The typical result is that conditioned responding declines. Thus, extinction appears to be the opposite of acquisition. Indeed, that is how extinction has been characterized in traditional theories of learning, such as the Rescorla-Wagner model (see Chapter 6). However, as the evidence described in the present chapter shows, this view of extinction is incorrect.

It is important to distinguish extinction from **forgetting.** Although both involve the loss of conditioned responding, forgetting results from the passage of time. Extinction, by contrast, occurs as a consequence of repeated presentations of the CS by itself or repeated instances of the instrumental response by itself. Thus, extinction is produced by a particular procedure, not merely the passage of time.

Effects of Extinction Procedures

Imagine looking forward to getting home after a hard day's work, then discovering that your key no longer opens the front door. This illustrates the basic procedure for extinction. A previously reinforced response (turning the key in the door) is no longer effective in producing the reinforcer (getting into your house). Such an unexpected absence of reinforcement produces both emotional and behavioral effects. The emotion you feel upon finding that your key no longer works is frustration and perhaps anger. Chances are you will not give up after your first attempt to open the door but will try several more times, perhaps jiggling the key in different ways. If none of these response variations work, you will eventually quit trying. This illustrates two basic behavioral effects of extinction. The most obvious is that responding decreases when the response no longer results in reinforcement. This is the primary behavioral effect of extinction, the effect that has occupied most of the attention of scientists. The other important behavioral consequence of extinction is an increase in response variability (Neuringer, Kornell, & Olufs, 2001). When your key failed to open the door on your first try, you jiggled the key in various ways in an effort to make it work. This increase in response variability is associated with the frustration of not receiving the expected reinforcement.

Extinction and Original Learning

Although extinction produces important behavioral and emotional effects, it does not reverse the effects of acquisition. Evidence that extinction does not erase what was originally learned has been obtained through studies of spontaneous recovery, renewal, reinstatement, and reinforcer devaluation effects. These various phenomena are described next.

Spontaneous Recovery

One of the hallmark features of extinction is that it dissipates with time. The consequence of this loss of the extinction effect over time is that the originally conditioned response returns if the subject is tested after a delay following the extinction procedure. This is referred to as **spontaneous recovery.** We previously encountered spontaneous recovery in connection with habituation. If a period of rest is introduced after the development of a habituation effect, the habituated response will "spontaneously" recover. A similar recovery of responding occurs with extinction in both Pavlovian and instrumental conditioning (Rescorla, 1996, 1997; Rosas & Bouton, 1996).

Figure 10.1 illustrates acquisition, extinction, and spontaneous recovery. During acquisition, conditioned responding increases as a function of trials. In extinction, responding declines. A period of rest is then instituted, followed by additional extinction trials. Notice that responding is higher after the period of rest than it was at the end of the first series of extinction trials. This is the phenomenon of spontaneous recovery. Spontaneous recovery typically does not restore responding to the same high levels that were evident during acquisition. However, the fact that responding recovers to any extent is evidence that extinction did not result in unlearning the conditioned response. Spontaneous recovery is one of the reasons that bad habits can return after attempts to extinguish them.

Renewal of Original Excitatory Conditioning

Another strong piece of evidence that extinction does not result in unlearning is the phenomenon of **renewal** identified by Mark Bouton and his colleagues. Renewal refers to a recovery of acquisition performance when the

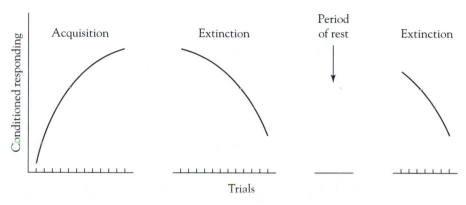

FIGURE 10.1   Illustration of spontaneous recovery following extinction.
During the acquisition phase, conditioned responding increases. In the subsequent
extinction phase, responding declines to the low level seen at the start of the acquisition phase. A period of rest is then introduced, during which training trials
are suspended. This results in a temporary recovery of the conditioned behavior.
(Note: Data are hypothetical.)

contextual cues that were present during extinction are changed. The change
may be a return to the context of original acquisition or a shift to a "neutral"
context. Renewal is particularly troublesome for behavior therapy because it
means that irrational fears that are extinguished in the context of a therapist's office can easily return when the subject moves to a different context.
Similarly, a bad drug habit that is extinguished in a residential treatment
center can be renewed when the client returns home.

The renewal effect was discovered during the course of research on transfer of training (Bouton, 1993). The basic question in these studies was how
learning that occurs in one situation transfers to other circumstances or contexts. For example, if you learn something in a noisy dormitory lounge, will
that learning transfer to a quiet classroom in which you have to take a test?
An equally important question concerns the transfer of extinction. If extinction is conducted in one situation so that the conditioned stimulus no
longer elicits conditioned responding in that context, will the CS also be ineffective in other situations?

Much of the research on the renewal effect has been conducted with laboratory rats. An example is provided in Figure 10.2. The participants received initial acquisition in an experimental chamber that had a particular
level of illumination and a particular odor. Let us call this conditioning
chamber Context A. As is typically the case, conditioned responding increased during the acquisition phase. The participants were then moved to

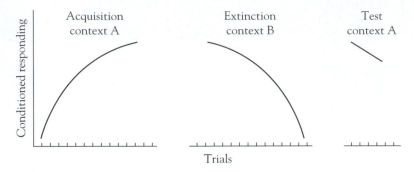

FIGURE 10.2   Illustration of the renewal effect.
Participants originally acquire the conditioned response in Context A. They then receive extinction training in Context B, which results in a decline of the conditioned response. In the third phase, they are returned to Context A for testing. The conditioned response is "renewed" when the participants are returned to Context A. (Note: Data are hypothetical.)

another chamber, which had less lighting and a different odor, and received an extinction procedure there. Let us call the second chamber Context B. As expected, responding declined in extinction. The subjects were then returned to Context A to see if the effects of extinction would transfer back to Context A.

If extinction involves the unlearning of a conditioned response, then returning to Context A after extinction in Context B should not result in recovery of the conditioned behavior. Contrary to that prediction, responding was restored when the participants were returned to Context A. This means that the effects of extinction training in Context B did not transfer back to the original training context. Rather, conditioned responding was "renewed" upon return to the context of original training.

Renewal effects occur because the memory of extinction is specific to the cues that were present during the extinction phase. Therefore, a shift away from the context of extinction disrupts retrieval of the memory of extinction, with the result that extinction performance is lost. But why should this restore behavior characteristic of original acquisition? To account for that, one has to make the added assumption that original acquisition performance generalizes from one context to another more easily than does extinction performance. This is indeed the case. Notice that in Figure 10.2, subjects responded as vigorously at the start of the extinction phase in Context B as they had at the end of the acquisition phase in Context A. This illustrates that a shift in context does not disrupt acquisition performance. It only disrupts extinction performance.

Why is it that original acquisition is minimally disrupted (if at all) by a change in context, whereas extinction performance is highly context specific? Bouton (1993, 1994) has suggested that contextual cues serve to disambiguate the significance of a conditioned stimulus. This function is similar to the function of semantic context in disambiguating the meaning of a word. Consider the word *cut*. *Cut* could refer to the physical procedure of creating two pieces, as in "The chef cut the carrots." Alternatively, it could refer to dropping a player from a team, as in "Johnny was cut from the team after the first game." The meaning of the word *cut* depends on the semantic context. A CS that has undergone excitatory conditioning and then extinction likewise has an ambiguous meaning, in that the CS could signify an impending US (acquisition) or the absence of the US (extinction). This ambiguity makes the CS more susceptible to contextual control. After acquisition training alone, the CS is not ambiguous because it only signifies one thing (impending US delivery). Such a CS is therefore not as susceptible to contextual control as one that has undergone both acquisition and extinction.

The renewal effect has important implications for behavior therapy, and unfortunately these implications are rather troubling. It suggests that even if a therapeutic procedure is effective in extinguishing a pathological fear or phobia in the relative safety of a therapist's office, the conditioned fear may easily return when the client encounters the fear CS in a different context. Equally problematic is the fact that the effects of excitatory conditioning readily generalize from one context to another (see Figure 10.2). Thus, if you acquire a pathological fear in one particular situation, the fear is likely to plague you in a variety of other places. But if you overcome your fear in a particular environment or context, this benefit will not generalize as readily. The renewal effect means that problems created by conditioning are likely to be much more widespread than the solutions or remedies for those problems. (For further discussion of the implications of the renewal effect for behavior therapy, see Bouton, 1988; Bouton & Nelson, 1998.)

REINSTATEMENT OF CONDITIONED EXCITATION

Another procedure that serves to restore responding to an extinguished conditioned stimulus is called **reinstatement.** Reinstatement refers to the recovery of excitatory responding to an extinguished stimulus produced by exposures to the unconditioned stimulus (see Figure 10.3). Consider, for example, learning an aversion to french fries because you got sick after eating some on a trip. Your aversion is then extinguished by nibbling on french fries without getting sick on a number of occasions. In fact, you may actually regain your enjoyment of french fries because of this extinction experience. The phenomenon of reinstatement suggests that if you were to become sick again for some reason, your aversion to french fries would return even if your illness

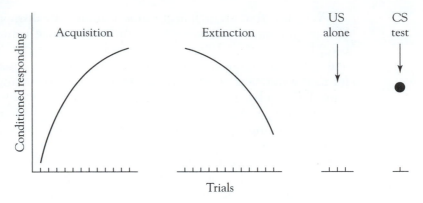

FIGURE 10.3   Illustration of the reinstatement effect.
After acquisition and extinction training, subjects receive exposures to the US alone. This is then followed by tests of responding to the CS. The US-alone presentations produce recovery in responding to the CS. (Note: Data are hypothetical.)

had nothing to do with eating fries. (For an analogous study with laboratory rats, see Schachtman, Brown, & Miller, 1985.)

As with renewal, reinstatement is a troublesome phenomenon for behavior therapy. Behavior therapy often involves trying to get clients to stop doing things that are problematic for them. Extinction may be one of the techniques for reducing behavior. Because of reinstatement, responses that are successfully extinguished during the course of therapeutic intervention can recur if the individual encounters the unconditioned stimulus again. For example, fear and anxiety acquired during the course of being in an abusive relationship (or living with an abusive parent) can return even after years of therapy if the individual encounters similar forms of abuse later in life.

SENSITIVITY TO US OR REINFORCER DEVALUATION

The persistence of original learning despite extinction has also been examined by testing the effects of reinforcer devaluation. As I described in Chapter 4, reinforcer or US devaluation in Pavlovian conditioning disrupts performance of the conditioned response if the CR was the product of S-S rather than S-R learning. Rescorla has used the US devaluation technique to determine whether the CS-US association established through Pavlovian conditioning persists through extinction. If extinction leaves intact a CS-US association, then US devaluation will disrupt responding to an extinguished CS, just as it disrupts responding to a CS that has not undergone extinction.

TABLE 10.1   Effects of US Devaluation on a Pavlovian CS Following Extinction (Rescorla 1996, Experiment 2)

Phase 1: Acquisition	Phase 2: Extinction	US Devaluation	Test
Group Ext			
CS1 → US1 and CS2 → US2	CS1 Ext and CS2 Ext	US1 →LiCl	CS1 and CS2
Group NotExt			
CS1 → US1 and CS2 → US2		US1 →LiCl	CS1 and CS2

CS1 and CS2 were a light and a tone (counterbalanced across subjects). US1 and US2 were sucrose and food pellets (counterbalanced across subjects and CSs). Before the US devaluation phase, both CS1 and CS2 were conditioned with a third US (polycose).

The outline of one experiment (Rescorla, 1996, Experiment 2) is presented in Table 10.1. Rats received appetitive conditioning with food and sucrose as the US. For each subject a light was paired with one US and a tone was paired with the other. (Which CS was paired with which US was counterbalanced across subjects, and each CS was always paired only with its own US.) As conditioning progressed, each subject came to insert its head in the food magazine as the conditioned response (focal search behavior). The rate of focal search during each CS was about 20 responses per minute at the end of the acquisition phase. Following acquisition, group Ext received extinction trials with both CS1 and CS2. This reduced responding to CS1 and CS2 to about 1 response per minute. The control group (NotExt) was placed in the experimental chamber during the extinction phase but did not get either CS1 or CS2 trials.

The extinction phase was followed by training in which all subjects had CS1 and CS2 paired with a new US (US3: polycose). This was done to make sure all subjects would show some responding to the CSs during the final test session. US3 was deliberately selected for retraining to be sure that retraining would not influence whatever associations each CS still had with US1 and US2. All of the subjects then had the value of US1 reduced by taste aversion conditioning. Presentations of US1 in the experimental chamber were followed by an injection that served to make the rats feel sick. After US devaluation, each subject was tested with CS1 and CS2.

The results of the first two presentations of CS1 and CS2 during the test session are summarized in Figure 10.4. Despite retraining with polycose as the

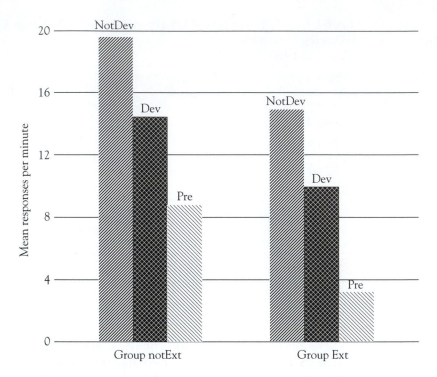

FIGURE 10.4 Susceptibility of a Pavlovian conditioned stimulus to the effects of US devaluation as a function of whether the CS had (or had not) undergone extinction previously.
Procedures are summarized in Table 10.1. Adapted from Rescorla, 1996.

US, responding to CS1 and CS2 in the extinction group was a bit lower than responding in the control group (NotExt). Nevertheless, the two groups showed equal sensitivity to US devaluation. In each group, responding to the CS whose associated US had been devaluated was lower than responding to the CS whose associated US had not been devaluated. This pattern of results could have occurred only if extinction allowed the original CS-US associations to remain intact. Thus, this pattern of results indicates that a CS-US association remains intact despite extinction of the CS.

One might argue that the conditioned stimulus in this experiment remained sensitive to devaluation of its associated US because not enough extinction trials were conducted. Six extinction sessions were conducted, with each CS presented eight times during each session. This was clearly enough to produce a major extinction effect, because, as I noted, responding declined from about 20 responses per minute to about 1 response per minute. Thus, extinction had a large impact. It is remarkable that despite so large an effect of extinction on conditioned responding, the extinction manipulation did not reduce the sensitivity of the subjects to US devaluation.

Experiments similar to the study of US devaluation in Pavlovian conditioning that I have just discussed have been conducted using instrumental conditioning procedures. In an instrumental conditioning procedure, subjects must perform a specified response in order to obtain a reinforcer outcome (R → O). As I explained in Chapter 7, if the instrumental conditioning procedure results in the learning of an R-O association, then devaluation of the reinforcer will produce a decline in the instrumental response. Studies have shown that this sensitivity to reinforcer devaluation also remains intact if the instrumental response is extinguished. As Rescorla (1993a) commented, "R-O associations, once trained, are relatively impervious to modification" (p. 244).

What Is Learned in Extinction?

If extinction does not involve "unlearning" and leaves R-O and S-S associations pretty much intact, why does responding decline in extinction procedures? In my discussion of Pavlovian conditioning, I reviewed evidence indicating that S-S associations or S-S learning are more important than S-R learning (see Chapter 4). In my discussion of instrumental conditioning, I reviewed evidence indicating that S-O and R-O associations are more important than the S-R association emphasized by Thorndike (see Chapter 7). These discussions reflect the major shift away from S-R mechanisms that occurred in contemporary learning theory during the last quarter of the twentieth century. This emphasis on S-S and R-O associations, however, creates a dilemma for theories of extinction.

INHIBITORY S-R ASSOCIATIONS

If conditioned behavior is supported primarily by S-S and R-O associations and these associations are not degraded during the course of extinction, why does extinction produce a decline in responding? In trying to answer this question, investigators have resurrected the importance of S-R associations. However, instead of focusing on excitatory S-R associations, as Thorndike originally did, contemporary investigators have come to the conclusion that nonreinforcement produces an **inhibitory S-R association.** That is, nonreinforcement of a response in the presence of a specific stimulus produces an inhibitory S-R association that serves to suppress that response whenever S is present. Consistent with the renewal effect, this hypothesis predicts that the effects of extinction will be highly specific to the context in which the response was extinguished.

Why should nonreinforcement produce an inhibitory S-R association? In answering this question, it is important to keep in mind that extinction involves a special type of nonreinforcement, namely, nonreinforcement after a history of reinforcement. Nonreinforcement without such a prior history is not extinction but is more akin to habituation. This is an important distinction, because the absence of a positive reinforcer is aversive only after a history of reinforcement. Thus, the emotional effects of nonreinforcement depend critically on the subject's prior history. If your partner never made you coffee in the morning, you will not be disappointed if the coffee is not ready when you get up. If you never received an allowance, you will not be disappointed when you don't get one. It is only the omission of an expected reward that creates disappointment or frustration. These emotional effects are presumed to play a critical role in the behavioral decline that occurs in extinction.

As I mentioned at the outset of this chapter, extinction involves both behavioral and emotional effects. The emotional reaction, technically called **frustration,** stems from the frustration that is triggered when an expected reinforcer is not forthcoming. Nonreinforcement in the face of the expectation of reward is assumed to trigger an unconditioned aversive frustrative reaction (Amsel, 1958). This aversive emotion serves to discourage responding during the course of extinction through the establishment of an inhibitory S-R association (Rescorla, 2001).

The establishment of an inhibitory S-R association during the course of extinction may be illustrated by an experiment whose procedures are outlined in Table 10.2. The subjects first received discrimination training in which a common response (Rc) was reinforced with food pellets whenever a light or noise stimulus (L or N) was present. This training was conducted so that nonreinforcement in the presence of L or N would elicit frustration when extinction was introduced. The targets of extinction were a lever-press and a chain-pull response (designated as R1 and R2, counterbalanced across subjects). To permit extinction of these responses, they were first reinforced, again with food pellets. Notice that the reinforcement of R1 and R2 did not occur in the presence of the light and noise stimuli. Therefore, this reinforcement training was not expected to establish any S-R associations involving the light and noise stimuli.

TABLE 10.2   Development of an Inhibitory S-R Association in Instrumental Extinction (Rescorla 1993b, Experiment 3)

Phase 1	Phase 2	Extinction	Test
N: Rc → P	R1 → P	N: R1$^-$	N: R1 vs. R2
L: Rc → P	R2 → P	L: R2$^-$	L: R1 vs. R2

N and L were noise and light discriminative stimuli; Rc was a common response (nose poking) for all subjects; P represents the food pellet reinforcer; R1 and R2 were lever press and chain pull, counterbalanced across subjects.

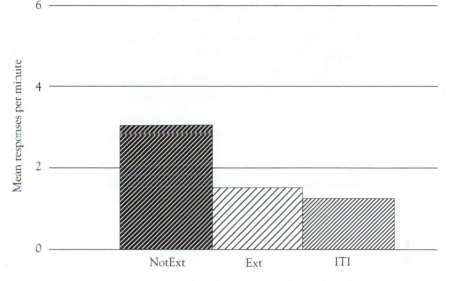

FIGURE 10.5 **Demonstration that extinction involves the acquisition of an inhibitory S-R association that is specific to the stimulus in the presence of which the response is nonreinforced.**
Procedures are summarized in Table 10.2. A particular response occurred less often during the stimulus with which the response had been extinguished than during an alternative stimulus. Adapted from Figure 7, page 333, in R. A. Rescorla, *Animal Learning & Behavior*, Vol. 21b. Copyright 1993 American Psychonomic Society, Inc. Reprinted by permission.

Extinction was conducted in the third phase of the experiment and consisted of presentations of L and N (to create the expectancy of reward), with R1 and R2 available but nonreinforced. The extinction phase presumably established inhibitory S-R associations involving L-R1 and N-R2. The presence of these associations was tested by giving subjects a choice between R1 and R2 in the presence of the L and N stimuli. If an inhibitory N-R1 association had been established during extinction, the subjects were predicted to make fewer R1 than R2 responses when tested with N. In a corresponding fashion, they were expected to make fewer R2 than R1 responses when tested with L. Notice that this differential response outcome cannot be explained in terms of changes in R-O or S-O associations, because such changes should have affected R1 and R2 equally.

The results of the experiment are presented in Figure 10.5. Responding is shown for the intertrial interval (ITI) and in the presence of the stimulus (L or N) with which the response had been extinguished or not. Responding during the stimulus with which the response had been extinguished was significantly less than responding during the alternate stimulus. Furthermore, the responding produced by the extinction stimulus was not significantly higher than that which occurred during the intertrial interval. These results indicate that the extinction procedure produced an inhibitory S-R association that was specific to a particular stimulus and response.

"Paradoxical" Reward Effects

If the decline in responding in extinction is due to the frustrative effects of an unexpected absence of reinforcement, then one would expect more rapid extinction following training that establishes greater expectations of reward. This is indeed the case and has led to a number of **paradoxical reward effects.**

OVERTRAINING EXTINCTION EFFECT

One of the paradoxical reward effects involves the effects of extensive reinforced training on subsequent extinction. The more training that is provided with reinforcement, the stronger will be the expectancy of reward that is learned; overtraining produces greater reward expectancy. For this reason, the frustrative effects of nonreinforcement will also be greater when extinction is introduced after overtraining. If the decline in responding in extinction is due to the frustrative effects of nonreward, more-extensive reinforcement training should produce more rapid extinction. This prediction has been confirmed (see Figure 10.6) and is called the **overtraining extinction effect** (Ishida & Papini, 1997).

The overtraining extinction effect is "paradoxical" because it involves fewer responses in extinction after more-extensive reinforcement training. Thinking casually, one might suppose that more-extensive reinforcement training would create a "stronger" response, one more resistant to extinction. But, in fact, the opposite is the case, especially when training involves continuous reinforcement. The more accustomed you become to receiving reinforcement, the more rapidly you will give up in the face of nonreinforcement.

MAGNITUDE OF REINFORCEMENT EXTINCTION EFFECT

Another paradoxical reward effect that reflects similar mechanisms is the **magnitude-of-reinforcement extinction effect.** This phenomenon reflects the fact that responding declines more rapidly in extinction following reinforcement with a larger reinforcer (see Figure 10.7), especially if training involves continuous reinforcement (Hulse, 1958; Wagner, 1961). The magnitude-of-reinforcement extinction effect is also readily accounted for in terms of the frustrative effects of nonreward. Nonreinforcement is apt to be more frustrative if the individual has come to expect a large reward than if the individual has come to expect a small reward. Consider two scenarios: In

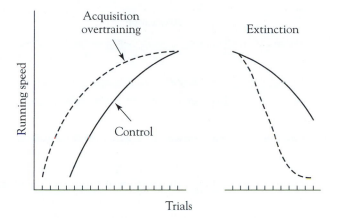

FIGURE 10.6   Illustration of the overtraining extinction effect.
During acquisition, two groups receive continuous reinforcement for performing an instrumental response. The overtraining group is trained until it reaches asymptote, and then training continues for additional trials. In contrast, the control group is trained only until it reaches asymptote. Both groups then receive extinction trials. Responding declines more rapidly for the overtrained group than for the control group. (Note: Data are hypothetical.)

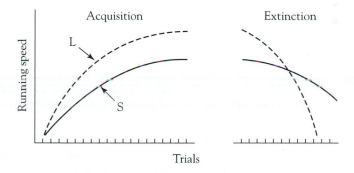

FIGURE 10.7   Illustration of the reward-magnitude extinction effect.
During the acquisition phase, one group of subjects is reinforced (on a continuous-reinforcement schedule) with a small reward (S), while another group is reinforced with a large reward (L). Both groups then receive extinction training. During the extinction phase, responding declines faster for group L than for group S. (Note: Data are hypothetical.)

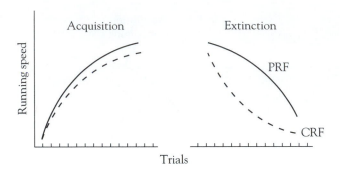

FIGURE 10.8   Illustration of the partial-reinforcement extinction effect.
During the acquisition phase, one group of subjects receives continuous reinforcement (CRF), while another group receives partial or intermittent reinforcement (PRF). Both groups then receive extinction training. During the extinction phase, responding declines faster for the CRF group than for the PRF group. (Note: Data are hypothetical.)

one you receive $100 per month from your parents to help with incidental expenses at college; in the other, you receive only $20 per month. In both cases your parents stop the payments when you drop out of school for a semester. This nonreinforcement will be more aversive if you had come to expect the larger monthly allowance.

PARTIAL-REINFORCEMENT EXTINCTION EFFECT

The most extensively investigated paradoxical reward effect is the **partial-reinforcement extinction effect.** A key factor that determines the vigor of both the behavioral and the emotional effects of an extinction procedure is the schedule of reinforcement that is in effect before extinction is introduced. Various subtle features of reinforcement schedules can influence the extinction of instrumental responses. However, the dominant schedule characteristic that determines extinction effects is whether the instrumental response is reinforced every time it occurs (**continuous reinforcement**) or only some of the times it occurs (**intermittent,** or **partial, reinforcement**). The general finding is that extinction is much slower and involves fewer frustration reactions if partial reinforcement rather than continuous reinforcement is in effect before introduction of the extinction procedure (see Figure 10.8). This phenomenon is called the partial-reinforcement extinction effect, or PREE.

The persistence in responding that is created by intermittent reinforcement can be remarkable. Habitual gamblers are slaves to intermittent reinforcement. Occasional winnings encourage them to continue gambling during long strings of losses. Intermittent reinforcement may also have undesirable consequences in parenting. Consider, for example, a child riding in a grocery cart while the parent is shopping. The child asks the parent to buy a piece of candy for him. The parent says no. The child asks again and again and then begins to throw a temper tantrum because the parent continues to say no. At this point, the parent is likely to give in to avoid public embarrassment. By finally buying the candy, the parent will have provided intermittent reinforcement for the repeated demands for candy. The parent will also have reinforced the tantrum behavior. The intermittent reinforcement of the requests for candy will make the child very persistent in asking for candy during future shopping trips.

MECHANISMS OF THE PARTIAL-REINFORCEMENT EXTINCTION EFFECT

Perhaps the most obvious explanation for the partial-reinforcement extinction effect is that the introduction of extinction is easier to detect after continuous reinforcement than after partial reinforcement. If you don't receive the reinforcer after each response during training, you may not immediately notice when reinforcers are omitted altogether during extinction. The absence of reinforcement is presumably much easier to detect after continuous reinforcement. This explanation of the PREE is called the **discrimination hypothesis.**

Although the discrimination hypothesis provides an intuitively reasonable explanation for the PREE, the partial-reinforcement extinction effect is not so straightforward. In an ingenious test of the discrimination hypothesis, Jenkins (1962) and Theios (1962) first trained one group of animals with partial reinforcement and another with continuous reinforcement. Both groups then received a phase of continuous reinforcement before extinction was introduced (see Table 10.3). Because the extinction procedure was introduced immediately after continuous-reinforcement training

TABLE 10.3   Design of the Jenkins/Theios Experiment to Test the Discrimination Hypothesis

Phase 1	Phase 2	Phase 3
Group PRF		
Partial reinforcement	Continuous reinforcement	Extinction
		Result: Slow extinction
Group CRF		
Continuous reinforcement	Continuous reinforcement	Extinction
		Result: Rapid extinction

for both groups, extinction should have been equally noticeable or discriminable for both. However, Jenkins and Theios found that the subjects that initially received partial-reinforcement training were slower to extinguish their behavior. These results indicate that the response persistence produced by partial reinforcement does not come from greater difficulty in detecting the start of extinction. Rather, it seems that subjects learn something long-lasting from partial reinforcement that is carried over through a phase of continuous reinforcement. Partial reinforcement seems to teach subjects not to give up in the face of failure, and this learned persistence is retained even if they subsequently experience an unbroken string of successes.

What do subjects learn during partial reinforcement that makes them more persistent in the face of a run of bad luck or failure? Numerous complicated experiments have been performed in order to answer this question. These studies indicate that partial reinforcement promotes persistence in two different ways. One explanation, **frustration theory,** is based on what subjects learn about the emotional effects of nonreward during partial-reinforcement training. The other explanation, **sequential theory,** is based on what subjects learn about the memory of nonreward.

Frustration Theory.   According to frustration theory, persistence in extinction results from learning something unusual, namely, to continue responding when you expect to be nonreinforced or frustrated (Amsel, 1958, 1992). Frustration theory assumes that intermittent reinforcement results in learning to respond in the face of expected nonreinforcement. However, this learning requires a considerable amount of experience with intermittent reinforcement.

Frustration theory characterizes the learning that occurs during the course of intermittent reinforcement in terms of stages (see Table 10.4). Partial reinforcement involves both rewarded and nonrewarded trials. Rewarded trials lead individuals to expect reinforcement, while nonrewarded trials lead them to expect the absence of reward. Consequently, intermittent reinforce-

TABLE 10.4   Stages of Acquisition in Frustration Theory

Partial Reinforcement

I. Expectancy of reward → Respond

Expectancy of nonreward → Don't respond

II. Expectancy of reward → Respond

Expectancy of nonreward → Respond

Continuous Reinforcement

I. Expectancy of reward → Respond

II. Expectancy of reward → Respond

ment leads to the learning of expectations both of reward and of nonreward. At first, the expectation of reward encourages subjects to respond, while the expectation of nonreward discourages responding. Thus, early in training, subjects receiving intermittent reinforcement are conflicted about what to do. Their expectations encourage opposite response tendencies. As training continues, however, this conflict is resolved in favor of responding.

The resolution of the conflict occurs because, in the typical partial-reinforcement schedule, reinforcement is not predictable. Therefore, the instrumental response ends up being reinforced on some of the occasions when the subject expects nonreward. As a result of such episodes, the instrumental response becomes conditioned to the expectation of nonreward. According to frustration theory, this is the key to persistent responding in extinction. With sufficient training, *intermittent reinforcement results in learning to make the instrumental response in anticipation of nonreward.* Once the response has become conditioned to the expectation of nonreward, responding persists when extinction is introduced.

By contrast, there is nothing about the experience of continuous reinforcement that encourages subjects to respond when they expect nonreward. With continuous reinforcement, subjects learn only to expect reward and to make the instrumental response when this reward expectancy is activated. Continuous reinforcement does not teach subjects to make the instrumental response when they expect nonreward, and therefore it does not produce persistence in extinction.

Sequential Theory.   Sequential theory was proposed by Capaldi (1967, 1971) and is heavily based on ideas related to memory. It assumes that subjects can remember whether or not they were reinforced for performing the instrumental response in the recent past. They remember both recently rewarded and recently nonrewarded trials. The theory further assumes that during intermittent-reinforcement training, the memory of nonreward becomes a cue for performing the instrumental response. According to sequential theory, this produces persistence in extinction. Precisely how this happens depends a great deal on the sequence of rewarded (R) and nonrewarded (N) trials that are administered in the intermittent-reinforcement schedule. This is why the theory is labeled "sequential."

Consider the following sequence of trials: RNNRRNR. In this sequence the subject is rewarded on the first trial, not rewarded on the next two trials, then rewarded twice, then not rewarded, and then rewarded again. The fourth and last trials are critical in this schedule and are therefore underlined. On the fourth trial, the subject is reinforced after receiving nonreward on the two preceding trials. It is assumed that the subject remembers the two nonrewarded trials when it is reinforced on the fourth trial. Because of this, the memory of two nonrewarded trials becomes a cue for responding. Responding in the face of the memory of nonreward is again reinforced on the last trial. On this trial, the animal is reinforced for responding during the memory of one nonrewarded trial. After enough experiences like these, the sub-ject learns to respond whenever it remembers not having gotten reinforce-ment on the preceding trials. This learning creates persistence of the instru-mental response in extinction.

Some have regarded frustration theory and sequential theory as compet-ing explanations of the partial-reinforcement extinction effect. Since the two mechanisms were originally proposed, however, a large and impressive body of evidence has been obtained in support of each theory. Therefore, it is inappropriate to regard one theory as correct and the other as incorrect. Rather, the two theories identify two different ways in which partial rein-forcement can promote persistence. Memory mechanisms may make more of a contribution when training trials are not separated by long intertrial inter-vals (thereby reducing the difficulty of remembering the outcome of the pre-ceding trial). In contrast, the emotional learning described by frustration theory is less sensitive to intertrial intervals and thus provides a better ex-planation of the PREE when widely spaced training trials are used. However, the prudent conclusion is that both mechanisms contribute to persistence in most situations.

Summary

Reinforcement procedures are not always permanent. The study of extinc-tion tells us what happens when a response is no longer reinforced or a CS is no longer paired with a US. Extinction produces two prominent behavioral changes: a decrease in the conditioned response and an increase in response variability. These changes depend on the previous circumstances of re-inforcement. Overtraining and the use of a large reinforcer produce faster decreases in responding during extinction, especially with continuous re-inforcement. In contrast, partial or intermittent reinforcement slows the re-sponse decline. The decrease in responding that occurs with extinction may look like the opposite of acquisition, but many lines of evidence indicate that extinction does not erase the effects of prior acquisition training. These phe-nomena include spontaneous recovery, renewal, and reinstatement. Extinc-tion also does not erase R-O and S-O associations. Rather, extinction ap-pears to involve the establishment of an inhibitory S-R association, based on the frustrative effects of nonreward.

Practice Questions

1. What are the primary effects of extinction?

2. What lines of evidence demonstrate that extinction does not involve unlearning?

3. How do acquisition and extinction effects transfer from one context to another? Why is one procedure more (or less) susceptible to changes in context?

4. If extinction does not involve unlearning, what produces the response suppression that is observed in extinction?

5. What are paradoxical reward effects and why are they "paradoxical"?

6. What mechanisms have been proposed to explain the partial-reinforcement-extinction effect?

7. What are some implications of recent findings about extinction for behavior therapy?

Suggested Readings

Amsel, A. (1992). *Frustration theory: An analysis of dispositional learning and memory*. Cambridge, UK: Cambridge University Press.

Bouton, M. E. (1994). Conditioning, remembering, and forgetting. *Journal of Experimental Psychology: Animal Behavior Processes, 20*, 219–231.

Bouton, M. E. (2001). Classical conditioning and clinical psychology. In N. J. Smelser & P. B. Baltes (Eds.), *Encyclopedia of the social and behavioral sciences*. Amsterdam: Elsevier Science.

Capaldi, E. J. (1971). Memory and learning: A sequential viewpoint. In W. K. Honig & P. H. R. James (Eds.), *Animal memory* (pp. 115–154). Orlando, FL: Academic Press.

Rescorla, R. A. (2001). Experimental extinction. In R. R. Mowrer & S. B. Klein (Eds.), *Contemporary learning theories* (pp. 119–154). Mahwah, NJ: Erlbaum.

Technical Terms

Continuous reinforcement

Discrimination hypothesis

Extinction

Forgetting

Frustration

Frustration theory

Inhibitory S-R association

Intermittent reinforcement

Magnitude-of-reinforcement extinction effect

Overtraining extinction effect

Paradoxical reward effect

Partial reinforcement

Partial-reinforcement extinction effect

Reinstatement

Renewal

Sequential theory

Spontaneous recovery

CHAPTER ELEVEN

Punishment

DID YOU KNOW THAT:

- Punishment does not have to involve physical pain.
- When properly applied, punishment can produce permanent suppression of behavior in a single trial.
- The effectiveness of punishment is substantially reduced by delivering punishment intermittently or with a delay.
- Mild punishment for an initial offense may immunize the individual to further punishment.
- Severe punishment for an initial offense may sensitize the individual to further punishment.
- The effectiveness of punishment is greatly increased by positive reinforcement of alternative behavior.
- Punishment facilitates responding if it signals positive reinforcement or if the punished response is a form of escape behavior.
- When one person punishes another out of anger or frustration, the parameters of effective punishment are usually violated, and no constructive changes in behavior are produced.

In discussing instrumental conditioning up to this point, I have relied primarily on examples of positive reinforcement—examples in which the instrumental response results in the delivery of an appetitive or "pleasant" event. It is common knowledge that instrumental behavior can also be controlled by aversive or "unpleasant" events. Perhaps the simplest aversive control procedure is **punishment.** In a punishment procedure, an aversive event is delivered contingent on the performance of an instrumental response. The expected or typical outcome is suppression of the punished behavior. However, the degree of response suppression depends on numerous factors, many of which are not intuitively obvious.

Punishment is the most controversial topic in conditioning and learning. It conjures up visions of cruelty and abuse and is the only conditioning procedure whose application is regulated by law. However, punishment need not involve unusual forms of physical cruelty or pain. A variety of aversive events have been used for punishment effectively, including verbal reprimands, monetary fines, placement in a time-out corner or a time-out room, loss of earned privileges or positive reinforcers, demerits, various restitution procedures, and even water mist or a squirt of lemon juice in the mouth. Electric shock is rarely used as a punisher with people, but it is common in animal research because with a shock stimulus, intensity and duration can be controlled more precisely than with other types of aversive events.

The stage for the punishment debate was set by Thorndike early in the twentieth century. Thorndike (1932) claimed that punishment is ineffective in producing significant and lasting changes in behavior and therefore should not be used. Based on his own studies, Skinner (1953) adopted a similar point of view. He argued that we should make every effort to eliminate the use of punishment in society because punishment is cruel and ineffective. Whether punishment is cruel cannot be decided by means of empirical evidence. However, the other aspect of the argument—that punishment is ineffective—can be tested experimentally. Contrary to the early claims of Thorndike and Skinner, such tests have indicated that punishment can be very effective in suppressing behavior, provided the punishment is properly applied.

Effective and Ineffective Punishment

Casual observation suggests that Thorndike's and Skinner's claims that punishment is ineffective may be correct. Violations of traffic laws are punished by fines and other unpleasant consequences. Nevertheless, we often see people going through red lights or driving faster than the posted speed limit. Grade-school children scolded by a teacher for not having their homework completed do not necessarily finish their next assignment on time. And a drug dealer apprehended for selling cocaine or heroin is likely to return to selling drugs once he is released from jail.

In contrast to the above examples, punishment is sometimes remarkably effective. A child who accidentally gets shocked while playing with an electric outlet is unlikely to poke his fingers into an outlet ever again. A person who falls and hurts herself rushing down a slippery staircase will slow down next time she has to negotiate the stairs. Someone who tips over a canoe by leaning too far to one side the first time out will be much more careful about staying in the middle of the canoe after that.

Why punishment is highly effective in suppressing behavior in some cases and ineffective in others has been the subject of extensive laboratory research, conducted mainly with rats and pigeons. In this chapter I will describe the most important findings with human examples. Keep in mind, however, that the empirical foundations of my claims come primarily from research with laboratory animals (Azrin & Holz, 1966; Church, 1969). Let us first consider the cases in which punishment fails.

WHEN PUNISHMENT FAILS

Why do drivers often exceed the speed limit even though speeding can result in a fine? Punishment in the enforcement of traffic laws is similar to punishment in much of the criminal justice system and in many social situations. In all of these cases, punishment is administered by an individual rather than being an automatic environmental consequence of a response. Unlike a canoe, which tips over automatically when someone leans too far to one side, drivers do not automatically get a ticket when they drive too fast. A police officer has to detect the transgression, and an officer of the court has to judge the severity of the offense and decide on what penalty to apply. Requiring officers to detect the response to be punished and administer the aversive stimulus can make punishment ineffective for a variety of reasons.

One consequence of requiring a police officer to detect speeders is that drivers are not caught every time they exceed the speed limit. In fact, the chances of getting caught are pretty slim. A driver may exceed the speed limit 50 times or more without getting caught for each time his speed is recorded by a patrol officer. Thus, *punishment is highly intermittent.*

On the rare occasion when a driver who is speeding is detected, chances are that he is not detected right away but only after he has been going too fast for some time. Thus, *punishment is delayed* after the initiation of the behavior targeted for punishment. Further delays in punishment occur because fines do not have to be paid right away. A ticket is issued that must be settled within a week or two. Tickets can also be appealed, and an appeal may take several months.

If the appeal is unsuccessful, punishment for the first offense is likely to be fairly mild. The driver will probably just have to pay a fine. More severe penalties are imposed only if the driver is repeatedly ticketed for speeding. Thus, *punishment is initially mild and increases in severity only after repeated offenses.* This gradual escalation of the severity of punishment is a fundamen-

TABLE 11.1   **Characteristics of Punishment**

For Driving Too Fast	For Poking Fingers into an Electric Outlet
Occurs intermittently	Occurs every time
Delayed	Immediate
Low-intensity aversive stimulus at first	High-intensity aversive stimulus every time
Signaled by a discriminative stimulus	Not signaled

tal aspect of societal uses of punishment. Someone who does something undesirable is first given a warning and a second chance. We get serious about punishing him only after repeated offenses.

Another reason punishment is not effective in discouraging speeding is that drivers can often tell when they are about to be clocked by a patrol officer. In some cities, the location of radar checkpoints is announced on the radio each morning. The presence of traffic police is also obvious from the distinctive markings of patrol cars. Furthermore, many drivers have radar detectors in their cars that signal the presence of a radar patrol. Patrol cars and radar detectors provide discriminative stimuli for punishment. Thus, *punishment is often signaled by a discriminative stimulus*. (See Table 11.1.)

WHEN PUNISHMENT SUCCEEDS

In contrast to the ineffectiveness of punishment in discouraging speeding, why does punishment work so well in discouraging a child from poking his fingers into an electric outlet? A child shocked while playing with an electric outlet is unlikely ever to do that again and may in fact develop a strong fear of outlets. What are the critical differences in the punishment contingencies involved in driving too fast and in playing with an electric outlet?

First, *punishment occurs consistently* for sticking your fingers into an electric outlet. Every time you do that, you will get shocked. If you touch an outlet and come in contact with the electrodes, you are sure to get shocked. The physical configuration of the outlet guarantees that punishment is delivered every time.

Second, *punishment is immediate*. As soon as you make contact with the electrodes, you get shocked. There is no elaborate detection or decision process involved to delay delivery of the aversive stimulus.

Third, *punishment is intense for the first transgression*. The outlet does not give you a warning the first time you touch the electrodes. The first offense is treated with the same severity as the tenth one. Each and every time you make the response, you get an intense shock.

Finally, punishment is not limited to times when a police officer or observer is watching. Thus, *punishment is not signaled* by a discriminative stimulus. There is no light or buzzer to tell you when the outlet will be "hot." No matter who is present in the room or what else may going on, sticking your fingers into the outlet will get you shocked. Severe and immediate punishment is always in effect for each occurrence of the target response.

Research Evidence on Punishment

All of the factors that characterize the punishment for touching the electrodes in an electric outlet have been found to be important in carefully conducted experimental work. Moreover, research has identified several additional factors that strongly determine the effectiveness of punishment. Ironically, much of the research was done under the leadership of one of Skinner's former students, Nathan Azrin (Azrin & Holz, 1966). Complementary studies were performed in a research program conducted by Church (1969). Azrin used pigeons for much of his research, whereas Church used laboratory rats. Contrary to the early claims of Thorndike and Skinner, these experiments demonstrated that punishment can be a highly effective technique for producing rapid and long-term changes in behavior.

RESPONSE-REINFORCER CONTINGENCY

Punishment is similar to positive reinforcement in that it involves a positive contingency between the instrumental response and the reinforcer. The reinforcer is delivered only if the organism has previously performed the target response. The primary difference between punishment and positive reinforcement is that in punishment the reinforcer is an aversive stimulus.

As with other instrumental conditioning procedures, a fundamental variable in punishment is the response-reinforcer contingency. This refers to the extent to which delivery of the aversive stimulus depends on the prior occurrence of the target response. If an aversive stimulus is administered independently of the target response, the procedure is a form of Pavlovian aversive conditioning rather than punishment. As we saw in Chapter 4, Pavlovian aversive conditioning results in the conditioning of fear, which is evident in freezing or the general suppression of ongoing behavior.

Some general suppression of ongoing behavior can result from punishment procedures as well. However, punishment also produces behavioral suppression specific to the target response (Camp, Raymond, & Church, 1967; Goodall, 1984). The specificity of the behavioral suppression depends on the contingency between the target response and the aversive reinforcer. The stronger the response-reinforcer contingency, the more specific is the response suppression produced by punishment.

RESPONSE-REINFORCER CONTIGUITY

As I previously described for positive reinforcement, the response-reinforcer contingency is just one aspect of the relation between an instrumental response and a reinforcer. Another important factor is the interval between the target response and delivery of the reinforcer. In a punishment procedure, this is the interval between the target response and the aversive consequence.

Response-reinforcer contiguity is just as important with punishment as it is with positive reinforcement. Punishment is most effective if the aversive stimulus is presented without delay after the target response (Camp et al., 1967). If punishment is delayed after the target response, some suppression of behavior may occur. However, the response suppression will not be specific to the punished response.

INTENSITY OF THE AVERSIVE STIMULUS

As one might suspect, the response-suppressing effects of punishment are directly related to the intensity of the aversive stimulus. Research with rats and pigeons has shown that low intensities of punishment produce only mild suppression of behavior. In contrast, dramatic suppressions of behavior may result from the use of intense aversive stimuli (Azrin, 1960). More important, the effects of the intensity of punishment depend largely on the participant's prior experience with punishment. In general, individuals tend to respond to a new level of punishment similar to how they responded during earlier encounters with punishment.

The historical effects of exposure to punishment can lead to somewhat unexpected results. Consider, for example, individuals who are initially exposed to a low intensity of punishment. Weak aversive stimuli produce only mild, if any, suppression of responding. Animals exposed to low-intensity punishment learn to continue to respond with little disruption in their behavior. Furthermore, their persistent responding in the face of mild punishment generalizes to higher intensities of aversive stimulation (Azrin, Holz, & Hake, 1963; Miller, 1960). As a result, the animals continue to respond when the intensity of punishment is increased. In a sense, exposure to mild aversive stimulation serves to immunize individuals against the effects of more-intense punishment (see Figure 11.1).

Interestingly, a history of exposure to intense punishment can have just the opposite effect. Initial exposure to intense punishment can increase the impact of subsequent mild punishment (see Figure 11.2). High-intensity aversive stimulation produces dramatic suppression of the punished response, and this severe suppression of responding persists when the intensity of the aversive stimulus is subsequently reduced (Church, 1969). Thus, mild punishment produces much more severe suppression of behavior in individuals who have previously received intense punishment than in individuals

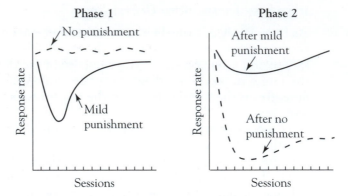

FIGURE 11.1 **Immunizing effects of prior experience with mild punishment.**
During Phase 1, one group of subjects is exposed to mild punishment while another group is permitted to respond without punishment. During Phase 2, both groups receive intense punishment. (Note: Data are hypothetical.)

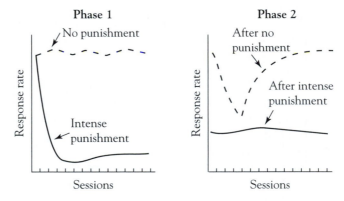

FIGURE 11.2 **Sensitizing effects of experience with intense punishment.**
During Phase 1, one group of subjects is exposed to intense punishment while another group is permitted to respond without punishment. During Phase 2, both groups receive mild punishment. (Data are hypothetical.)

who were not punished previously. Exposure to intense punishment sensitizes the participant to subsequent mild aversive stimulation.

SIGNALED PUNISHMENT

Some punishment contingencies are always in effect. However, more commonly (particularly in the case of punishment administered by a teacher or patrol officer), the punishment contingency is only in effect in the presence of particular stimuli. If punishment is signaled by a distinctive stimulus, the procedure is called **discriminative punishment.** A child, for example, may be reprimanded for running through the living room when her parents are home but not when her grandparents are in charge. In this case, punishment would be signaled by cues associated with the presence of the child's parents. The parents would be discriminative stimuli for punishment.

As you might suspect, a child reprimanded by her parents but not by her grandparents will avoid running through the living room when her parents are home but will not show such restraint when the grandparents are in charge. Discriminative-punishment procedures result in discriminative suppression of behavior (Dinsmoor, 1952). Responding becomes suppressed in the presence of the discriminative stimulus, but continues unabated when the discriminative stimulus is absent.

Discriminative control of a punished response can be problematic. A parent may try to get a child not to use foul language by punishing him whenever he curses. This may discourage the child from cursing in the presence of the parent but will not stop him from cursing around his friends. The suppression of foul language will be under discriminative control, and the parent's goal will not be achieved.

In other cases, the discriminative punishment is not problematic. If a child starts talking loudly during a religious service, she is likely to be reprimanded. If the punishment procedure is effective, the child will cease talking during the service, but this will not stop her from talking enthusiastically elsewhere. Having the response suppressed only under the discriminative-stimulus control of the church service is not a problem.

PUNISHMENT AND MECHANISMS MAINTAINING THE PUNISHED RESPONSE

Punishment procedures are applied to responses that already occur for one reason or another. Typically, punished responses are maintained by some form of positive reinforcement. This turns out to be very important, because the effects of punishment depend on the type of reinforcement and schedule of reinforcement that support the target response.

A child may talk during a church service to attract attention or to enjoy the camaraderie that comes from talking with a friend. If the child is reprimanded for talking, the aversiveness of the reprimand is pitted against the enjoyment of the attention and camaraderie. The outcome of the punishment procedure depends on how the individual solves this cost-benefit problem. Laboratory research with nonhuman subjects has shown that, in general, punishment will be less effective if the target response is reinforced often than if the target response is reinforced only once in a while (Church & Raymond, 1967).

The outcome of punishment also depends on the particular schedule of positive reinforcement that maintains the target response. With variable- and fixed-interval schedules, punishment reduces the overall level of responding but does not change the temporal distribution of behavior (e.g., Azrin & Holz, 1961). In contrast, if the instrumental response is maintained on a fixed-ratio schedule of reinforcement, punishment tends to increase the postreinforcement pause (Azrin, 1959; Dardano & Sauerbrunn, 1964).

PUNISHMENT AND REINFORCEMENT OF ALTERNATIVE BEHAVIOR

As we saw in the preceding section, the outcome of punishment procedures can be analyzed in terms of the relative costs and benefits of performing the target response. This cost-benefit analysis involves not only the punished response but also other activities the individual may perform. A powerful technique for increasing the effects of punishment is to provide positive reinforcement for some other behavior (Perry & Parke, 1975). Effective parents are well aware of this principle. Punishing children on a long car ride for quarreling among themselves is relatively ineffective if the children are not given much else to do. Punishment of quarreling is much more effective if it is accompanied by an alternative reinforced activity, such as listening to a story or playing with a new toy.

PARADOXICAL EFFECTS OF PUNISHMENT

The factors that I have described so far determine the extent to which punishment will suppress the target response. Punishment will not be very effective if the punished response is maintained by a powerful schedule of positive reinforcement, if there is no positive reinforcement for alternative behavior, or if the punishment is mild, delayed, and involves a weak response-reinforcer contingency. Weak punishment parameters make punishment ineffective. Under some circumstances, punishment may even produce the opposite of what is intended—facilitation rather than suppression of responding.

Punishment as a Signal for Positive Reinforcement.   Paradoxical facilitation of responding can occur when punishment serves as a signal for positive reinforcement (Holz & Azrin, 1961). Attention, for example, is a powerful source of reinforcement for children. A child may be ignored by his parents

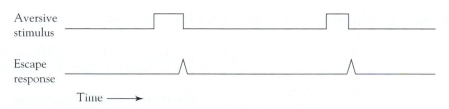

F I G U R E   1 1 . 3   Diagram of an escape or negative-reinforcement procedure.
The escape response occurs during the aversive stimulus and results in its termination.

---

most of the time as long as he is not doing anything dangerous or disruptive. If he starts playing with matches, he is severely reprimanded and sent to his room. Will punishment suppress the target response in this case? Not likely. Notice that the child receives attention from his parents only after he does something bad and is being punished. Under these circumstances, punishment can become a signal for positive reinforcement, with the outcome that the child will seek out punishment as a way of obtaining attention.

Punishment of Escape Behavior.   Paradoxical effects can also occur if punishment is applied to an escape response. An escape response serves to terminate an aversive stimulus. When a response terminates an aversive stimulus, thereby increasing the probability of the response, the stimulus is called a **negative reinforcer** and the operation is called **negative reinforcement.** (I will have more to say about negative reinforcement in Chapter 12.)

Negative reinforcement is highly constrained because before an organism can terminate an aversive stimulus, the aversive stimulus must be present or turned on. Thus, an escape response is performed in the presence of an aversive stimulus (see Figure 11.3). This makes the presence of the aversive stimulus a discriminative cue for the escape response.

Punishment of an escape response facilitates rather than suppresses responding (e.g., Dean & Pittman, 1991). This paradoxical effect occurs because the aversive stimulus used to punish the response preserves the conditions that motivated the behavior in the first place. Hence, the escape response persists even though it is being punished.

Paradoxical effects of punishment are not common, and they should not encourage us to jump to the conclusion that punishment produces unpredictable results. Rather, if a paradoxical effect of punishment is observed, one should examine the situation carefully to determine whether punishment had come to serve as a signal for positive reinforcement. If that does not seem likely, perhaps the target response was previously reinforced as an escape response.

Can and Should We Create a Society Free of Punishment?

As I noted at the beginning of this chapter, both Thorndike and Skinner advocated that punishment not be used, because they regarded punishment as ineffective in producing significant and lasting changes in behavior. Their recommendation was fine, but their reasoning was wrong. Laboratory experiments have shown that punishment can be highly effective in decreasing undesired behavior. Does this mean that we should go ahead and use punishment whenever we are interested in discouraging some activity? Or should we work to build a society entirely free of punishment? Answers to these questions depend in part on what one considers to be just and ethical human conduct. Ethical questions are outside the scope of this discussion. We can consider, however, how empirical evidence about the effectiveness of punishment may inform the decisions we make about societal uses of punishment.

First, can we create a punishment-free environment? It's unlikely. Punishment is an inevitable consequence of various aspects of the physical and biological environment. If you mishandle a cat, the cat will scratch you. If you don't hold your glass steady as you pour from a pitcher, you will spill and get your clothes wet. If you lift a pot out of the oven without a pot holder, you will burn yourself. It would be impossible to redesign our environment so as to eliminate all sources of punishment.

Given that punishment cannot be eliminated entirely, what kinds of punishment should we try to get rid of, and would doing that be sensible? The kind of punishment that people in our culture find most objectionable is physical pain inflicted by one person in an effort to control the behavior of someone else. We have laws against the use of corporal punishment in schools. We also have laws against child abuse and spousal abuse. Such laws are justified on moral and ethical grounds. Do such laws also make sense from the perspective of empirical principles of punishment? I think so.

Interpersonal interactions involving punishment require one individual to inflict pain on another. An important factor is the willingness of the person administering the punishment to hurt the recipient. A parent may claim to be punishing a child for having received a poor grade in school, or a husband may say that he is punishing his wife for getting home late. However, whether or not the punishment takes place is often related to the emotional state of the person who administers the punishment. People are more likely to administer punishment if they are frustrated and angry; and under such circumstances, principles of effective punishment are probably farthest from their mind. (For a recent discussion of contextual moderators of punishment practices, see Gershoff, 2002.)

If punishment is administered out of frustration and anger, it is not likely to be linked to an undesired response. A poor grade on a school assignment may not aggravate a parent every time, and so the punishment is likely to be intermittent. Frustrative punishment is also likely to occur sometime after the target response has taken place. A parent may become abusive when a child brings home a poor report card, even though the responses that contributed to the poor grades occurred over a period of weeks earlier.

Furthermore, frustrative punishment is often under discriminative stimulus control, with the discriminative stimulus being unrelated to the punished behavior. A parent may become upset by a poor report card when the parent's emotional resources are strained by events entirely unrelated to the child's behavior. The parent may be irritable because of stresses at work, ill health, or drug abuse. Under these circumstances, the likelihood of punishment will be signaled by the parent's irritability, and the child will learn that she can get her report card signed without being punished if she just waits until the next day or the weekend.

Another shortcoming of frustrative punishment is that it is rarely accompanied by positive reinforcement of alternative behavior. When a parent punishes a child out of irritability and anger, the parent is not likely to have the presence of mind to accompany the punishment with a programmatic effort to provide positive reinforcement for more constructive activities.

Punishment as an act of aggression and frustration violates many of the parameters of effective punishment and therefore does not produce constructive changes in behavior. Because punishment out of frustration is poorly related to the targeted behavior, frustrative punishment is abusive and cannot be justified as a systematic behavior modification procedure. To avoid administering punishment out of frustration, a reasonable rule of thumb is not to administer punishment on impulse.

Alternatives to Punishment

Abusive punishment cannot be justified on either ethical or empirical grounds. But undesired responses are bound to occur in homes, classrooms, and other settings. What are we to do about them? What alternatives are there to abusive punishment? Unfortunately, there are no easy answers. It has become clear that whatever procedure is adopted to suppress undesired responses, that procedure must be applied as part of a systematic program of intervention that considers not only the response to be suppressed but also the other activities of the individual and its other sources of reinforcement. We discussed in Chapter 9 how the effects of positive reinforcement depend on a broader behavioral context. The same thing is very much the case for punishment.

TIME-OUT

A popular alternative to physical punishment in educational settings is the **time-out** procedure. In fact, many classrooms have a time-out chair where a student has to sit if he is being punished. In a time-out procedure, the consequence of making an undesired response is not a physically aversive event but time-out from sources of positive reinforcement. A teenager who is "grounded" for a week for having taken the family car without permission is undergoing a form of the time-out procedure. Time-out is also being used when a child is told to "go to your room" as a form of punishment.

As with other instrumental conditioning procedures, the effectiveness of time-out depends on the delay between the target response and the time-out consequence. The effectiveness of the procedure also depends on how consistently it is applied. In addition, time-out involves some special considerations. To be effective, the procedure must result in a substantial reduction in the rate of positive reinforcement.

Whether a substantial reduction in reinforcement is experienced in time-out depends on how much reinforcement was available beforehand as compared with how much reinforcement is available in the time-out situation. Time-out is unlikely to suppress behavior if the individual is not getting much positive reinforcement anyway. A child who is not enjoying any aspect of being in a classroom will not experience much of a loss of reinforcement when he is put in time-out. One must also make sure that the time-out situation is actually devoid of reinforcement. A child who has many fun things to do in her room will not be discouraged by being sent to her room as a form of time-out.

DIFFERENTIAL REINFORCEMENT OF OTHER BEHAVIOR

Another alternative to abusive punishment is **differential reinforcement of other behavior** (abbreviated DRO). A DRO procedure involves a negative contingency between a target response and a reinforcer. I have previously discussed learning produced by a negative contingency in connection with inhibitory Pavlovian conditioning. There the negative contingency was between a conditioned and an unconditioned stimulus. The inhibitory CS indicated that the US would not occur. In a DRO procedure, the negative contingency is between a target instrumental response and presentations of a reinforcing stimulus. Occurrence of the target response leads to the omission of the reinforcer.

In a DRO procedure, the reinforcer is scheduled to be delivered periodically, every 30 seconds, for example. Occurrence of the target response causes cancellation of these scheduled reinforcers for a specified period. Thus, the target response may result in reinforcement being cancelled for the next 20 seconds. This serves to suppress the target response.

Cancelling a teenager's weekly allowance because she stayed out too late one night is an example of a DRO schedule. The allowance is provided on a regular basis. However, the occurrence of a target undesired response results in suspension of the allowance for a specified period.

DRO is different from the time-out procedure described in the preceding section in several respects. One important difference is that reinforcers are not cancelled by having the individual go to a specific time-out chair or time-out room. In a DRO procedure, previously scheduled reinforcers are simply omitted for a certain amount of time after the target response. Another important difference is that in the DRO procedure, reinforcers are explicitly provided when the target response does not occur. Thus, activities other than the target behavior are explicitly reinforced. This is why the procedure is called differential reinforcement of other behavior. It does not matter what those "other" behaviors are. But because organisms are always doing something, alternatives to the target response are reinforced in a DRO procedure.

A DRO procedure is more difficult to administer than the more common time-out procedure because it requires providing a reinforcer periodically when the target response is not made. To employ a DRO procedure, a convenient reinforcer must be identified and arrangements must be made to deliver the reinforcer over long periods of time. Thus, the DRO procedure requires interacting with the organism for long periods of time even if the response of interest does not occur.

Summary

In a punishment procedure, an aversive stimulus is presented contingent on the instrumental response. Punishment is highly effective in suppressing the target response if it is administered without delay, at a high intensity from the beginning, and each time the target response is made. The effectiveness of punishment can be further increased by providing positive reinforcement for alternative activities. Exposure to mild punishment at the beginning can result in learned resistance to the suppressive effects of more intense punishment, and signaling punishment can limit the response suppression to the presence of the signal. Punishment can result in a paradoxical increase in responding if it serves as a signal for positive reinforcement or is applied to escape behavior that is aversively motivated.

In daily life, the use of punishment is often related to the emotional state of the person who administers the aversive stimulus. People are likely to use punishment when they are frustrated and angry. Under these circumstances, many of the parameters of effective punishment are violated, with the result that no constructive changes in behavior are produced. Problems with the use of punishment have encouraged the use of alternatives such as time-out and differential reinforcement of other behavior. Successful application of any response-suppression procedure requires considering not only the undesired response but also the individual's other activities and other sources of reinforcement.

Practice Questions

1. What factors make punishment of drivers who exceed the speed limit ineffective?

2. What factors make punishment effective in the case of putting your finger into an electric outlet?

3. What is the relation between Pavlovian conditioned fear and instrumental punishment effects?

4. What is the effect of delaying the punishing stimulus?

5. What are the effects of the intensity of the punishing stimulus and its method of introduction?

6. What is discriminative punishment and what are its effects?

7. How is punishment related to positive reinforcement?

8. Under what circumstances does punishment increase responding?

9. What alternatives to punishment are there for discouraging an undesired response?

Suggested Readings

Azrin, N. H., & Holz, W. C. (1966). Punishment. In W. K. Honig (Ed.), *Operant behavior: Areas of research and application* (pp. 380–447). New York: Appleton-Century-Crofts.

Church, R. M. (1969). Response suppression. In B. A. Campbell & R. M. Church (Eds.), *Punishment and aversive behavior* (pp. 111–156). New York: Appleton-Century-Crofts.

Gershoff, E. T. (2002). Corporal punishment by parents and associated child behaviors and experiences: A meta-analysis and theoretical review. *Psychological Bulletin, 128,* 539–579.

Repp, A. C., & Singh, N. N. (Eds.). (1990). *Perspectives on the use of non-aversive and aversive interventions for persons with developmental disabilities.* Sycamore, IL: Sycamore.

Technical Terms

Differential reinforcement of other
  behavior
Discriminative punishment
Negative reinforcement

Negative reinforcer
Punishment
Time-out

CHAPTER TWELVE

Avoidance Learning

DID YOU KNOW THAT:

- Avoidance is a form of instrumental conditioning in which the instrumental response prevents the delivery of an aversive stimulus.

- No major theory assumes that avoidance behavior is reinforced by the absence of the avoided aversive stimulus.

- Although avoidance is a form of instrumental behavior, theories of avoidance learning rely heavily on concepts from Pavlovian conditioning.

- In many situations, avoidance learning is assumed to involve learning about internal temporal cues and proprioceptive or feedback cues.

- Avoidance behavior is strongly determined by the preexisting defensive behavior of the organism.

Punishment is just one of the major forms of instrumental conditioning that involve aversive stimuli. Another form of aversive control is avoidance conditioning. In punishment procedures, performance of the instrumental response results in the presentation of an aversive stimulus. In avoidance conditioning, performance of the instrumental response prevents or blocks the presentation of the aversive event.

We do a lot of things that prevent something bad from happening. Putting out one's hand when approaching a door prevents the discomfort of walking into a closed door; grabbing a handrail prevents the discomfort of slipping on a flight of stairs; slowing down while driving prevents a collision with the car in front of you; putting on a coat prevents you from catching a chill. All of these are avoidance responses.

As with other forms of instrumental conditioning, avoidance procedures involve a contingency between an instrumental response and a motivating or reinforcing stimulus. Avoidance conditioning differs from positive reinforcement in two ways. First, the motivating or reinforcing event is an unpleasant or **aversive stimulus.** Second, the contingency between the instrumental response and the motivating stimulus is negative. With a negative contingency, if the organism performs the instrumental response, the aversive event is not delivered. Thus, by responding, the participant prevents the delivery of the aversive reinforcer.

Since I have already discussed various instrumental conditioning procedures, and since people are highly familiar with avoidance learning from personal experience, one might suppose that analyses of avoidance conditioning would be fairly straightforward, if not self-evident. Unfortunately, this is not the case. In fact, avoidance learning has been one of the most difficult forms of learning to analyze and explain. Because of thorny conceptual problems involved in avoidance learning, much of the research has been motivated by theoretical rather than practical considerations. This is in sharp contrast to research on punishment, which has been dominated by practical considerations.

Dominant Questions in the Analysis of Avoidance Learning

Avoidance procedures are clear enough: the participant performs an instrumental response that prevents the delivery of an aversive stimulus. However, it is not clear what aspect of the avoidance procedure reinforces the instrumental response. A successful avoidance response prevents the delivery of the aversive stimulus. Therefore, a successful avoidance response is followed by nothing. Mowrer and Lamoreaux (1942) pointed out that this raises a major theoretical question in the analysis of avoidance learning: *How can "nothing" reinforce behavior and produce learning?*

Various hypotheses and theories have been offered to explain how "nothing" can reinforce avoidance responding. The hypotheses and theories differ in many ways. However, all of the major explanations reject the common-sense idea that avoidance responses occur because they prevent the delivery of the aversive event. As we shall see, a number of ingenious proposals have been offered in an effort to explain avoidance learning without relying on the theoretically vacuous idea that "nothing" serves as a reinforcer.

The second major question in analyses of avoidance behavior is, *How are Pavlovian conditioning processes involved in avoidance learning?* As we have seen, Pavlovian conditioning processes have also been discussed in analyses of positively reinforced instrumental behavior (see Chapter 7). However, Pavlovian conditioning concepts have not dominated thinking about positively reinforced instrumental behavior as much as they have dominated analyses of avoidance learning. Historically, avoidance learning was regarded as a special case of Pavlovian conditioning. In fact, to this day some accounts of avoidance learning regard avoidance behavior as entirely the product of Pavlovian conditioning mechanisms.

Origins of the Study of Avoidance Learning

Avoidance learning was first investigated by the Russian scientist Bechterev (1913), who set out to study the conditioning of motor rather than glandular responses. The procedure Bechterev devised was fairly simple. He asked people to place a finger on metal electrodes resting on a table. A mild current could be passed through the electrodes, and this caused the participant to lift his finger. Thus, the unconditioned response was finger withdrawal. To turn the situation into one involving classical conditioning, Bechterev presented a brief warning stimulus immediately before the shock on each trial. As you might suspect, the participants quickly learned to lift their fingers when the CS was presented, and this was measured as the conditioned response.

Although Bechterev considered his finger-withdrawal technique to be a convenient way to study Pavlovian conditioning, more careful consideration of his procedure shows that in fact it was an instrumental rather than a Pavlovian procedure. Recall that the electrodes rested on the surface of a table; they were not attached to the participant's finger. Therefore, if the participant lifted his finger in response to the CS, he could entirely avoid getting shocked. This differs from standard Pavlovian conditioning procedures, in which the occurrence of the conditioned response does not alter the delivery of the US. Bechterev had inadvertently given his participants control over presentation of the unconditioned stimulus. This made the finger-withdrawal technique an instrumental rather than a Pavlovian conditioning procedure.

Contemporary Avoidance Conditioning Procedures

Two types of avoidance conditioning procedures are commonly used in contemporary research: the discriminated avoidance procedure and the nondiscriminated, or free-operant, avoidance procedure.

DISCRIMINATED AVOIDANCE

Without knowing it, Bechterev invented what has come to be known as the **discriminated avoidance** procedure. In a discriminated avoidance procedure, the response-reinforcer contingency is not always in effect. Rather, responding prevents delivery of the reinforcer only during discrete periods or trials when a CS or warning stimulus is presented. As illustrated in Figure 12.1, what happens during these trials depends on the participant's behavior. If the participant responds, the conditioned stimulus is turned off and the aversive US is not delivered. In contrast, if the participant fails to respond during the conditioned stimulus, the CS continues to be presented for its full duration and ends in the presentation of the aversive US. Thus, a discriminated avoidance procedure involves two types of trials, response trials and no-response trials, and the aversive US only occurs on trials without a response.

Since Bechterev's research, the discriminated avoidance procedure has been adapted for use with laboratory animals. In fact, most of the research on the theoretical mechanisms of avoidance learning has been done with laboratory rats. Typically the aversive unconditioned stimulus has been mild electric shock, because stimulus intensity and duration can be controlled more easily with shock than with other aversive stimuli. In addition, shock

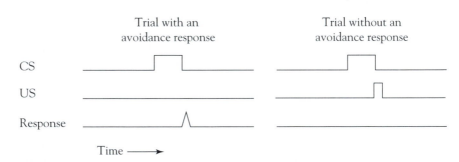

FIGURE 12.1   Diagram of the discriminated, or signaled, avoidance procedure.
If the organism responds during the warning signal or CS, the conditioned stimulus is turned off and the aversive US is not delivered. In contrast, if the organism fails to respond during the warning signal or CS, the CS continues to be presented for its full duration and ends in the presentation of the aversive US.

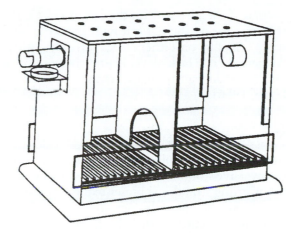

FIGURE 12.2   Shuttle box used in studies of avoidance learning.
The animal has to cross from one compartment to the other to avoid mild shock through the grid floor.

is unlike any other aversive stimulus the animals are likely to have encountered (or learned about) before participating in the experiment.

In some experiments, rats must press a response lever during the CS to avoid receiving the shock. In other experiments, they must run from one side to the other of a **shuttle box.** Figure 12.2 illustrates a typical shuttle box. It consists of a rectangular chamber divided into two compartments. The rat is allowed to move from one compartment to the other through an open doorway. Mild shock is administered through a grid floor. Each trial starts with presentation of a CS, a light or a tone, on one side of the apparatus. If the rat moves to the other side before the end of the CS, the shock does not occur. If the shuttle avoidance response is not made, the mild shock is turned on and remains on until the rat escapes to the other side.

The shuttle box can be used to implement either a one-way or a two-way avoidance procedure. In a **one-way avoidance** procedure, the participant is always placed in the same compartment at the start of each trial (e.g., the left side). Because each trial starts on the same side (left), the avoidance response always entails going in the same direction (left to right).

Notice that in a one-way avoidance procedure, the side the participant starts on is always potentially dangerous, because if the rat doesn't run to the other side it gets shocked. In contrast, the other side is always safe. The animal never gets shocked on the other side. Thus, a one-way avoidance procedure has a consistently safe side and a consistently dangerous side. This makes the one-way avoidance task rather easy to learn.

In a **two-way avoidance** procedure, trials can start either on the left side or the right side, depending on which compartment the animal happens to occupy. If the rat starts on the left, it must go to the right to avoid shock. If the rat starts on the right, it must go to the left side to avoid shock. Because trials can start on either side, both sides of the shuttle box are potentially dangerous. The lack of a consistently safe side makes the two-way avoidance task more difficult to learn than the one-way procedure (Theios, Lynch, & Lowe, 1966).

NONDISCRIMINATED OR FREE-OPERANT AVOIDANCE

In discriminated avoidance procedures, responding is effective in preventing the aversive stimulus only if the response occurs during the trial period, when the warning stimulus is presented. Responses made during the intertrial interval have no effect. In fact, in many studies the participants are removed from the apparatus during the intertrial interval. In contrast to such traditional discrete-trial procedures, Sidman (1953) devised a **nondiscriminated** or **free-operant avoidance** procedure.

Sidman's free-operant procedure was developed in the Skinnerian or operant tradition. In this tradition, trials are not restricted to periods when a discrete stimulus is present, and the participant can repeat the instrumental response at any time. On a fixed-ratio schedule in a Skinner box, for example, responses made at any time count toward completion of the ratio requirement. Sidman extended these features of operant methodology to the study of avoidance behavior.

In the free-operant avoidance procedure, an explicit warning stimulus is not used, and there are no discrete trials. The avoidance response may be performed at any time, and responding always provides some measure of benefit. Changing the oil in your car is an example. Changing the oil is an avoidance response that prevents engine problems. If you wait until the problems develop, you will encounter costly repairs. The best thing to do is to change the oil before any sign of engine difficulty. The recommended interval is every 3,000 miles. Thus, each oil change buys you 3,000 miles of trouble-free driving. You can change the oil after driving just 1,000 miles or drive 800 additional miles. Provided you change the oil before you have driven 3,000 miles, you won't have to do it again for the next 3,000 miles. Changing the oil in your car is just one example of a safety or health practice that involves doing something before signs of danger are evident. All of these are examples of free-operant avoidance contingencies.

In the laboratory, free-operant avoidance procedures employ a brief shock that is programmed to occur at set intervals. For example, the shock may be scheduled to occur every 15 seconds in the absence of an avoidance response. This is the shock-shock interval, or **S-S interval.** Performance of the avoidance response creates a period of safety, during which no shocks are given. The safe period may be 30 seconds. This is the response-shock interval, or **R-S interval** (see Figure 12.3). Whether a shock occurs at the end of the R-S interval or at the end of the S-S interval, it is not preceded by an explicit warning signal.

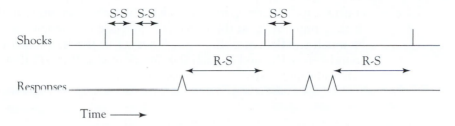

FIGURE 12.3   Diagram of a nondiscriminated, or free-operant, avoidance procedure.

As long as the animal fails to respond, a brief shock is scheduled to occur periodically, as set by the S-S interval. Each occurrence of the avoidance response creates a period without shock, as set by the R-S interval.

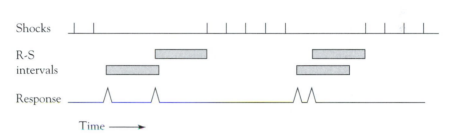

FIGURE 12.4   Effect of repeating the avoidance response early or late in an R-S interval in a free-operant avoidance procedure.

The R-S intervals are indicated by the shaded horizontal bars. On the left, the response was repeated late in an R-S interval; on the right, the response was repeated early in an R-S interval. Notice that the total time without shocks is longer if the response is repeated late in an R-S interval.

An important aspect of free-operant avoidance procedures is that the R-S interval is reset and starts over again each time the avoidance response is made. Thus, if the R-S interval is 30 seconds, each response resets the R-S interval and starts the 30-second period of safety all over again. Because of this feature, each occurrence of the avoidance response provides some benefit, just as each oil change provides some benefit. However, the degree of benefit depends on exactly when the response is made.

If the participant responds when the R-S interval is already in effect, the R-S interval will start over again, and time left on the R-S clock will be lost. The net benefit of responding will depend on whether the response occurs early or late in the R-S interval (see Figure 12.4). If the participant responds late in the R-S interval, it will lose only a small amount of time remaining on the R-S clock, and the net benefit of responding will be substantial. In contrast, if the participant responds early in the R-S interval, it will lose a lot of time remaining on the R-S clock, and the net benefit of responding will be much smaller. In either case, however, if the individual manages to respond before the end of each R-S interval, it will reset all of the R-S intervals and thereby successfully avoid all shocks.

Theoretical Approaches to Avoidance Learning

Because research on avoidance learning emerged from investigations of classical conditioning, classical conditioning has been very important in the analysis of avoidance learning. Initially, in fact, avoidance learning was considered to be entirely due to classical conditioning. As I noted earlier, Bechterev considered his finger-withdrawal task to be a classical conditioning procedure. In keeping with that interpretation, he considered the avoidance response to be a classically conditioned response to the warning signal, much like salivation conditioned to a visual cue paired with food. According to this interpretation, the fact that the avoidance response prevented the delivery of the aversive US was considered to be irrelevant to the acquisition of avoidance behavior.

TEST OF THE ROLE OF THE INSTRUMENTAL CONTINGENCY

The idea that preventing the aversive stimulus is irrelevant to avoidance learning is counterintuitive and has been found to be wrong. A powerful test of the idea was conducted by Brogden, Lipman, and Culler (1938), who studied the avoidance conditioning of guinea pigs in a running wheel apparatus. The design of the experiment is outlined in Table 12.1. Each trial started with a tone CS or warning signal. One group of subjects received a strictly Pavlovian conditioning procedure. For them, the warning signal always ended in a brief shock through the grid floor of the running wheel. A second group (the instrumental group) received a conventional discriminated avoidance procedure. If they rotated the wheel during the warning signal, the CS was turned off and the shock scheduled on that trial was omitted.

TABLE 12.1   Outline of the Brogden, Lipman, and Culler (1938) Experiment

---

Pavlovian Group

CS → Shock on all trials

Instrumental Group

CS → Shock if subject did not respond

CS → No shock, if subject responded

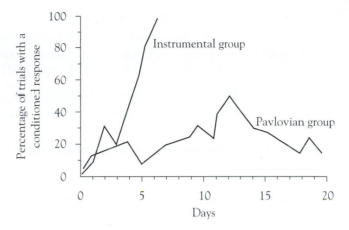

FIGURE 12.5   Results of the experiment by Brogden et al. (1938).
The Pavlovian group received a pure Pavlovian conditioning procedure. The instrumental group received a discriminated avoidance procedure.

Notice that from the perspective of Pavlovian conditioning, the instrumental group received a rather poor conditioning procedure. For the instrumental group, pairings of the warning signal with shock occurred only some of the time, namely, on trials when they did not respond. In contrast, for the Pavlovian group, the warning signal ended in shock on every trial. Therefore, if Pavlovian conditioning had been entirely responsible for avoidance learning, the Pavlovian group should have shown higher rates of responding than the instrumental group.

The results turned out just the opposite. The Pavlovian group responded significantly less often than the instrumental group. Within eight sessions, the subjects given the instrumental procedure were responding on 100 percent of the trials. In contrast, the Pavlovian group responded on just 20–30 percent of the trials, even after extensive training (see Figure 12.5).

The results of the study by Brogden et al. indicated clearly that the instrumental contingency makes a significant contribution to avoidance learning. Although the empirical result was unambiguous, the two dominant questions about avoidance learning remained unresolved. The experiment left no doubt that response consequences are important, but the reinforcer for avoidance responding remained unidentified. Successful avoidance responses were followed by nothing, and the experiment provided no hints about how "nothing" could serve as an effective reinforcer. Moreover, the experiment failed to clarify the role Pavlovian conditioning might play in avoidance learning. Was Pavlovian conditioning entirely irrelevant? If Pavlovian conditioning was not irrelevant, how was it involved?

THE TWO-FACTOR THEORY OF AVOIDANCE

The questions left unresolved by the Brogden et al. experiment were answered by the **two-factor theory** of avoidance behavior that was proposed about 10 years later by O. H. Mowrer (Mowrer, 1947; see also Miller, 1951). According to this theory, avoidance learning involves both classical and instrumental conditioning processes (hence the name "two-factor" theory). However, Mowrer did not describe either of these processes in ways that are intuitively obvious.

Let us first consider the classical conditioning process in the two-factor theory. Instead of thinking of classical conditioning as being directly responsible for the avoidance response (as Bechterev had thought), Mowrer proposed that this process results in the conditioning of a hypothetical emotional state called fear. On trials when the avoidance response does not occur, the CS or warning stimulus is paired with the aversive US, and this is assumed to result in the conditioning of fear to the warning stimulus.

Conditioned fear is presumably an unpleasant or aversive state. Therefore, the reduction or elimination of fear is assumed to be reinforcing. Fear reduction brings into play the second process in the two-factor theory. On trials when the avoidance response is made, the response turns off the warning stimulus and prevents the delivery of the US. Turning off the warning stimulus is assumed to result in the reduction of conditioned fear, and this fear reduction is assumed to provide reinforcement for the avoidance response. Thus, the second factor in the two-factor theory of avoidance is instrumental conditioning of the avoidance response through fear reduction.

Notice that according to the two-factor theory, avoidance behavior is not reinforced by "nothing" occurring after the avoidance response. Rather, the behavior is reinforced by fear reduction. Fear reduction is a form of **negative reinforcement** (removal of an aversive stimulus contingent on behavior). In the two-factor theory, the instrumental response is considered to be an escape response—a response that escapes fear. Instead of focusing on the fact that avoidance behavior prevents delivery of the aversive US, the two-factor theory treats avoidance behavior as a special type of escape behavior. (For an earlier discussion of escape behavior, see Chapter 11.)

Interactions between the Classical and Instrumental Factors.   The two-factor theory provides answers to many questions about avoidance learning. The answers were innovative when they were first proposed and have shaped the course of research on avoidance conditioning ever since. According to the theory, both Pavlovian and instrumental processes contribute to avoidance learning. Furthermore, the two processes are interdependent in various ways.

Before fear reduction can provide instrumental reinforcement for the avoidance response, fear must first become conditioned to the warning stimulus. Thus, classical conditioning of fear is a prerequisite for the instrumental component of the two-factor theory. The instrumental process depends on the integrity of the Pavlovian process.

The Pavlovian process is in turn influenced by the instrumental contingency, but in this case the influence is disruptive. Each time the avoidance response occurs, the aversive US is omitted, and the warning stimulus ends up being presented without the US. According to the principles of Pavlovian conditioning, this should result in extinction of the fear that had been conditioned to the warning stimulus. Thus, frequent avoidance responding should result in Pavlovian extinction of conditioned fear.

Extinction of fear in turn undermines the effectiveness of fear reduction as a source of instrumental reinforcement. If the instrumental avoidance response is no longer followed by fear reduction, the response will undergo extinction. As the avoidance response becomes extinguished, the warning stimulus will again end in presentation of the aversive US. This in turn should reactivate conditioning of fear to the warning signal. Once fear has become reconditioned to the warning stimulus, fear reduction can again serve as an effective reinforcer for instrumental responding. Thus, according to the two-factor theory, avoidance behavior is determined by a continually changing dynamic interaction of Pavlovian and instrumental processes.

Challenges to the Two-Factor Theory.   Many predictions of the two-factor theory have been substantiated. Despite these successes, however, the theory has been challenged by several striking results. One set of findings that has been challenging (but not fatal) for the two-factor theory is the phenomenon of free-operant avoidance behavior. As I noted earlier, in a free-operant avoidance procedure, shocks occur periodically without an explicit warning stimulus, and each occurrence of the avoidance response initiates a period of safety (the R-S interval). Since the mechanisms of the two-factor theory seem to require a warning stimulus, it is not obvious how the two-factor theory can explain free-operant avoidance behavior.

Another challenging phenomenon for the two-factor theory is the common observation that once well learned, avoidance responding persists at high levels for long periods of time even though shocks are no longer delivered. As noted above, a long string of avoidance responses should result in Pavlovian extinction of fear, which in turn should result in extinction of the instrumental avoidance response. This does not seem to happen (Solomon, Kamin, & Wynne, 1953).

A third major challenge for the two-factor theory is the fact that after participants become proficient in avoiding the aversive US, they do not seem to be very fearful. In fact, levels of conditioned fear often decline with increased proficiency in avoidance responding (Mineka & Gino, 1980). Common experience also suggests that little if any fear exists once an avoidance response becomes well learned. Steering a car so that it does not drift off the road is basically avoidance behavior; a competent driver avoids letting the car get too close to the side of the road or another lane of traffic. Yet proficient drivers show no fear under normal traffic conditions.

Conditioned Temporal Cues

Findings that are difficult to explain in terms of the two-factor theory of avoidance have encouraged modifications and additions to the theory. Efforts to integrate new findings with the two-factor theory have often involved postulating internal stimuli and ascribing important functions to these internal cues. For example, one approach to explaining nondiscriminated or free-operant avoidance behavior in terms of the two-factor theory involves assuming that internal cues related to the passage of time acquire conditioned aversive properties (Anger, 1963).

Recall that in a nondiscriminated avoidance procedure, explicit warning stimuli are not provided before each shock. However, shocks occur at predictable times. Free-operant avoidance procedures are constructed from two types of intervals (S-S intervals and R-S intervals), both of which are of fixed duration. In both S-S and R-S intervals, shock occurs when the intervals have been completed. Therefore, the passage of time is predictive of when the next shock will occur.

Free-operant avoidance learning can be explained in terms of the two-factor theory by assuming that individuals use the passage of time as a cue for when the next shock will occur. Animals (including people) are quite good at responding on the basis of the passage of time (Bradshaw & Szabadi, 1997). Time stimuli are referred to as **temporal cues.**

Temporal cues characteristic of the end of the S-S and R-S intervals are different from temporal cues characteristic of the beginning of these intervals. At first, participants probably do not distinguish between the beginning and end of the S-S and R-S intervals. However, they soon learn the difference, because early and late temporal cues have different consequences. Temporal cues that characterize the beginning of the S-S and R-S intervals are never paired with shock. If shock occurs, it always occurs at the end of these intervals. As a consequence of this differential reinforcement, participants can learn to distinguish the early and late temporal cues.

Temporal cues characteristic of the end of an S-S or R-S interval are paired with shock and presumably acquire conditioned aversive properties. Each avoidance response starts a new R-S interval and thereby reduces the conditioned aversiveness created by temporal cues characteristic of the end of the S-S and R-S intervals (see Figure 12.6). In this way, an avoidance response can result in reduction of conditioned fear and satisfy the tenets of the two-factor theory.

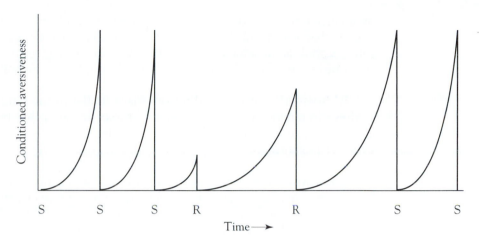

FIGURE 12.6 **The presumed conditioned aversiveness of temporal cues during R-S and S-S intervals in a free-operant avoidance procedure.**
R, occurrence of the avoidance response; S, occurrence of a brief shock. Notice the low levels of conditioned aversiveness at the beginning of each S-S and R-S interval, and high levels of aversiveness at the end of these intervals. Each occurrence of the response always reduces the conditioned aversiveness of temporal cues because each response starts a new R-S interval.

SAFETY SIGNALS IN AVOIDANCE LEARNING

The next explanation of avoidance learning that we shall consider — the **safety signal** hypothesis — also resulted from a consideration of internal cues that participants may experience during the course of avoidance conditioning. However, instead of focusing on cues that predict danger, the safety signal hypothesis focuses on signals for the absence of shock, or signals for safety (Dinsmoor, 1977).

In an avoidance procedure, periods of safety are best predicted by the occurrence of the avoidance response. After all, avoidance behavior cancels the delivery of an aversive stimulus. We know from biology that the movements of muscles and joints that are involved in making responses can give rise to internal **proprioceptive cues.** Such cues are also called response feedback cues, or simply **feedback cues.** The feedback cues that are produced by an avoidance response are followed by a predictable period without the aversive US, a predictable period of safety. As we saw in Chapter 5, stimuli that reliably predict the absence of a US may acquire Pavlovian conditioned inhibitory properties. Therefore, feedback cues generated by avoidance responses may also acquire Pavlovian conditioned inhibitory properties.

The safety signal explanation of avoidance learning is based on these ideas. According to the safety signal hypothesis, feedback cues from the avoidance response acquire Pavlovian conditioned inhibitory properties and thereby become signals for safety. In a situation involving potential danger, safety signals are assumed to be reinforcing. According to the safety signal hypothesis, avoidance behavior is positively reinforced by conditioned inhibitory safety signals.

Although the safety signal hypothesis is similar to the temporal cue hypothesis in relying on stimuli internal to the organism, it has been more accessible to experimental verification. The safety signal hypothesis has been evaluated by introducing an external stimulus (e.g., a brief tone) at the time the interoceptive feedback cue is presumed to occur. That is, a brief tone is presented when the participant performs the avoidance response. If the safety signal hypothesis is correct, such an exteroceptive cue should acquire conditioned inhibitory properties. Moreover, these conditioned inhibitory properties should make the feedback stimuli effective as a positive reinforcer for instrumental behavior. Both of these predictions have been confirmed (e.g., Morris, 1974, 1975; Weisman & Litner, 1972).

A less obvious prediction is that avoidance learning should be facilitated by increasing the salience of safety signal feedback cues. Consistent with this prediction, the introduction of an external-response feedback stimulus (which is presumably more salient than internal proprioceptive cues) substantially facilitates avoidance learning (e.g., D'Amato, Fazzaro, & Etkin, 1968).

The safety signal hypothesis is not incompatible with the two-factor theory and need not be viewed as an alternative to that theory. Rather, positive reinforcement through a conditioned inhibitory safety signal may be considered a third factor in avoidance learning that operates in combination with classical conditioning of fear and instrumental reinforcement through fear reduction.

AVOIDANCE LEARNING AND UNCONDITIONED DEFENSIVE BEHAVIOR

As I noted in Chapter 2, learning procedures are superimposed on an organism's preexisting behavioral tendencies, tendencies that an organism brings to a learning situation. Learned responses are the product of an interaction between the conditioning procedures used and the organism's preexisting behavioral structure. The two-factor theory and safety signal mechanisms are based on a simple view of what an organism brings to an aversive conditioning situation. For these learning mechanisms to operate, all we must assume is that the organism finds some stimulus aversive. Given an aversive stimulus, fear can become conditioned to a cue that predicts the aversive event, safety can become conditioned to a cue that predicts the absence of the aversive event, and fear reduction and safety can serve as reinforcers for any instrumental behavior.

About 30 years ago, it started to become evident that the preexisting behavioral tendencies organisms bring to an avoidance conditioning situation are much more complex than is presumed by the two-factor theory and the safety signal hypothesis. Organisms come into an avoidance conditioning situation not only with certain stimuli they find aversive but also with a rich behavioral repertoire for dealing with aversive situations. The existence of this unconditioned defensive behavior repertoire was first emphasized by Bolles (1970).

Bolles suggested that organisms could not survive with just the ability to detect aversive stimuli and the ability to learn about them through the Pavlovian and instrumental conditioning mechanisms presumed by traditional theories. The mechanisms of the two-factor theory and safety signal learning require extensive training to generate avoidance responses. An animal first has to learn about signals for danger and signals for safety. It then has to learn what instrumental responses are required to turn off the danger signals and produce the safety signals.

Bolles pointed out that in their natural habitat, animals may not have time to learn about danger and safety signals. An animal being pursued by a predator must avoid the danger successfully the first time, because otherwise it may not be alive for a second or third trial. Since dangerous situations require effective coping mechanisms without much opportunity for practice, Bolles suggested that organisms respond to aversive situations with a hierarchy of unconditioned defensive responses, which he called **species-specific defense reactions,** or **SSDRs.**

The SSDR Theory of Avoidance.   Because SSDRs are unconditioned responses to aversive stimuli, they are assumed to predominate during the initial stages of avoidance training. SSDRs are responses such as freezing, fleeing, and fighting. Bolles suggested that which particular SSDR occurs depends on the nature of the aversive stimulus and the response opportunities provided by the environment. If a familiar and effective means of escape is available, the animal is most likely to try to flee when it encounters the aversive stimulus. Without a familiar escape route, freezing will be the predominant defensive response. In social situations, fighting may predominate.

In addition to describing what animals are likely to do initially in an aversive situation, the SSDR theory also specified how an avoidance conditioning procedure can shape the future actions of the organism. In contrast to the negative- and positive-reinforcement mechanisms of earlier theories, the SSDR theory presumed that defensive responses were shaped and selected by punishment.

If the particular species-specific defense reaction that occurred during the first few trials of an avoidance conditioning procedure was not effective in preventing the aversive US, the aversive stimulus would be applied and the SSDR would end up being punished. Suppression by punishment of the first SSDR the animal made would then result in a switch to the next-most-likely SSDR in that situation. If this second response also turned out to be ineffective in preventing delivery of the aversive US, it would be punished and suppressed as well. This in turn would result in switching to the third SSDR in the response hierarchy.

According to the SSDR theory, the participant would eventually end up performing the required avoidance response as its ineffective SSDRs became suppressed by punishment. The required avoidance response was assumed to emerge not because it was reinforced by shock avoidance, fear reduction, or safety signals. Rather, the required avoidance response presumably emerged because it was the only response that was not followed by the aversive US and thus the only response not suppressed by punishment.

The SSDR theory advanced our knowledge of avoidance learning a great deal, because it emphasized that avoidance learning is influenced by the pre-existing defensive behavior of the organism. However, details of the SSDR theory have not survived subsequent empirical scrutiny. Punishment has not been found to be effective in suppressing SSDRs (e.g., Bolles & Riley, 1973). In addition, SSDRs appear to be organized by the likelihood that injury is about to happen rather than by response opportunities provided by the environment (Fanselow, 1997).

The Predatory Imminence Continuum.   Animals do one thing when they perceive a low likelihood of injury and other things when the likelihood of injury is higher. The different defensive responses that are elicited by different degrees of perceived danger constitute the **predatory imminence** continuum (Fanselow, 1997; Fanselow & Lester, 1988).

The predatory imminence continuum has been investigated most extensively in laboratory rats (Fanselow, 1989, 1994). Rats are preyed upon by various attackers, including snakes. Different modes of defensive behavior are activated depending on the rat's perceived likelihood of injury (see Figure 12.7). The pre-encounter response mode is activated if during the course of its foraging, a rat wanders into an area where there is some chance of finding a snake, but the snake has not been encountered yet. In the pre-encounter mode, the rat may move to a safer area. If a safer area is not available, the rat will become more cautious in its foraging. It will rarely go out of its burrow, and on those few excursions it will eat larger meals (Fanselow, Lester, & Helmstetter, 1988).

If the pre-encounter defensive responses are not successful and the rat encounters the snake, the predator-encounter response mode will be activated. In the predator-encounter mode, freezing is the predominant response. Finally, if this defensive behavior is also unsuccessful and the rat is attacked by the snake, the predator-contact response mode will be activated. In the predator-contact mode, the rat will suddenly leap into the air and strike out at the snake. This is called a circa strike response (see Figure 12.7).

Pre-existing behavioral tendencies are likely to predominate during early avoidance conditioning trials, before much learning has taken place. With continued training, the Pavlovian and instrumental mechanisms presumed by the two-factor theory and the safety signal hypothesis will come into play.

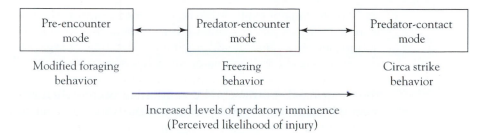

FIGURE 12.7   **The predatory imminence continuum.**
Different modes of defensive behavior are activated at different levels of predatory imminence. The pre-encounter mode represents the defensive behavior of an animal before it encounters a predator. The predator-encounter mode represents defensive behavior after the animal has encountered a predator. The predator-contact mode represents its behavior after the predator has made physical contact.

However, the predatory imminence continuum is also likely to be reflected in the behavioral manifestations of the learning processes that are activated by an avoidance procedure.

As I noted in Chapter 4, conditioning involves incorporating new stimuli into a preexisting behavior system. In an avoidance conditioning situation, the aversive US involves the highest level of predatory imminence and activates the predator-contact response mode. The warning stimulus that occurs before the aversive US is highly predictive of the US and activates the predator-encounter mode. We may expect responses such as freezing that are characteristic of the predator-encounter mode to develop to conditioned stimuli that become associated with an unconditioned aversive event. In contrast, safety signals should elicit recuperative and relaxation responses, because they signal the total absence of predatory imminence. These considerations illustrate that even when organisms learn about an aversive situation, their behavior is heavily influenced by the preexisting organization of their defensive behavior system.

Summary

Studies of avoidance learning originated in studies of classical conditioning and relied on a discrete-trial method in which a warning signal ended in a brief shock unless the avoidance response was made. Subsequently, free-operant avoidance procedures that did not employ explicit warning signals were developed. Regardless of which method is used, however, avoidance learning is puzzling, because the consequence of an avoidance response is that nothing happens. How can "nothing" motivate learning?

The first major explanation of avoidance learning, the two-factor theory, assumed that avoidance behavior is the result of a dynamic reciprocal interaction between classical and instrumental conditioning. According to this theory, classical conditioning occurs when the participant fails to make the avoidance response and the warning signal is followed by an aversive US. On the other hand, instrumental conditioning occurs when the avoidance response is made, because this terminates the warning signal and reduces conditioned fear. Subsequent research has identified a third factor, safety signal learning, that also contributes to avoidance learning. According to the safety signal hypothesis, cues that accompany the omission of the US in an avoidance procedure become conditioned inhibitors of fear and provide instrumental reinforcement for the avoidance response.

Much of the experimental evidence on avoidance learning is compatible with the two-factor theory supplemented by safety signal learning, especially when temporal and proprioceptive cues are taken into account. However, these mechanisms require numerous conditioning trials to develop. Therefore, these mechanisms are of little help to an animal that encounters a dangerous predator and has to defend itself successfully the first time or face death or dismemberment. In response to these selective pressures, animals have evolved with a rich unconditioned defensive behavioral repertoire. The current view is that unconditioned species-specific defense reactions are organized by predatory imminence, with different defensive response modes activated by different levels of perceived danger from predatory attack.

Practice Questions

1. What are the two primary issues that theories of avoidance learning have to address?

2. What is a discriminated avoidance procedure?

3. What is a nondiscriminated avoidance procedure?

4. What are the basic concepts of the two-factor theory of avoidance? How does this theory treat the two primary avoidance problems?

5. How do classical and instrumental conditioning interact in avoidance learning, according to the two-factor theory?

6. What findings challenge the two-factor theory of avoidance?

7. How is the concept of temporal cues helpful in explaining free-operant avoidance behavior?

8. How does the safety signal hypothesis operate?

9. What are SSDRs and how are they involved in avoidance situations?

Suggested Readings

Bolles, R. C. (1972b). The avoidance learning problem. In G. H. Bower (Ed.), *The psychology of learning and motivation* (Vol. 6). Orlando, FL: Academic Press.

Bouton, M. E., Mineka, S., & Barlow, D. H. (2001). A modern learning theory perspective on the etiology of panic disorder. *Psychological Review, 108,* 4–32.

Fanselow, M. S. (1997). Species-specific defense reactions: Retrospect and prospect. In M. E. Bouton & M. S. Fanselow (Eds.), *Learning, motivation, and cognition* (pp. 321–341). Washington, DC: American Psychological Association.

Fanselow, M. S., & Lester, L. S. (1988). A functional behavioristic approach to aversively motivated behavior: Predatory imminence as a determinant of the topography of defensive behavior. In R. C. Bolles & M. D. Beecher (Eds.), *Evolution and learning* (pp. 185–212). Hillsdale, NJ: Erlbaum.

Herrnstein, R. J. (1969). Method and theory in the study of avoidance. *Psychological Review, 87,* 49–69.

McAllister, D. E., & McAllister, W. R. (1991). Fear theory and aversively motivated behavior: Some controversial issues. In M. R. Denny (Ed.), *Fear, avoidance, and phobias* (pp. 135–163). Hillsdale, NJ: Erlbaum.

Technical Terms

Aversive stimulus	R-S interval
Discriminated avoidance	S-S interval
Feedback cue	Safety signal
Free-operant avoidance	Shuttle box
Negative reinforcement	Species-specific defense response
Nondiscriminated avoidance	SSDR
One-way avoidance	Temporal cues
Predatory imminence	Two-factor theory
Proprioceptive cue	Two-way avoidance

CHAPTER THIRTEEN

Stimulus Control of Behavior

DID YOU KNOW THAT:

- Differential responding is used to identify control of behavior by a particular stimulus.
- Even simple stimuli have many features or dimensions.
- Control of behavior by one training stimulus often generalizes to other similar stimuli.
- Stimulus generalization and stimulus discrimination are complementary concepts.
- Generalization of behavior from one stimulus to another depends on the individual's training history with the stimuli.
- Discrimination training produces differential responding and increases the steepness of generalization gradients.
- Equivalence training leads to responding in the same manner to physically different stimuli.
- The learning of words and perceptual concepts involves an interplay between different levels of discrimination and generalization learning.

Throughout the book, we have seen various aspects of behavior that are controlled by environmental events. Elicited behavior and responding that results from Pavlovian conditioning are obvious examples. As we saw in Chapter 7, instrumental behavior can also be regarded as responding that occurs because of the presence of antecedent stimuli. These antecedent stimuli may activate the instrumental response directly or may activate a representation of the response-reinforcer relation.

Clearly much of learned behavior occurs because of the presence of particular environmental events. Up to this point, however, our discussion of learning has left two critical issues about the stimulus control of behavior unanswered. The first concerns the measurement of stimulus control: How can we determine to what extent a specific stimulus or feature of the environment is responsible for a particular response? Are some types of stimuli more important than others in controlling a particular response? If so, how can we measure such differences in the degree of stimulus control?

Once we know how to measure stimulus control, we can tackle the second issue, which concerns the determinants of stimulus control. What determines which stimulus will gain control over a particular response and what determines the degree of stimulus control? Why does a response come to be controlled more by one feature of the environment rather than another?

Questions about stimulus control arise in part because of the complexity of environmental events. Even something as simple as a dial tone on the telephone is a complex stimulus with multiple features. The tone can be characterized in terms of its loudness, pitch, how suddenly it begins and ends, tonal complexity, and location in space. How do we determine which of these stimulus features is critical, and what makes those features critical?

Measurement of Stimulus Control

Analyzing the stimulus control of behavior in a new situation or new species is not unlike trying to figure out what is happening if you were a visitor from a different culture or a different planet. Assume that you are a creature from Mars seeing cars, streets, and traffic lights on earth for the first time. Periodically the cars go past a traffic light. At other times they stop and wait. You want to figure out what makes the drivers stop some of the time and continue moving at other times. How might you approach this problem?

The first step would be to formulate a hypothesis or guess about what is going on. The possibilities are limited only by your imagination. Perhaps drivers stop because a sensor in the road near an intersection signals an on-board computer to stop the car. Alternatively, drivers may be sending signals to each other, with a particular gesture indicating "stop" and another indicating "go." Another possibility is that the drivers come to a stop when they need a short break and continue when they have rested a bit. Or there may be an elaborate schedule, known to all drivers, according to which they have to stop at certain times of day and are allowed to continue at other times. Yet another possibility is that stops and starts are controlled by the traffic lights.

IDENTIFYING RELEVANT STIMULI

How could you determine which stimulus causes cars to stop at an intersection? The various possibilities may be tested in different ways. For example, you may test whether drivers are signaling each other by comparing what happens when there is just one car on the road with what happens when several cars are present at the same time. To determine whether the traffic lights have anything to do with it, you could see whether the cars are less likely to stop when the traffic lights are covered up. To determine whether sensors in the road are relevant, you could try to find the sensors and see what happens when they are deactivated.

Notice that each of these tests involves observing the behavior of interest in the presence and absence of the stimulus that we guessed might be responsible for the behavior. To test whether the drivers were signaling each other to stop, we compared stopping when such signals could not have been transmitted (when there was only one car on the road) with a situation in which such signals could have occurred (when there were several cars on the road at the same time). In testing the possibility that the traffic lights were responsible for the stops and starts, we observed what happened when the lights were covered up. These examples illustrate a basic manipulation involved in the measurement of stimulus control: *The stimulus control of behavior is measured by comparing the behavior of interest in the presence and absence of the test stimulus.*

If the presence/absence of the test stimulus does not produce differences in responding, we may conclude that the stimulus does not control the behavior in question. Cars are just as likely to stop at a traffic light whether or not there are other cars on the road. Therefore, we may conclude that stops and starts are not cued by signals between drivers. In contrast, cars are much more likely to stop when the traffic lights are visible than when they are covered up. This provides evidence that the traffic lights control the behavior of interest and illustrates the basic criterion for the stimulus control of behavior: *A response is said to be under the control of a particular stimulus if the response is altered by changes in that stimulus.*

A change in responding related to changes in a stimulus is called **differential responding.** Which possible stimulus is responsible for the target behavior is identified by differential responding related to changes in that stimulus. If responding is altered by changes in a stimulus, that stimulus is involved in the control of the behavior. If responding is not altered by changes in a stimulus, that stimulus is not relevant to the control of the behavior.

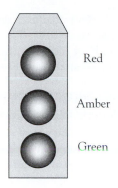

FIGURE 13.1   **Stimulus features of traffic lights.**
The lights differ in both color and position.

IDENTIFYING RELEVANT STIMULUS FEATURES

Determining that stops and starts on a road are somehow controlled by traffic lights is progress. However, many details must be filled in for us to know exactly how drivers respond to traffic lights. For example, traffic lights are often arranged in a vertical array, with the red light on top and the green light on the bottom (see Figure 13.1). Which feature is important, the color of the light or its position? Do drivers stop when they see a red light, or do they stop when the light on top is illuminated?

The strategy for identifying relevant stimulus features is similar to the strategy for identifying relevant stimuli. To determine whether a particular stimulus feature is important, we have to vary that feature without altering other cues and see whether the behavior of interest changes in turn. To determine whether color rather than position is important in traffic lights, we have to test red and green lights presented in the same position. To determine whether the position rather than color is important, we have to test lights of the same color in different positions.

When we vary one feature of a stimulus while keeping all others constant, we are testing the importance of a particular **stimulus dimension** for the behavior in question. Different stimulus dimensions may be important for different drivers. Drivers who are color-blind must focus on the position of the illuminated light. Some other drivers respond primarily to the color of traffic lights. Still others may respond to both the color and the position of the light. Thus, substantial individual differences in stimulus control may occur in response to the same situation.

MEASUREMENT OF THE DEGREE OF STIMULUS CONTROL

Determining whether a response is influenced by the presence/absence of a stimulus tells us whether the stimulus is of any relevance to the behavior. However, the presence/absence test does not tell us how precisely the behavior is tuned to a particular stimulus feature. Continuing with the traffic light example, let us assume that a driver stops whenever he sees a red traffic light. What shade of red does the light have to be? To answer this question, we would have to test the driver with a range of colors, including several different shades of red.

The wavelength of red light is at the long end of the visual spectrum. Shorter wavelengths of light appear less red and more orange. As the wavelength of light becomes even shorter, the light appears more and more yellow. A detailed test of stimulus control by different colors requires systematically presenting lights of different wavelengths.

Stimulus Generalization Gradients.   Several different outcomes may occur if a variety of test colors ranging from deep red to deep yellow are presented. If the driver were paying very close attention to color, he would stop only if the light had a perfect red color. Lights with a tinge of orange would not cause the driver to stop. This possibility is illustrated by Curve A in Figure 13.2. At the other extreme, the driver may stop when he sees any color that has even a vague resemblance to red. This possibility is illustrated by Curve C in Figure 13.2. An intermediate outcome is shown by Curve B. In this case, the driver's behavior exhibits considerable sensitivity to differences in color, but responding is not as closely limited to a particular shade of red as in Curve A.

Each of the curves in Figure 13.2 is a **stimulus generalization gradient.** We previously encountered the concept of stimulus generalization in connection with habituation (see Figure 3.3). Generalization gradients can be obtained for any stimulus feature — stimulus position, size, brightness, shape, height, and so forth. As Figure 13.2 illustrates, the gradients may be very steep (Curve A) or rather shallow (Curve C). The steepness or slope of the generalization gradient indicates how closely the behavior is controlled by the stimulus feature in question. A steep generalization gradient indicates strong control by the stimulus feature or dimension. A shallow or flat generalization gradient indicates weak stimulus control.

Stimulus Generalization and Stimulus Discrimination.   Stimulus generalization gradients involve two important phenomena: generalization and discrimination. In **stimulus generalization,** the responding that occurs with one stimulus is also observed when a different stimulus is presented. Points 1 and 2 in Figure 13.3 illustrate the phenomenon of stimulus generalization. Behavior that occurred at Point 1 also occurred at Point 2, or generalized to Point 2. Generalization of responding signifies similar responding to different stimuli.

Stimulus discrimination is the opposite of stimulus generalization. Here changes in a stimulus result in different levels of responding. Points 1 and 3 in Figure 13.3 illustrate the phenomenon of stimulus discrimination. More responding occurred to the stimulus at Point 1 than to the stimulus at Point 3.

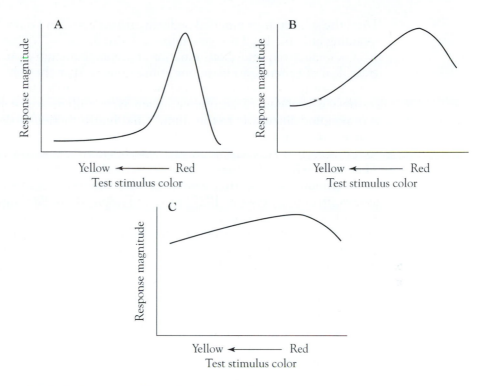

FIGURE 13.2   Hypothetical stimulus generalization gradients indicating different degrees of control of responding by the color of a stimulus.
Curve A illustrates strongest stimulus control by color; Curve C illustrates weakest stimulus control by color.

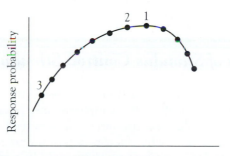

FIGURE 13.3   A hypothetical generalization gradient for responding to different colored stimuli.
Points 1 and 2 illustrate the phenomenon of stimulus generalization. Points 1 and 3 illustrate the phenomenon of stimulus discrimination.

Thus, the subject discriminated or distinguished between Points 1 and 3. Responding at Point 1 did not generalize to Point 3.

Generalization and discrimination are complementary phenomena. A great deal of generalization among stimuli means that the subject responds the same way to these stimuli, and hence there is little discrimination. In contrast, a great deal of discrimination among stimuli means that the subject is responding differently to the stimuli, and hence there is little generalization among them.

Theories of Generalization.   Why do individuals respond similarly to different stimuli? Why do they generalize from one stimulus to another? Early investigators (e.g., Pavlov, 1927) proposed a spread-of-effect interpretation. According to this idea, responses conditioned to one stimulus generalize to other cues because the effects of training spread from the original training stimulus to other similar stimuli. When a child first learns the word for cow, she is likely to use the word *cow* not only when she sees a cow but also when she sees a bull, and perhaps even a horse. According to the spread-of-effect interpretation, such generalization occurs because bulls and horses are similar to cows, and the learned response to cows spreads to other similar animals.

The spread-of-effect interpretation was challenged by Lashley and Wade (1946), who proposed that organisms respond similarly to different stimuli because they have not learned to distinguish between them. According to their idea, a child will use the word *cow* when she sees cows, bulls, and horses because she has not yet learned to distinguish among these different animals.

The Lashley-Wade hypothesis suggests that stimulus generalization can be limited by appropriate training. I will describe evidence confirming this prediction when I describe learning factors that determine the degree of stimulus control later in this chapter. Before we get to that, however, let us consider how features of a stimulus and features of the organism determine stimulus control.

Determinants of Stimulus Control: Stimulus and Organismic Factors

Having determined how to measure the stimulus control of behavior, and having identified the complementary phenomena of stimulus generalization and stimulus discrimination, we are ready to tackle the second major question, namely, what factors determine which features of a stimulus will gain control over a particular response? In addressing this question, we will first consider factors related to the type of stimulus and organism involved.

SENSORY CAPACITY

Perhaps the most obvious factor determining whether a particular stimulus feature will influence behavior is the sensory capacity of the organism. An organism cannot respond to a stimulus if it lacks the sense organs needed to detect the stimulus. People are unable to respond to radio waves, ultraviolet light, and sounds above about 20,000 cycles per second (cps) because they lack the sense organs to detect such stimuli. Dogs, in contrast, are able to hear sounds of much higher frequency than human beings and are therefore capable of responding to ultrasounds that are inaudible to people.

Sensory capacity sets a limit on the kinds of stimuli that can come to control an organism's behavior. However, sensory capacity is merely a precondition for stimulus control. It does not ensure that behavior will be influenced by a particular stimulus feature. People with a normal sense of smell have the capacity to distinguish the aroma of various red wines. However, to a novice in wine tasting all red wines smell alike. Sensory capacity is just the starting point for bringing behavior under the control of a particular stimulus feature.

SENSORY ORIENTATION

Another prerequisite for stimulus control is the sensory orientation of the organism. For a stimulus to gain control over some aspect of an individual's behavior, the stimulus must be accessible to the relevant sense organ. If you have a cold and have to breathe through your mouth, olfactory stimuli are not likely to reach the nasal epithelium, and you will be unable to make fine distinctions among different odors.

Some stimuli, such as sounds and overall levels of illumination, spread throughout an environment. Therefore, such stimuli are likely to be encountered whether or not the individual is oriented toward the source of the stimulus. For this reason, tones and overhead lights are popular stimuli in learning experiments. In contrast, a localized visual cue may present a problem because it is encountered only if the individual is facing toward it. For example, if you are watching for traffic signs on the right side of a road, you may miss a sign placed on the left side.

STIMULUS INTENSITY OR SALIENCE

Other things being equal, behavior is more likely to come under the control of intense or salient stimuli than weak ones (e.g., Kamin, 1965). In fact, the presence of an intense stimulus can interfere with the control of behavior by a weaker cue. This phenomenon, first identified by Pavlov (1927), is referred to as **overshadowing.**

In one demonstration of overshadowing (Kamin, 1969), two groups of rats were compared in their acquisition of conditioned fear to a fairly soft 50 dB noise using the conditioned suppression procedure (see Table 13.1). For the overshadowing group, the noise CS was presented simultaneously with a light on each conditioning trial. For the control group, the noise was presented without the light. After eight conditioning trials, the fear response of both groups was measured to the noise CS presented alone.

TABLE 13.1   Experimental Design to Demonstrate Overshadowing

Conditioning	Testing	Result
Overshadowing Group		
Noise + Light → Shock	Noise	Weak fear of noise
Control Group		
Noise → Shock	Noise	Strong fear of noise

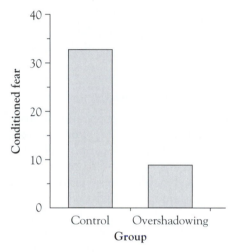

FIGURE 13.4   Levels of conditioned fear elicited by a 50 dB noise CS after pairings with foot shock in which the CS was presented simultaneously with a light CS (overshadowing) or without the light (control).
Based on Kamin, 1969.

The results of the noise-alone test trials are summarized in Figure 13.4. A substantial level of conditioned fear was observed to the noise in the control group. In contrast, much less fear occurred in the overshadowing group. This outcome indicates that the presence of the light during the conditioning trials interfered with or "overshadowed" the development of conditioned fear to the noise CS. The light also elicited considerable conditioned fear in the overshadowing group (not shown). In fact, it is this conditioning of the light that created interference with conditioning the noise CS.

MOTIVATIONAL FACTORS

The extent to which behavior comes under the control of a particular stimulus is also determined by the motivational state of the organism. Motivational factors in the stimulus control of behavior have not been investigated extensively. However, the available evidence indicates that attention can be shifted away from one type of stimulus to another by a change in motivation. LoLordo and his associates have found, for example, that pigeons conditioned with food as the reinforcer come to respond to visual cues more than to auditory cues. In contrast, pigeons conditioned to avoid pain are more likely to respond to auditory cues than to visual cues (Foree & LoLordo, 1973; Shapiro, Jacobs, & LoLordo, 1980).

The motivational state of the organism appears to activate a stimulus filter that biases the attention of the organism in favor of certain types of cues. When pigeons are hungry and motivated to find food, they are especially sensitive to visual cues. In contrast, when pigeons are fearful and motivated to avoid danger, they are especially sensitive to auditory cues. For other species, these motivational influences may take different forms. A species that hunts for live prey at night, for example, may be especially attentive to auditory cues when it is hungry.

Determinants of Stimulus Control: Learning Factors

Given the required sensory capacity and sensory orientation, perhaps the most important factor determining the extent to which behavior will be controlled by a particular stimulus is the significance or validity of that stimulus. As Pavlov pointed out, biologically significant stimuli (such as food for a hungry animal) can control behavior unconditionally or without prior training. In addition, stimuli that are not significant at the outset can become important through association with stimuli or events that are already significant.

PAVLOVIAN AND INSTRUMENTAL CONDITIONING

An initially ineffective stimulus can come to control behavior through either a direct or an indirect association with an unconditioned stimulus (US). As I discussed in Chapter 4, simple Pavlovian conditioning procedures make an initially ineffective stimulus (the CS) significant by establishing an association between that event and the US. Stimulus significance can also be established through instrumental conditioning, with either positive or negative reinforcement.

In the case of positive reinforcement, the reinforcer (O) is presented contingent on a response (R) in the presence of an initially neutral stimulus (S). The three-term S-R-O instrumental contingency increases the significance of stimulus S by establishing an association between S and the reinforcing outcome O or by having stimulus S signal when the response will be reinforced (see Chapter 7). The situation is similar in the case of negative reinforcement (see Chapter 12). In the discriminated avoidance procedure, for example, the instrumental response results in avoidance of aversive stimulation only if the response occurs in the presence of a warning signal, and this makes the warning signal significant to the organism.

Simple Pavlovian and instrumental conditioning procedures increase the control of behavior by an initially ineffective stimulus, but such procedures do not determine which feature(s) of that stimulus will become most effective. Consider, for example, a compound stimulus with both auditory and visual features. Whether the visual or the auditory component will gain predominant control over the conditioned response will depend on the stimulus and organismic factors that I described in the preceding section. If the organism has a keen sense of sight but poor hearing, the visual component will predominate. If both senses are adequate and the organism is motivated by fear, the auditory component may be more important. If the visual component is more intense or salient than the auditory feature, the visual component may overshadow the auditory component.

How about stimulus features that cannot be distinguished on the basis of sensory capacity, sensory orientation, stimulus intensity, or motivation? How can they come to control differential responding? Consider, for example, a car that has been recently filled with gas and one that is about to run out of gas. There is little difference between these two types of cars in terms of the modality and intensity of the stimuli a driver encounters. The only difference is the fuel gauge indicator points to F or E, and that difference may be merely an inch. Nevertheless, the difference between having plenty of gas and being nearly empty is highly significant to drivers. People also respond very differently to seeing the word *fire* as compared to the word *hire*, even though the visual features of these two words are nearly identical. How do such highly similar stimuli come to control dramatically different responses? The answer rests with conditioning procedures that provide differential reinforcement in the presence of different stimuli.

STIMULUS DISCRIMINATION TRAINING

Procedures that provide differential reinforcement in the presence of different stimuli are called stimulus discrimination procedures. Stimulus discrimination training can be conducted with either Pavlovian or instrumental methods. Simple cases of Pavlovian and instrumental conditioning involve only one CS or stimulus condition. In contrast, stimulus discrimination training requires two conditioned stimuli. One of these is called the S^+ and the other is called the S^-. Any two stimuli that are initially ineffective in generating the conditioned or instrumental response may serve as S^+ and S^-. For example, S^+ and S^- may be the letters *f* and *h*, a tone and a buzzer, or a light and a noise. Each trial involves presenting only one of the discriminative stimuli, and trials with the S^+ and the S^- are presented in a random sequence.

In a Pavlovian discrimination procedure, each presentation of S^+ is paired with the unconditioned stimulus. In contrast, the unconditioned

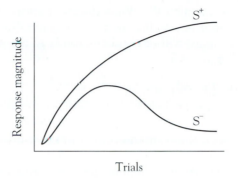

FIGURE 13.5 **Typical results of a Pavlovian discrimination training procedure in which S⁺ is paired with a US and S⁻ is presented equally often alone.** The conditioned responding that develops initially to S⁺ generalizes to S⁻. However, with continued training, a strong discrimination develops between S⁺ and S⁻.

stimulus is omitted on trials when S⁻ occurs. Thus, S⁺ and S⁻ are associated with different outcomes or differential reinforcement. S⁺ and S⁻ may be two orange cats, for example, one rather friendly and the other aloof. The friendly cat (S⁺) is paired with tactile pleasure because she allows people to pet her. The aloof cat (S⁻) does not let people pet her and is therefore not paired with the positive tactile US.

Typical results of a discrimination procedure are illustrated in Figure 13.5. Early in training, the conditioned response comes to be elicited by the S⁺, and this responding generalizes to S⁻. The outcome is that the participant responds to some extent to both the S⁺ and the S⁻ at this stage of training. With continued discrimination training, responding to S⁺ continues to increase, whereas responding to S⁻ gradually declines. The final result is that the participant responds much more to S⁺ than to S⁻. A strong distinction develops between S⁺ and S⁻. At this point, the two stimuli are said to be discriminated.

Let's consider again our two cats, one friendly and the other aloof. As you start to associate one of the cats with tactile pleasure, any affection that you develop for her may generalize to the other cat. However, as you have additional pleasant encounters with one cat but not with the other, your affection for the friendly cat will increase and your response to the aloof cat will decline. You will come to distinguish one cat from the other.

Discrimination training can be conducted in an analogous fashion with instrumental conditioning. In this case, the instrumental response is reinforced on trials when S⁺ is presented (S⁺ → R → O). In contrast, the response is not reinforced when a different stimulus (S⁻) is presented (S⁻ → R → noO). Thus, S⁺ and S⁻ are again associated with differential reinforcement. As with Pavlovian discrimination procedures, during initial stages of training, responding to S^+ may generalize to S^-. However, eventually the participant will respond vigorously to S^+ and little, if at all, to S^-, as shown in Figure 13.5.

In all stimulus discrimination procedures, different stimuli are associated with different outcomes. In the preceding examples, differential reinforcement was provided by the delivery versus omission of the US or the reinforcer. The presence versus absence of reinforcement represents a common but special case in discrimination training procedures. Any form of differential reinforcement can be used in discrimination training.

Infants, for example, quickly learn to discriminate mom from dad. This does not occur because mom is a source of reinforcement whereas dad is not. Both mom and dad provide pleasure for the infant, but they are likely to provide different types of pleasure. One parent may provide more tactile comfort and nutritional reinforcement, whereas the other may provide mostly sensory reinforcement in the form of tickling or physical play. Each type of reinforcer is associated with a different parent, which leads the infant to discriminate between the parents.

MULTIPLE SCHEDULES OF REINFORCEMENT

Differential reinforcement may also be programmed in terms of different schedules of reinforcement in the presence of different stimuli. For example, a variable-interval schedule may be in effect in the presence of a high-pitch tone (Stimulus A), and a fixed-interval schedule may be in effect in the presence of a low-pitch tone (Stimulus B). Such a procedure is called a **multiple schedule of reinforcement.** As a result of training on a multiple VI-FI schedule of reinforcement, participants will come to respond to Stimulus A in a manner typical of variable-interval performance and will respond to Stimulus B in a manner typical of fixed-interval performance.

Listening to different instructors in different classes, for example, is reinforced on a multiple schedule. The reinforcer is the new information provided in each class. Some professors say lots of new things during their classes, thereby reinforcing listening behavior on a dense variable-interval schedule. Other professors predictably make just four or five important points during a lecture and spend about 10 minutes elaborating each point. This reinforces listening behavior on what is akin to a fixed-interval schedule. Each schedule of reinforcement is in effect in the presence of the distinct stimuli of each professor and class. Across both classes, therefore, listening behavior is reinforced on a multiple schedule that produces differential listening behavior. Students will listen at a steady rate without predictable pauses in the class where listening is reinforced on a dense VI schedule and will show post-reinforcement lapses in attention in the class where listening is reinforced on an FI schedule.

TABLE 13.2   Outline of Experiment by Jenkins and Harrison

Training	Test
Group D: Discrimination Training	
S$^+$ (1000 cps tone): Pecks → Food	Tones of various frequencies
S$^-$ (no tone): Pecks → no Food	
Group C: No Discrimination Training	
1000 cps tone: Pecks → Food	Tones of various frequencies
Tone always present during training	

DIFFERENTIAL REINFORCEMENT AND STIMULUS CONTROL

Differential reinforcement in the presence of S$^+$ and S$^-$ produces differential responding to those stimuli. Interestingly, these effects may extend far beyond the actual stimuli that were used in the discrimination procedure. The far-reaching effects of discrimination training were first identified in a landmark experiment by Jenkins and Harrison (1960). They compared the stimulus control of pecking behavior in two groups of pigeons (see Table 13.2). Group D was first conditioned to discriminate between the presence and absence of a tone. These pigeons were reinforced for pecking a response key whenever a tone with a frequency of 1000 Hz was turned on (S$^+$) and were not reinforced when the tone was absent (S$^-$). The control group (Group C) received similar reinforcement for pecking the response key, but for them the tone was on continuously during the training sessions. Thus, Group C did not receive differential reinforcement associated with the tone.

After this contrasting training had taken place, the responses of both groups were measured in a test of stimulus generalization. Tones of various frequencies were presented during the test session. The results are summarized in Figure 13.6. The control group, Group C, which did not receive discrimination training, responded vigorously to the tone that had been present during training (the 1000 Hz tone). They also responded vigorously to most of the other tones, which they encountered for the first time during the generalization test. Thus, in the absence of discrimination training, a fairly flat generalization gradient was obtained. This indicates that the frequency of the tones did not gain much control over the behavior of these birds.

The results were dramatically different for the pigeons in Group D, which were first trained to discriminate between the presence and absence of the 1000 Hz tone. These birds showed a steep generalization gradient. They responded a great deal to the 1000 Hz tone (the S$^+$), but their behavior quickly dropped off when tones of other frequencies were presented. This is a remarkable outcome, because the other tones had not been presented during discrimination training. None of the other tones had served as the S$^-$

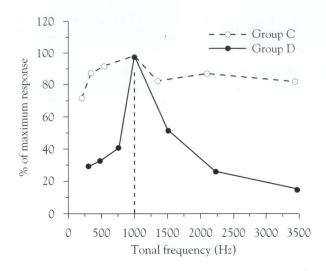

FIGURE 13.6   Effects of discrimination training on control of the pecking behavior of pigeons by the frequency of different tones.
Prior to the generalization test, Group D received discrimination training in which the S⁺ was a 1000 Hz tone and the S⁻ was the absence of the tone. In contrast, Group C received only reinforcement for key-pecking in the presence of the 1000 Hz tone. Based on Jenkins & Harrison, 1960.

in the discrimination procedure. Even though Group D had not encountered nonreinforcement in the presence of tones during training, tones other than S⁺ did not support much pecking behavior.

The results presented in Figure 13.6 show that the shape of a generalization gradient can be altered by discrimination training. Discrimination training not only produces differential responding to S⁺ and S⁻ but also increases the steepness of generalization gradients. Thus, the effects of discrimination training extend beyond the specific stimuli that are used as S⁺ and S⁻.

INTERDIMENSIONAL VERSUS INTRADIMENSIONAL DISCRIMINATIONS

So far we have stressed the importance of differential reinforcement in discrimination training procedures. The nature of the S⁺ and S⁻ stimuli also determines the outcome of discrimination training. The similarities and differences between S⁺ and S⁻ are especially important. If S⁺ and S⁻ differ in several respects, the discrimination is called an **interdimensional discrimination.** If S⁺ and S⁻ differ in only one respect, the discrimination is called an **intradimensional discrimination.**

Interdimensional Discriminations.   Perhaps the most common forms of interdimensional discrimination training are simple Pavlovian or discrete-trial instrumental conditioning procedures, although we don't usually think of these as involving discrimination training. A simple Pavlovian procedure involves just one CS and one US. Presentations of the CS end in delivery of the US. In contrast, the US is not delivered when the CS is absent. Thus, the discrimination is between times when the CS is present and times when the CS is absent (the intertrial interval). All of the features of the CS (its modality, intensity, and location) serve to distinguish the CS from its absence. Therefore, this is an interdimensional discrimination.

In discrete-trial instrumental conditioning, the participant is reinforced for responding in the presence of particular stimuli (e.g., the stimuli of a runway), and responding is not reinforced in the absence of these cues. Thus, simple discrete-trial instrumental conditioning similarly involves a discrimination between the stimuli that define a trial and those that are encountered during the intertrial interval. Because numerous stimulus features distinguish the trial stimuli from the intertrial interval, this is also an interdimensional discrimination.

Interdimensional discriminations can be also set up between discrete stimuli serving as S^+ and S^-. The discrimination between a red and a green traffic light I discussed earlier in this chapter is an interdimensional discrimination, because red and green traffic lights differ in both color and position. The discrimination learned by an infant between mom and dad is also an interdimensional discrimination. Mom and dad differ in many respects, including visual features, differences in how each holds the infant, differences in voice, differences in the time of day each is likely to interact with the infant, and so on.

Intradimensional Discriminations.   *Interdimensional* discriminations are effective in establishing stimulus control. However, they do not establish a high degree of control over behavior by any particular stimulus feature. For example, since many things distinguish mom from dad, the infant may not respond a great deal to any one distinguishing feature. The most effective way to establish control by a specific stimulus feature is through *intradimensional* discrimination training (Jenkins & Harrison, 1960, 1962). In intradimensional discrimination training, the stimuli associated with differential reinforcement differ in only one respect.

Many forms of expert performance involve intradimensional discriminations. Reading, for example, requires discriminating between letters that differ in only one respect. The letters *E* and *F* differ only in the horizontal bottom stem, which is present in *E* but not in *F*. The physical difference is very small, but the differential consequences in terms of meaning can be substantial. The letters *B* and *P* and *M* and *N* are other pairs that are similar physically but differ greatly in significance. Learning to read requires learning many intradimensional discriminations of this sort.

One of the interesting things about learning fine intradimensional discriminations is that the participant is not likely to be aware of the physical difference between the stimuli at the outset of training. Initially, the letters E and F may appear the same to a child. The child may recognize E and F as being different from O but may not be able to tell the difference between E and F. The child may come to recognize the visual difference between the two letters only after being taught to say one thing when shown E and something else when shown F. *Differential reinforcement serves to focus attention on physical differences that are otherwise ignored.*

Similar effects occur in the acquisition of other forms of expertise. Children learning to sing may not be able to tell at first when they are singing in tune or off-key. However, this skill develops through differential reinforcement from a teacher. Likewise, budding ballerinas learn to pay close attention to proprioceptive cues indicating the precise position of their arms and legs, and billiard players learn to make precise judgments about angles and trajectories. Intradimensional discrimination training brings behavior under precise control of small variations in a stimulus, thereby serving to increase sensitivity to these small stimulus variations. Thus, sensitivity to variations in environmental stimuli depends not only on sensory capacity but also on one's history of discrimination training.

STIMULUS EQUIVALENCE TRAINING

As we have seen, discrimination procedures foster differential responding and steeper generalization gradients. There are situations, however, in which just the opposite is desired, that is, situations in which physically different stimuli must be treated the same way. Consider, for example, the same word written in different fonts and sizes. If you are concerned about the meaning of the word, you must treat the word as having the same meaning regardless of the font or size in which it is written. This raises the question: Are there learning procedures that promote responding to different stimuli in the same manner? Are there learning procedures that increase stimulus generalization?

In a discrimination procedure, stimuli are treated differently — they have different consequences. The differential treatment or significance of the stimuli leads organisms to respond to them as distinct from each other. What would happen if two stimuli were treated in the same or equivalent fashion? Would such a procedure lead organisms to respond to the stimuli as similar or equivalent? The answer seems to be "yes." Just as discrimination training encourages differential responding, **stimulus equivalence** training encourages generalized responding.

There are several approaches available for promoting generalization rather than discrimination among stimuli. One approach is to arrange the same consequence for responding to various physically different stimuli. This is frequently done in perceptual-concept learning. For example, pigeons can be trained to respond in a similar fashion to different photographs, all of which include water in some form (ocean, lake, puddle, stream) (Herrnstein, Loveland, & Cable, 1976). The basic training strategy is to reinforce the

TABLE 13.3   Outline of Equivalence Experiment

Training Phase 1	Training Phase 2	Test
Equivalence Group		
Noise → Food Clicker → Food	Noise → Shock	Conditioned fear to noise generalizes to clicker.
Control Group		
Noise → no Food Clicker → Food	Noise → Shock	Conditioned fear to noise does not generalize to clicker.

same response (pecking a response key) in the presence of various pictures containing water, and not to reinforce that response when photographs without water appear. Herrnstein et al. trained such a discrimination using 500–700 photographs of various scenes in New England. Once the pigeons learned the water/no-water discrimination, their behavior generalized to novel photographs that had not been presented during training.

Investigators have also explored the possibility that functional equivalence between two different stimuli might be established by linking each of the distinct cues with a common third stimulus. In an experiment by Honey and Hall (1989), for example, rats first received presentations of two different auditory cues, a noise and a clicker (see Table 13.3). For one group of animals, both the noise and the clicker were paired with food. The common food outcome was expected to create functional equivalence between the noise and clicker stimuli. The control group also received presentations of the noise and the clicker, but for this group, only the clicker was paired with food. Both groups then had the noise paired with mild foot shock, resulting in the conditioning of fear to the noise. The investigators were interested in the extent to which this conditioned fear of the noise would generalize to the clicker. Significantly more generalization occurred in the equivalence-trained animals than in the control group. The equivalence-trained animals were more apt to treat the clicker and noise similarly than the control group.

The concept of equivalence class has been particularly important in analyses of language. The written word *apple*, for example, derives its meaning from the fact that it is in an equivalence class that includes the spoken word *apple* as well as a photograph or drawing of an apple and an actual apple you can eat. All of these physically different stimuli are treated as functionally equivalent and interchangeable once the meaning of the word has been learned. For example, you should be able to say the word *apple* when you see a picture of one, and you should be able to pick out the picture if asked to identify what the word *apple* signifies.

Generally, individuals with better verbal skills learn equivalence classes more easily. This has encouraged some investigators to suggest that verbal skill and the formation of equivalence classes are integrally related (see Horne & Lowe, 1996, 1997, and related commentary).

Shaping of Discriminations and Perceptual-Concept Learning

As the discussion in the preceding section indicates, the stimulus control of behavior is not fixed by an organism's sensory capacity but can be shaped by experience. Whether an organism responds in the same manner to certain stimuli or responds differentially depends on its training history. The flexibility and modifiability of stimulus control are critical for learning words and perceptual concepts. **Perceptual concepts** are the means by which organisms categorize the various stimuli they encounter in their world so as to respond similarly to some of them and differently to others.

Consider the perceptual category that consists of various types of dogs. In calling greyhounds, poodles, and dachshunds all "dogs," a child has to ignore differences in the overall size, speed, fur quality, and other features that characterize these breeds. On the other hand, the category "dogs" requires distinguishing greyhounds, poodles, and dachshunds from other mammals such as cats, ferrets, and beavers. Thus, the learning of a perceptual category involves an interplay between generalization and discrimination. The child has to learn to ignore differences among various distinctive dog breeds (stimulus generalization) at the same time that she learns to tell the difference between dogs and other mammals (stimulus discrimination).

The exact interplay between generalization and discrimination learning depends on the level of the perceptual category. "Dog" is an intermediate-level category. A higher-level category is "mammal"; a lower-level category is a specific type of dog, such as "greyhound." Although various types of dogs differ in numerous respects, dogs are more similar to one another than are animals belonging to the higher-level category "mammals." Therefore, learning the category "mammal" requires more generalizations than learning the category "dog." On the other hand, more discrimination learning is required for the lower-level category "greyhound." In responding to an animal as a "greyhound," one must learn to distinguish greyhounds from other breeds of dogs.

Successful navigation of the environment requires learning to respond to certain stimuli in the same manner despite their differences (generalization) while responding differentially to other cues (discrimination). Contingencies of reinforcement serve to shape an organism's stimulus generalization and discrimination performance and thereby serve to coordinate the organism's behavior with its ecological niche.

Summary

Organisms must learn not only what to do but when and where to do it. When and where a response is made involves the stimulus control of behavior. Stimulus control is identified by differential responding and can be precisely measured by the steepness of generalization gradients. The extent to which a stimulus influences behavior depends on stimulus and organismic variables such as sensory capacity, sensory orientation, stimulus intensity, and the organism's motivational state. Stimuli that cannot be differentiated on the basis of these factors may gain control over behavior as a result of differential reinforcement.

Discrimination training may involve either *inter*dimensional or *intra*-dimensional stimuli. Intradimensional discrimination training produces more-precise stimulus control than interdimensional training and is the basis for various forms of expert performance. However, learning fine discriminations is not always useful. Sometimes you have to learn to treat physically different objects in the same fashion. This is accomplished by stimulus equivalence learning. Stimulus equivalence is important in learning words and in perceptual-concept learning. Both of these require a precise balance between discrimination learning and stimulus generalization or equivalence. For example, more-precise discriminations are required for low-level perceptual concepts and more stimulus generalization is required for higher-level concepts.

Practice Questions

1. What is the definition of *stimulus control*, and how is stimulus control measured?

2. What is the relationship between stimulus discrimination and stimulus generalization?

3. How do Pavlov's views differ from those of Lashley and Wade concerning the mechanisms of stimulus generalization?

4. What features of an organism determine which stimuli can come to control its behavior?

5. How can the steepness of a generalization gradient be increased by learning?

6. Which view of stimulus generalization (Pavlov's or Lashley & Wade's) is supported by evidence that the stimulus control can be shaped by learning?

7. What is the most effective way to bring behavior under the control of small variations in a stimulus?

8. What is a multiple schedule, and why does it increase stimulus control?

9. What types of discrimination procedures are there and how do they differ?

10. How can subjects be trained to treat different stimuli in the same manner?

Suggested Readings

Balsam, P. D. (1988). Selection, representation, and equivalence of controlling stimuli. In R. C. Atkinson, R. J. Herrnstein, G. Lindzey, & R. D. Luce (Eds.), *Stevens' handbook of experimental psychology* (Vol. 2, pp. 111–166). New York: Wiley.

Horne, P. J., & Lowe, C. F. (1997). Toward a theory of verbal behavior. *Journal of the Experimental Analysis of Behavior*, 68, 271–296.

Pearce, J. M. (1994). Discrimination and categorization. In N. J. Mackintosh (Ed.), *Animal learning and cognition* (pp. 109–134). San Diego: Academic Press.

Sidman, M. (2000). Equivalence relations and the reinforcement contingency. *Journal of the Experimental Analysis of Behavior*, 74, 127–146.

Wasserman, E. A., & Astley, S. L. (1994). A behavioral analysis of concepts: Its application to pigeons and children. In D. L. Medin (Ed.), *The psychology of learning and motivation* (Vol. 31, pp. 73–132). San Diego: Academic Press.

Technical Terms

Differential responding	S^-
Interdimensional discrimination	Stimulus dimension
Intradimensional discrimination	Stimulus discrimination
Multiple schedule of reinforcement	Stimulus equivalence
Overshadowing	Stimulus generalization
Perceptual concept	Stimulus generalization gradient
S^+	

CHAPTER FOURTEEN

Memory Mechanisms

DID YOU KNOW THAT:

- Learning and memory are integrally related.
- Tasks testing memory mechanisms have to be specially designed so that they cannot be solved without the use of memory.
- Memory for even simple stimuli is not a passive or automatic process.
- Memory can improve with learning.
- Memory can be brought under stimulus control.
- Memory can be prospective and involve future rather than past events.
- Failures of memory can be caused by remembering too much or by not remembering enough.
- Seemingly trivial aspects of a learning situation can stimulate retrieval of what was learned.

In Chapter 13, I described mechanisms responsible for the control of behavior by stimuli an organism encounters in its environment. This chapter deals with how behavior can be controlled by events that occurred at an earlier time but are no longer present. Past events influence behavior through memory mechanisms.

Philosophers and scientists have been interested in how people remember things since the time of the ancient Greeks. Studies of memory continue today as a prominent aspect of contemporary research in human cognitive psychology. In contrast, systematic investigations of memory mechanisms in nonhuman animals have a much shorter history. Only in the last 30 years has much experimental research on memory been conducted with various species of animals (Honig & James, 1971; Kendrick, Rilling, & Denny, 1986; Medin, Roberts, & Davis, 1976; Spear & Riccio, 1994).

Why should anyone study memory mechanisms in nonhuman animal species? Why should we care about how rats or pigeons remember things? Animal research on memory mechanisms is important for several reasons. It promises to inform us about the evolution of cognitive processes (Sherry & Schachter, 1987). Such research is also essential for investigations of the physiological bases of memory, for the development and testing of drugs that influence memory, and for the development of systems of artificial intelligence that mimic living organisms. Finally, studies of memory mechanisms promise to help us understand basic mechanisms of conditioning and learning (e.g., Miller, Kasprow, & Schachtman, 1986).

Learning and memory are integrally related; one cannot have one without the other. In fact, research on memory mechanisms in animals makes extensive use of the basic conditioning procedures that I have described in earlier chapters. This makes the discussion of memory research appropriate at the end of a book on basic conditioning procedures. However, a fundamental question arises: If all learning involves memory, what distinguishes studies of memory from studies of learning? The answer is that studies of memory focus on a different stage of information processing than studies of learning.

Stages of Information Processing

Memory involves the delayed effects of experience. For experience with stimuli and responses to influence behavior some time later, three things have to happen. First, information about the stimuli and responses has to be acquired and encoded in the nervous system in some fashion. This is the **acquisition stage** of information processing. Once encoded, the information has to be stored for later use. This is the retention stage of information processing. Finally, when the information is needed at the end of the **retention interval,** it has to be recovered from storage. This is the **retrieval stage.**

Acquisition, retention, and retrieval are involved in all studies of learning as well as all studies of memory. However, which stage is the focus of interest depends on whether one is primarily concerned with learning pro-

TABLE 14.1   Differences between Experiments on Learning
and Experiments on Memory

Phase	Learning Experiments	Memory Experiments
Acquisition	Varied	Constant
Retention interval	Constant (long)	Varied (short and long)
Retrieval	Constant	Varied

cesses or memory processes (see Table 14.1). Studies of learning focus on the acquisition stage. In studies of learning, the circumstances of acquisition are manipulated or varied while the conditions of retention and retrieval are kept constant. By contrast, in studies of memory, the conditions of acquisition are kept constant while the retention interval and the conditions of retrieval are varied.

The Matching-to-Sample Procedure

A variety of different techniques have been used to study memory mechanisms in animals. Memory procedures often require special controls to ensure that the participant's behavior is determined by its past experience rather than by some clue that is inadvertently presented in the test situation. In addition, special procedures must be designed to isolate particular memory processes. To facilitate illustration of these complexities, I will describe one technique for the study of memory mechanisms in detail — the **matching-to-sample procedure.**

Matching to sample is perhaps the most versatile procedure for the study of memory mechanisms. It can be used to investigate memory for a variety of different kinds of stimuli and can be adapted to address a variety of different research questions. Although our discussion will focus on the matching-to-sample technique, the conceptual issues involved are relevant to all other memory tasks as well.

In the matching-to-sample procedure, the participant is first exposed to a sample stimulus. The sample is then removed for a retention interval. After the retention interval, the participant receives a multiple-choice memory test. Several alternatives are presented, one of which is the same as the sample stimulus that was presented at the start of the trial. If the participant selects the previously presented sample, it is reinforced.

The matching procedure has been used with species as diverse as dolphins, rats, and people (Baron & Menich, 1985; Forestell & Herman, 1988; Wallace, Steinert, Scobie, & Spear, 1980), and the procedure has been adapted for various types of sample stimuli, including visual, auditory, and spatial cues. Figure 14.1 illustrates a version of the procedure for use with pigeons.

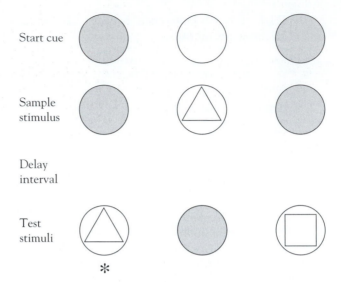

FIGURE 14.1   Illustration of a matching-to-sample trial used with pigeons.
The trial begins with the center key illuminated by a white light as a start cue. At this point, the side keys are dark. The sample stimulus (a triangle) is then presented, also on the center key. The sample is then turned off, and a retention interval begins. At the end of the retention interval, the subject receives two test stimuli on the side keys, one of which matches the sample stimulus. Pecks at the matching test cue are reinforced, as indicated by the asterisk.

Pigeons are typically tested in a Skinner box that is provided with three response keys arranged in a row. Each trial begins with a start cue, which might be illumination of the center key with a white light. One peck at the start cue results in presentation of the sample stimulus on the center key. In our example, the sample stimulus is a triangle. After a few seconds, the sample stimulus is turned off and a retention interval begins. At the end of the retention interval, the pigeon receives two test stimuli on the side keys. One of the test stimuli is the same as the previously presented sample (a triangle), whereas the other is different (a square). Pecks at the matching stimulus are reinforced. Pecks at the alternate test stimulus have no consequence.

SIMULTANEOUS AND DELAYED MATCHING TO SAMPLE

As you might suspect, the difficulty of a matching-to-sample procedure depends in part on the duration of the retention interval (Grant, 1976). To facilitate learning of a matching task, it is useful to begin training without a retention interval. Such a procedure is called **simultaneous matching to**

sample. In simultaneous matching to sample, each trial begins with a start cue on the center key. This is followed by presentation of the sample stimulus on the center key. The test stimuli are then presented on the side keys while the sample remains on the center key. Because the sample stimulus is visible at the same time as the test stimuli, the procedure is called simultaneous matching to sample.

After the participants have learned to make the accurate choice in a simultaneous matching procedure, a retention interval can be introduced between presentation of the sample and presentation of the test stimuli, as illustrated in Figure 14.1. Because, in this case, the test stimuli are delayed after presentation of the sample, the procedure is called **delayed matching to sample.**

PROCEDURAL CONTROLS FOR MEMORY

Introducing a retention interval is necessary to ensure that the participant remembers something about the sample stimulus in order to respond accurately when the test choices are presented. However, having a retention interval in the procedure is not sufficient to ensure that the participant is using memory based on the sample stimulus. The sample and test stimuli must also be varied from one trial to the next.

Consider, for example, a procedure in which every trial was exactly the same as the trial illustrated in Figure 14.1. To respond accurately with repetitions of this trial, the pigeon would simply have to learn to peck the left key when the side keys were illuminated. The pigeon would not have to remember anything about the shape of the visual cue that was projected on any of the response keys.

To force pigeons to pay attention to and remember information about the specific stimuli that are presented in a matching procedure, the sample stimulus used and the position of the test stimuli must be varied across training trials. Figure 14.2 illustrates various types of trials in a matching procedure involving two shape stimuli (triangle and square) and two pattern stimuli (a vertical grid and a horizontal grid). There are eight possible trial types. With each sample stimulus, two types of test trials can be designed, one with the correct stimulus on the left and one with the correct stimulus on the right. If the eight trial types appear randomly during training, the participant cannot be consistently accurate unless it uses information based on the sample to guide its choice of responses.

Types of Memory

Memory is not a homogeneous process. There are different kinds of memory based on the kind of information that is remembered, the types of manipulations that influence the nature of the memory, and how long the memory lasts. In research with laboratory animals, distinctions between reference and

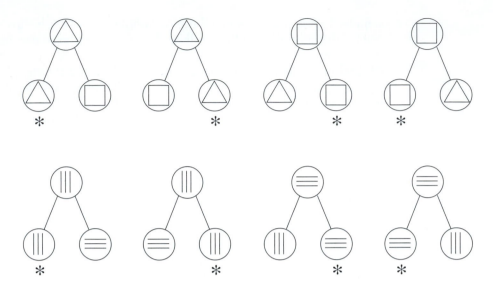

FIGURE 14.2 Eight different types of trials used to make sure that participants in a matching-to-sample procedure are responding on the basis of information obtained from the sample stimulus.
For each trial type, the sample is presented on top, and the two choice stimuli are presented below. The correct choice is identified by an asterisk.

working memory, active and passive memory, and prospective and retrospective memory have received special attention. (These distinctions have also been made in the human memory literature, but the terms used there are not always the same.)

REFERENCE MEMORY AND WORKING MEMORY

What kinds of memory are required to respond successfully in a matching-to-sample procedure? In our discussion of procedural controls for memory, we were concerned with making sure that responses to the test stimuli on a particular trial depended on what the participant remembered from the sample stimulus that was presented on that trial. Such memory is called **working memory.**

Working memory is retention of information that is needed to respond successfully on one trial or task but is not useful in responding on the next trial or task. Because the sample stimulus is varied from one trial to the next in a matching procedure (see Figure 14.2), information from the sample presented on one trial does not help in choosing the correct test stimulus on the next trial. Thus, working memory is of limited duration.

The control procedures that we discussed previously (variations in the sample stimulus and in the location of the correct choice stimulus) ensure that matching-to-sample procedures involve working memory. However, to respond successfully, participants must remember more than just information from the sample on a particular trial. They also must remember general features of the matching procedure that remain constant from one trial to the next. For example, pigeons must remember to peck the start cue and to peck one of the test stimuli after the retention interval. In addition, they must remember that correct responses are reinforced and where to obtain the reinforcer once it is delivered. Such memory is called **reference memory.** Because reference memory involves constant features of a task, it is of considerably longer duration than working memory.

The distinction between working memory and reference memory is applicable to all sorts of situations. Baking a cake, for example, involves both working memory and reference memory. As you prepare the batter, you must remember which ingredients you have already included and which ones to add next. This kind of information is useful only for the cake you are preparing; it will not help you bake the next cake. Therefore, such information involves working memory.

To bake a cake, you must also have some general information about cooking. You must know about cake pans, ovens, various ingredients, and how to measure and mix those ingredients. These general skills are useful not just for the cake you happen to be baking but also for any future cakes you might want to make. Therefore, such information involves reference memory.

ACTIVE MEMORY AND PASSIVE MEMORY

Working memory and reference memory are distinguished by the type of information that is retained and by how long the information is remembered. Memory mechanisms can also be distinguished by the kinds of procedures that influence them. A fundamental issue is whether memory can be modified or influenced by other psychological processes. This is the basis for the distinction between active memory and passive memory.

Passive memory processes are assumed to be automatic and not subject to modification by other psychological processes. A prominent passive memory process that has been considered in matching-to-sample experiments is the trace-decay hypothesis (Roberts & Grant, 1976). According to this hypothesis, presentation of a sample stimulus activates a neural trace that automatically decays after the end of the stimulus. Information about the sample is available only as long as the trace is sufficiently strong. The gradual fading or decay of the neural trace is assumed to produce progressively less-accurate recall.

The initial strength of a neural trace is assumed to depend only on the physical intensity and duration of the sample stimulus. (More-intense and longer stimuli presumably activate stronger neural traces.) However, regard-less of its initial strength, a neural trace is assumed to gradually fade with time. Consistent with these assumptions, pigeons respond less accurately in delayed matching-to-sample procedures as the retention interval between the sample stimulus and the choice test is increased; in addition, responding is more accurate with longer sample stimuli (Grant, 1976).

According to the trace-decay hypothesis, information about the sample is lost automatically during the retention interval, and nothing can be done about that. However, several lines of evidence suggest that memory loss is not an automatic, passive process that is immune to modification by other psychological processes. Contrary to the trace-decay hypothesis, memory for a sample stimulus improves with practice (D'Amato, 1973). Memory can also be improved by making the stimulus surprising (Maki, 1979). Yet an-other line of evidence suggests that memory mechanisms can be brought un-der stimulus control (Grant & Soldat, 1995; Roper, Kaiser, & Zentall, 1995). Animals can be conditioned to remember a sample stimulus in one situation but not in another. Finally, accuracy in delayed matching to sample depends not only on the delay interval used during testing but also on the delay in-terval used during training (Sargisson & White, 2001). Subjects that receive longer delays between the sample and the choice stimuli during the training trials perform more accurately during subsequent tests with long delays.

The preponderance of evidence suggests that working memory in a matching-to-sample procedure does not decay automatically with longer de-lays, as is assumed by the trace-decay hypothesis. Rather, the memory can be influenced by a number of psychological processes, including practice, sur-prisingness, stimulus control, and training with longer intervals.

RETROSPECTIVE MEMORY AND PROSPECTIVE MEMORY

So far, we have established that the matching-to-sample task involves both working memory and reference memory, and that working memory is best characterized as an active rather than passive process. Another important issue concerns the contents of working memory, that is, what the organism remembers during the retention interval that enables it to make the correct choice at the end of a trial.

Retrospective Memory.   The most obvious possibility is that information about the sample stimulus is retained during the retention interval, thus en-abling the participant to select the correct test stimulus. Presumably, the memory of the sample is compared to each of the test stimuli at the end of the trial to determine which alternative best resembles the sample. The par-ticipant then selects the test stimulus that best matches the sample.

Remembering attributes of the sample stimulus is a form of **retrospective memory.** Retrospective memory is memory of stimuli or events that were en-countered previously.

Retrospective memory is perhaps the most obvious possibility for the contents of working memory in a matching task. However, a hypothesis may be obvious and still be incorrect. What else might a participant keep in mind during the retention interval that would enable it to respond correctly during the choice test?

Prospective Memory.   Recall that, in the typical matching procedure, a limited number of different trial types are repeated over and over again in random order. Figure 14.2, for example, illustrates a procedure in which there are four possible sample stimuli: a triangle, a square, a vertical grid, and a horizontal grid. For each sample, there is a unique correct test stimulus. Because of this, the matching procedure involves pairs of sample and test stimuli.

Let us represent a sample stimulus as S and a test stimulus as T. Different sample-test stimulus pairs may then be represented as S1-T1, S2-T2, S3-T3, and so on. Given these S-T pairings, participants could select the correct choice stimulus in a matching task by thinking of T after presentation of the sample S and storing that information during the retention interval. This involves keeping in memory information about a future stimulus and is called **prospective memory.** Prospective memory involves remembering something that is predicted to occur in the future, or prospectively.

Deciding between Retrospection and Prospection.   Retrospective memory involves remembering the sample stimulus S during the retention interval. Prospective memory involves remembering the test stimulus T during the retention interval. How can we distinguish between these possibilities experimentally?

In a matching-to-sample procedure, the sample stimulus S and the correct test stimulus T are the same. If the sample is a triangle, the correct test stimulus is also a triangle. This makes it virtually impossible to decide whether information stored during the retention interval concerns stimulus S or stimulus T. To distinguish between retrospective and prospective memory, we must change the matching procedure somewhat, so that T is not the same physical stimulus as S. Such a procedure is called *symbolic matching to sample*.

A symbolic matching procedure is illustrated in the left column of Figure 14.3. Each row represents a different trial type in the procedure. The procedure is based on symbolic relationships between sample and test stimuli rather than the identity relationship. In Figure 14.3, responding to the vertical grid is reinforced after presentation of a triangle as the sample stimulus, and responding to the horizontal grid is reinforced after presentation of a square as the sample. In a sense, the vertical grid is a symbol for the triangle sample, and the horizontal grid is a symbol for the square sample.

As with the standard matching procedure, in a symbolic matching task the correct test stimulus appears equally often on the left and the right, and there is a delay between the sample and the test stimuli. Therefore, the task

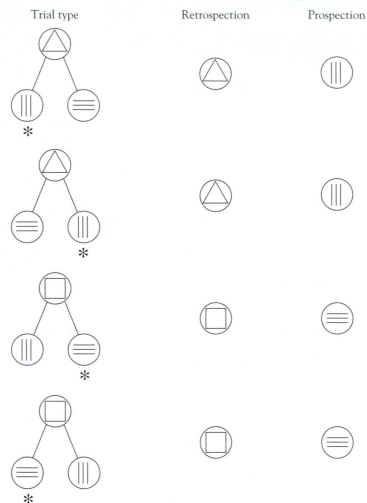

Contents of working memory

Trial type   Retrospection   Prospection

FIGURE 14.3   Diagram of a symbolic matching-to-sample procedure and illustration of the difference between retrospective and prospective working memory.

For each trial type, the test stimuli are shown below the sample stimulus, and the correct test stimulus is indicated by an asterisk.

involves working memory, just as the standard matching procedure does. However, with symbolic matching, different things are remembered depending on whether the memory is retrospective or prospective. The differences are shown in the center and right columns of Figure 14.3. On trials with the triangle as the sample, retrospective memory involves retention of information about the triangle. In contrast, prospective memory involves retention of information about the vertical-grid test stimulus, which is the correct choice after a triangle sample. On trials with the square as the sample, retrospective memory involves remembering the square, whereas prospective memory involves remembering the horizontal grid.

Using symbolic matching-to-sample tasks, investigators have found that pigeons use prospective rather than retrospective memory (e.g., Roitblat, 1980; Santi & Roberts, 1985). Research using other kinds of memory tasks has also provided evidence of prospective memory. However, not all instances of working memory involve prospection, or memory for events that are predicted to occur in the future. Whether organisms remember a past event (retrospection) or a future event (prospection) appears to depend on which form of memory is more efficient in solving a particular task (Cook, Brown, & Riley, 1985; Zentall, Steirn, & Jackson-Smith, 1990).

Sources of Memory Failure

Instances of the failure of memory can tell us as much about memory mechanisms as instances of successful remembering. Memory may fail for a variety of reasons. You may not remember something because you never encoded or learned the information in the first place. Memory failure may also result from failure to effectively retrieve information that was successfully encoded or stored. Finally, you may perform poorly in a memory task because you remember several different things and are unable to choose correctly among these alternatives. The following sections provide examples of each of these sources of memory failure in the context of investigations of interference and retrieval failure.

INTERFERENCE

Memory failure due to interference has been extensively investigated in both human and animal studies. Interference refers to memory failure resulting from exposure to stimuli or events that are extraneous, and sometimes contradictory, to the memory task the individual is tested on. If you were presented with a single visual pattern in an otherwise darkened room, you would show good retention of that stimulus several minutes later. In contrast, if you saw numerous visual stimuli before and after the stimulus that you were tested on, your memory for the test item would be much worse. Exposure to

TABLE 14.2   Distinction between Proactive and Retroactive Interference

Proactive interference

Extraneous events → Target task → Memory test

Retroactive interference

Target task → Extraneous events → Memory test

various visual stimuli before and after the test item would interfere with your memory for the test item.

What kind of interference effect occurs depends on whether the interfering events take place before or after the event on which the participant is to be tested (see Table 14.2). If the extraneous stimuli that disrupt memory occur before the target event, the phenomenon is called **proactive interference.** In proactive interference, the interfering stimuli act forward, or proactively, to disrupt memory for the target event. Consider, for example, going to a sociology class that deals with the issue of punishment from the standpoint of the penal system and then attending a psychology class in which punishment is discussed from the perspective of conditioning procedures. You would be experiencing proactive interference if what you learned in the sociology class disrupted your memory of the information that was presented in the psychology class.

Memory disruptions can also work in the opposite direction. Something you encounter later can act backward to disrupt your memory of something you learned earlier. This is called **retroactive interference.** You might be at a party, for example, where you first talk to Jane and then talk with Janice. When you think back on the experience the next day, you may have difficulty remembering Jane's name because of your later interactions with Janice. Information about Janice would act backward or retroactively to disrupt memory of Jane.

Proactive Interference in Matching to Sample.   Both proactive and retroactive interference have been investigated in animal studies using delayed matching-to-sample procedures. In early studies of proactive interference, an explicit extraneous stimulus was presented before the start of a matching trial (and thus before presentation of the sample stimulus for that trial). Subjects performed less accurately on trials preceded by the extraneous stimulus than on control trials conducted in the absence of the extraneous stimulus (Medin, 1980).

Proactive interference is a fairly general phenomenon and may occur even in the absence of the presentation of an explicit extraneous stimulus. The matching-to-sample task involves repeated training trials. If these trials are presented close enough together, what occurs on one trial can disrupt performance on the next trial. Thus, proactive interference may occur because of the close scheduling of successive training trials (Edhouse & White, 1988; Jitsumori, Wright, & Shyan, 1989).

To see how proactive interference may develop between training trials, let us consider again the matching-to-sample task that was summarized in Figure 14.2. In this task, one of four sample stimuli could occur on a particular trial (triangle, square, vertical grid, or horizontal grid). Let us assume that the subject receives a trial in which the triangle is the sample stimulus and the correct choice, and this is followed by a trial in which the square is the sample and correct choice. To respond accurately on the trial with the square sample, the subject must disregard the fact that the triangle was correct on the preceding trial. If the subject fails to disregard what was correct on the preceding trial, it may make an error on the square trial by choosing the triangle (see Figure 14.2).

Proactive interference caused by earlier matching trials is particularly interesting because in this case, subjects perform poorly on a memory task not because they remember too little but because they remember too much. The disruption of performance is caused by remembering what happened on an earlier trial and confusing that with the correct response on the current trial. This phenomenon illustrates the general rule that memory failure can occur for a variety of reasons, not all of which involve the loss of information over time.

Retroactive Interference in Matching to Sample.   Retroactive interference has been investigated by presenting extraneous stimuli during the retention interval after the presentation of the sample stimulus. In some studies with pigeons, for example, the sample and choice stimuli were various visual cues projected on pecking keys. As a test for retroactive interference, on designated trials the house lights were turned on during the delay interval after presentation of the sample stimulus; on other trials, the pigeons spent the delay interval in darkness. Illumination of the house lights during the retention interval exposed the pigeons to various visual features of the experimental chamber and produced retroactive interference. The birds were less likely to select the correct test stimulus after illumination of the house lights during the delay interval than if they spent the delay interval in darkness (Roberts & Grant, 1978; see also Grant, 1988).

In contrast to proactive interference, which results from remembering too much, retroactive interference seems to result from failure to retain required information during the delay interval. Presentation of extraneous stimuli during the delay interval disrupts the rehearsal processes that are required to effectively store information based on the sample, resulting in poor performance during the memory test (Wright, Urcuioli, Sands, & Santiago, 1981).

RETRIEVAL FAILURE

Studies of proactive and retroactive interference illustrate two different causes of poor performance in a memory task. Proactive interference may result from remembering too much and confusing the sample stimulus on the current trial with what was correct on the previous trial. In contrast, retroactive interference is usually the result of not remembering enough. Yet another common reason for poor performance on a memory task is the subject's inability to effectively retrieve information that it previously learned.

If poor performance on a memory task is due to retrieval failure, then procedures that facilitate retrieval should facilitate performance. Retrieval of information is facilitated by exposure to stimuli that were previously associated with the target information. Such stimuli are called **retrieval cues.**

Remarkably insignificant features of the environment may become associated with a learning task and facilitate retrieval of information relevant to that task. In one study (Borovsky & Rovee-Collier, 1990), for example, 6-month-old infants received an instrumental conditioning procedure in their playpen at home (see Figure 14.4). Each infant was placed in a baby seat in the playpen with a mobile positioned overhead in plain view. The mobile was gently attached to one foot of the infant with a satin ribbon. By moving its foot, the infant could make the mobile move. Thus, the instrumental response was a leg movement, and the reinforcer was movement of the mobile.

Infants readily learned the leg-movement task but showed substantial forgetting in as little as 24 hours. Does this rapid forgetting reflect failure to effectively acquire or encode the instrumental contingency, or failure to retrieve what was learned the day before? If the instrumental response was not learned effectively in the first place, then there is nothing one can do to counteract the poor performance that is evident 24 hours later. In contrast, if the forgetting was due to retrieval failure, then the presentation of retrieval or reminder cues should restore the performance.

What might be an effective retrieval cue for the infants in this situation? Borovsky and Rovee-Collier (1990) found that the pattern of the cloth liner that covered the sides of the playpen served as an effective retrieval cue for the instrumental response. Sometimes the liner for the playpen had a striped pattern; on other occasions the liner had a square pattern. Infants for whom the striped pattern was in the playpen during training responded better 24 hours later if they were tested with the striped liner than if they were tested with the square liner. The reverse results were obtained with infants for whom the other liner was used during original training.

The results of this experiment are remarkable because nothing was done to direct the attention of the infants to the cloth liners. The square and striped patterns were both familiar to the infants, and the patterns were not predictive of reinforcement. They served as background cues rather than as discriminative stimuli. Nevertheless, the pattern present during original training became associated with the instrumental task and helped to retrieve information about the task during the memory test 24 hours later.

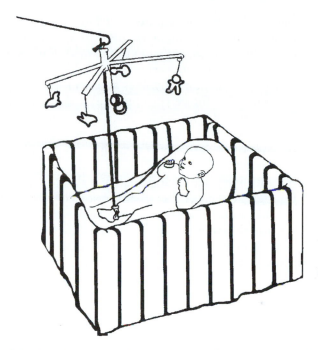

FIGURE 14.4   Experimental situation used by Borovsky and Rovee-Collier (1990) to study the effects of retrieval cues on the memory of human infants for an instrumental conditioning task.
The instrumental response was moving a leg, and the reinforcer was consequent movement of a mobile located in the infant's view.

A variety of different stimuli have been found to be effective as retrieval cues in various learning situations, including exposure to a conditioned stimulus in extinction (Gordon & Mowrer, 1980), internal cues induced by psychoactive drugs (Spear, Smith, Bryan, Gordon, Timmons, & Chiszar, 1980), and exposure to the nonreinforced stimulus in a discrimination procedure (Campbell & Randall, 1976). In addition, retrieval cues have been found to counteract a variety of instances of failed memory, including forgotten early life experiences (Richardson, Riccio, & Jonke, 1983) and amnesia caused by electroconvulsive shock (Gordon & Mowrer, 1980).

Summary

Learning and memory are integrally related; but studies of learning focus on the acquisition stage of information processing, whereas studies of memory focus on the retention and retrieval stages. Working memory is used to retain information that is required just long enough to complete a trial or job. In contrast, reference memory involves aspects of the task or trial that remain constant from one occasion to the next. Early studies considered memory to be passive and retrospective. However, more-recent evidence suggests that in many cases memory involves active processes and that the stored information concerns future (prospective) rather than past (retrospective) events.

Studies of what individuals forget can tell us as much about memory mechanisms as studies of successful performance. Memory failure may occur because of proactive or retroactive interference or because of retrieval failure. Proactive interference is often due to remembering both useful and irrelevant information and not being able to select between these. Retroactive interference can be due to disruptions of rehearsal processes needed for successful memory. Proper rehearsal, however, does not guarantee good memory. Information that is properly retained may not be retrieved during a memory test. Retrieval cues, some of which may be seemingly trivial features of the training situation, can facilitate memory performance in cases of retrieval failure.

Practice Questions

1. What is the relationship between learning and memory?

2. Why study memory mechanisms in nonhuman animals?

3. What are the fundamental features of the matching-to-sample procedure? How does the procedure ensure that responding is based on memory rather than an inadvertent cue?

4. What is the difference between prospective and retrospective memory?

5. How is identity matching to sample different from symbolic matching to sample?

6. What are possible causes of memory failure?

Suggested Readings

Kendrick, D. F., Rilling, M. E., & Denny, M. R. (Eds.). (1986). *Theories of animal memory*. Hillsdale, NJ: Erlbaum.

Miller, R. R., Kasprow, W. J., & Schachtman, T. R. (1986). Retrieval variability: Sources and consequences. *American Journal of Psychology, 99*, 145–218.

Spear, N. E., & Riccio, D. C. (1994). *Memory: Phenomena and principles*. Boston: Allyn & Bacon.

Technical Terms

Acquisition stage
Delayed matching to sample
Matching-to-sample procedure
Proactive interference
Prospective memory
Reference memory
Retention interval

Retrieval cues
Retrieval stage
Retroactive interference
Retrospective memory
Simultaneous matching to sample
Working memory

Glossary

Acquired drive   A source of motivation for instrumental behavior caused by the presentation of a stimulus that was previously conditioned with a primary, or unconditioned, reinforcer.

Acquisition stage   The first stage necessary for memory performance in which information about the stimuli and responses is encoded in the nervous system in some fashion.

Afferent neuron   A neuron that transmits messages from sense organs to the central nervous system.

Appetitive behavior   The initial component of an elicited behavior sequence. Appetitive behavior is variable, occurs in response to general spatial cues, and serves to bring the organism in contact with releasing stimuli that elicit consummatory responses.

Appetitive conditioning   A type of conditioning in which the unconditioned stimulus or reinforcer is a pleasant event, a stimulus the subject tends to approach.

Associative learning   Learning in which one event (a stimulus or a response) becomes linked to another, with the result that the first event activates a representation of the second.

Autoshaping   Same as *Sign tracking*.

Aversive conditioning   A type of conditioning in which the unconditioned stimulus or reinforcer is an unpleasant event, a stimulus that elicits aversion and withdrawal responses.

Aversive stimulus   Noxious or unpleasant stimulus that elicits aversion and/or withdrawal responses.

Behavior   The observable actions of an organism.

Behavioral bliss point   The optimal distribution of activities in the absence of constraints or limitations imposed by an instrumental conditioning procedure.

Behavioral regulation   A mechanism that focuses on the allocation or distribution of an animal's responses. It is assumed that animals work to maintain an optimal distribution of activities.

Behavior system   A sequence of response modes and corresponding behavioral and physiological control mechanisms that are activated in a coordinated manner to achieve particular functions such as feeding or defense against predation.

Between-subjects experiment   An experimental design in which two or more independent groups of participants are compared. The focus is on differences in the average performance of the various groups rather than the behavior of the individual participants.

Blocking effect   Interference with the conditioning of a novel stimulus because of the presence of a previously conditioned stimulus.

Chained schedule   A schedule of reinforcement in which the primary reinforcer is delivered only after the subject has performed a sequence of responses, with each response performed in the presence of a different stimulus.

Comparator hypothesis   The idea that conditioned responding depends on a comparison between the associative strength of the conditioned stimulus (CS) and the associative strength of other cues present during training of the target CS.

Compound stimulus test   A test procedure that identifies a stimulus as a conditioned inhibitor if that stimulus reduces responding elicited by a conditioned excitatory stimulus.

Concurrent schedule   A reinforcement procedure in which the subject can choose one of two or more simple reinforcement schedules that are available simultaneously. Concurrent schedules allow for the measurement of choice between simple schedule alternatives.

Conditioned drive   A drive state induced by the presentation of a stimulus that was previously conditioned with a primary, or unconditioned, reinforcer.

Conditioned inhibition   A type of Pavlovian conditioning in which the conditioned stimulus becomes a signal for the absence of the unconditioned stimulus.

Conditioned reinforcer   A stimulus that becomes an effective reinforcer because of its association with a primary, or unconditioned, reinforcer.

Conditioned response   A response that comes to be made to the conditioned stimulus as a result of classical conditioning.

Conditioned stimulus   A stimulus that initially does not elicit a conditioned response or activate a representation of an unconditioned stimulus but comes to do so after pairings with an unconditioned stimulus.

Conditioned suppression   An aversive Pavlovian conditioning procedure in which conditioned responding is measured by the suppression of positively reinforced instrumental behavior.

Constraints on learning   A limitation on learning resulting from the evolutionary history of the organism.

Consummatory behavior   Behavior that brings an elicited behavior sequence to an end; behavior that consummates or finishes a sequence of elicited responses.

Contingency   A measure of the extent to which two events are linked, or the extent to which the occurrence of one event depends on the other, and vice versa.

Continuous reinforcement   A schedule of reinforcement in which every occurrence of the instrumental response produces the reinforcer. Abbreviated *CRF*.

Control condition   A condition in which subjects do not receive a training procedure but are treated the same way in all other respects as subjects that are trained. Performance in the control condition is compared to performance in the experimental condition in the basic learning experiment.

CS-US interval   Same as *Interstimulus interval*.

CS-US relevance   Facilitated learning that occurs with certain combinations of conditioned and unconditioned stimuli (e.g., taste and illness) as compared with other combinations (e.g., taste and shock).

Cumulative record   A graphical representation of the cumulative number of occurrences of a particular response as a function of the passage of time. The horizontal distance on the record represents the passage of time, the vertical distance represents the total number of responses that have occurred up to a particular point in time, and the slope represents the rate of responding.

Delayed conditioning   A Pavlovian conditioning procedure in which the conditioned stimulus begins before the unconditioned stimulus on each trial.

Delayed matching to sample   A procedure in which subjects are reinforced for responding to a test stimulus that is the same as a previously presented sample stimulus.

Differential probability principle   See *Premack principle*.

Differential reinforcement of other behavior   An instrumental conditioning procedure in which a positive reinforcer is periodically delivered, but only if the participant fails to perform a particular response. Abbreviated *DRO*.

Differential responding   Responding in different ways or at different rates in the presence of different stimuli.

Directed forgetting   Stimulus control of memory, achieved by presenting a cue indicating when subjects will, or will not, be required to remember something.

Discrete-trial method   A method of instrumental conditioning in which the subject can perform the instrumental response only during specified periods, usually determined either by placement of the subject in an experimental chamber or by presentation of a stimulus.

Discriminated avoidance   An avoidance conditioning procedure in which the occurrence of an aversive unconditioned stimulus is signaled by a conditioned stimulus or warning signal.

Responding during the conditioned stimulus terminates that stimulus and prevents the delivery of the aversive unconditioned stimulus.

Discrimination hypothesis   An explanation of the partial reinforcement extinction effect according to which extinction is slower after partial reinforcement than after continuous reinforcement because the onset of extinction is more difficult to detect following partial reinforcement.

Discriminative control   A control procedure for Pavlovian conditioning in which one conditioned stimulus (the CS^+) is paired with the unconditioned stimulus, whereas another conditioned stimulus (the CS^-) is presented without the unconditioned stimulus. The development of responding during the CS^+ but not during the CS^- is considered evidence of Pavlovian conditioning.

Discriminative punishment   A type of punishment procedure in which responses are punished in the presence of a discriminative stimulus but not when the discriminative stimulus is absent.

Dishabituation   Recovery of a habituated response as a result of presentation of a strong extraneous stimulus.

Disinhibition   Recovery of a partly extinguished conditioned response as a result of presentation of a novel stimulus.

Drive reduction theory   A theory of reinforcement according to which reinforcers are effective because they reduce the subject's drive state and return the subject to homeostasis.

Drive state   A motivational state that exists when a system is not at its homeostatic level. Return of the system to its homeostatic level reduces the drive state.

Efferent neuron   A neuron that transmits impulses from the central nervous system to muscles.

Elicited behavior   A specific behavior or action pattern that occurs reliably upon presentation of a particular stimulus (its eliciting stimulus).

Equipotentiality   The idea that the rate of learning is independent of the combination of stimuli, reinforcers, or responses that are involved with the conditioning procedure.

Ethology   A specialization in biology concerned with the analysis of species-typical behavior patterns that evolve in natural habitats.

Evolution   Change in a physical or behavioral trait that occurs across successive generations because of differential reproductive success.

Experimental condition   A condition in which subjects receive a training procedure. Performance in the experimental condition is compared to performance in the control condition in the basic learning experiment.

Experimental observation   Observation of behavior under conditions specifically designed by an investigator to test particular factors or variables that might influence the learning or performance of the behavior.

External inhibition   Same as *Disinhibition*.

Extinction (in classical conditioning)   Reduction of a learned response that occurs because the conditioned stimulus is no longer paired with the unconditioned stimulus. Also, the procedure of repeatedly presenting a conditioned stimulus without the unconditioned stimulus.

Extinction (in instrumental conditioning)   Reduction in instrumental responding that occurs because the response is no longer followed by the reinforcer. Also, the procedure of no longer reinforcing the instrumental response.

Facilitation   A Pavlovian conditioning procedure in which a conditioned stimulus is presented on trials when a second stimulus is paired with a US but not on trials when the second stimulus is presented alone. In such a procedure, one cue designates when another cue will be reinforced.

Fatigue   A temporary decrease in behavior caused by repeated or excessive use of the muscles involved in the behavior.

Feedback cue   A stimulus that results from the performance of a response.

Feedback function   The relation between rates of responding and rates of reinforcement allowed by a particular reinforcement schedule.

Fixed-interval schedule   A reinforcement schedule in which reinforcement is delivered for the first response that occurs after a fixed amount of time following the last reinforcer.

Fixed-ratio schedule   A reinforcement schedule in which a fixed number of responses must occur in order for the next response to be reinforced.

Flavor neophobia   An aversion caused by the unfamiliarity of the flavor of a new food.

Focal search mode   A response mode in the feeding system that is activated once a potential source of food has been identified.

Forgetting   A reduction of a learned response that occurs because of the passage of time, not because of particular experiences

Free-operant avoidance   Same as *Nondiscriminated avoidance*.

Free-operant method   A method of instrumental conditioning that permits repeated performance of the instrumental response, in contrast to the discrete-trial method.

Frustration   An aversive emotional reaction that results from the unexpected absence of reinforcement.

Frustration theory   A theory of the partial reinforcement extinction effect according to which extinction is retarded after partial reinforcement because the instrumental response becomes conditioned to the anticipation of frustrative nonreward.

General search mode   The initial response mode of the feeding system. In this mode, the organism reacts to general features of the environment with responses that enable it to come in contact with a variety of potential sources of food.

Habituation effect   A progressive decrease in the vigor of an elicited response that may occur with repeated presentations of the eliciting stimulus.

Heterogeneous chain   A sequence of different responses, each of which is performed in the presence of a different stimulus, and possibly on a different schedule of reinforcement.

Higher-order stimulus relation   A relation in which a stimulus signals a relationship between two other stimuli rather than signaling just the presence or absence of another stimulus. In a higher-order Pavlovian relation, one CS signals whether or not another CS is paired with a US.

Homeostatic level   The optimal or defended level of a physiological or behavioral system.

Homeostasis   A process by which a physiological system is maintained at a target or optimal level. Deviations from this level trigger adjustments that return the system to the target level.

Homogeneous chain   A behavior sequence in which each component involves the same response, but each component occurs in the presence of a different stimulus and involves a different schedule requirement.

Hydraulic model   A model in ethology according to which certain factors lead to the buildup of a particular type of motivation or drive that increases the likelihood of corresponding modal action patterns. Performance of the modal action patterns reduces or discharges the motivational state.

Inhibitory S-R association   An S-R association in which presentation of the stimulus inhibits the associated response.

Instrumental behavior   An activity that is effective in producing a particular consequence or reinforcer.

Instrumental conditioning   Conditioning that results from the relation between behavior and its consequences.

Interdimensional discrimination   A discrimination between two stimuli that differ in several different respects.

Intermittent reinforcement   A schedule of reinforcement in which only some of the occurrences of the instrumental response are reinforced. The instrumental response is reinforced occasionally, or intermittently. Also called *Partial reinforcement*.

Interneuron   A neuron in the spinal cord that transmits impulses from afferent (or sensory) to efferent (or motor) neurons.

Interstimulus interval   The interval in a Pavlovian conditioning procedure between the start of the conditioned stimulus and the start of the unconditioned stimulus.

Interval schedule   A reinforcement schedule in which a response is reinforced only if it occurs more than a set amount of time after the last delivery of the reinforcer.

Intradimensional discrimination   A discrimination between stimuli that differ in only one stimulus characteristic, such as color, brightness, or pitch.

I/T ratio   Ratio between the intertrial interval (I) and the CS or trial (T) duration.

Latent inhibition effect   Retardation of Pavlovian conditioning that occurs because of prior CS preexposure or presentations of the conditioned stimulus by itself.

Law of Effect   A rule for instrumental behavior, proposed by Thorndike, according to which reinforcement of an instrumental response strengthens the association between the response and the stimulus in the presence of which the response occurred.

Learning   An enduring change in the mechanisms of behavior involving specific stimuli and/or responses that results from prior experience with those stimuli and responses.

Long-delay learning   A classical conditioning procedure in which the conditioned stimulus is presented long before the unconditioned stimulus on each conditioning trial.

Long-term habituation   A type of habituation that results in a response decrement that lasts for a week or more.

Long-term sensitization   A form of sensitization that is persistent or slow to decay.

Magnitude-of-reinforcement extinction effect   Less persistence of instrumental behavior in extinction following training with a large reinforcer than following training with a small or moderate reinforcer.

Marking stimulus   A brief visual or auditory cue presented after an instrumental response that makes the instrumental response more memorable and helps overcome the deleterious effect of delayed reinforcement.

Matching law   A rule for instrumental behavior, proposed by Herrnstein, according to which the relative rate of response on a particular response alternative equals the relative rate of reinforcement for that response alternative.

Matching to sample   A procedure in which subjects are reinforced for selecting a stimulus that corresponds to the sample presented on that trial.

Maturation   A change in behavior caused by physical or physiological development.

Memory   A theoretical term used to characterize instances in which behavior at one point in time is determined by some aspect of experience at an earlier point in time.

Memory retrieval   The recovery of information from a memory store.

Modal action pattern   A response pattern that occurs in much the same fashion most of the time and in most members of a species. Modal action patterns are often used as basic units of behavior in ethological investigations of behavior.

Motivation   A hypothetical state that increases the probability of a coordinated set of activities or activates a system of behaviors that functions to satisfy a goal such as feeding, predatory defense, infant care, or copulation.

Motor neuron   Same as *Efferent neuron*.

Multiple schedule of reinforcement   A procedure in which different reinforcement schedules are in effect in the presence of different stimuli presented in succession. Generally, each stimulus comes to evoke a pattern of responding that corresponds to whatever reinforcement schedule is in effect in the presence of that stimulus.

Naturalistic observation   Observation of behavior as it occurs under natural conditions, in the absence of interventions or manipulations introduced by the investigator.

Negative reinforcement   An instrumental conditioning procedure in which there is a negative contingency between the instrumental response and an aversive stimulus. If the instrumental response is performed, the aversive stimulus is terminated or prevented from occurring; if the instrumental response is not performed, the aversive stimulus is presented.

Negative reinforcer   Same as *Aversive stimulus*.

Nondiscriminated avoidance   An avoidance conditioning procedure in which the aversive stimulus is not signaled by an external warning signal. In the absence of avoidance behavior, the aversive stimulus occurs periodically, as set by the S-S interval. Each occurrence of the avoidance response prevents the delivery of the aversive stimulus for a fixed period (called the R-S interval).

One-way avoidance   An avoidance conditioning procedure in which the required instrumental response is always to cross from one compartment of a shuttle box to the other in the same direction.

Operant behavior   Behavior that is defined by the effect it produces in the environment. Examples include pressing a lever and opening a door. Any sequence of movements that depresses the lever or opens the door constitutes an instance of that particular operant.

Operant conditioning   A form of instrumental conditioning in which the response is defined by the effect it produces on the environment.

Opponent process   A compensatory mechanism that ensures that deviations of a system from a preferred or homeostatic level are counteracted so as to return the system to its preferred level.

Orienting response   A reaction to a novel stimulus that usually involves turning toward the source of the stimulus.

Outcome   Same as *Reinforcer*.

Overshadowing   Interference with the conditioning of a stimulus due to the simultaneous presence of another stimulus that is easier to condition.

Overtraining extinction effect   Less persistence of instrumental behavior in extinction following extensive training with reinforcement (overtraining) than following only moderate levels of reinforcement training.

Paradoxical reward effect   A phenomenon in which there is more responding in extinction following training with fewer, more intermittent, or smaller reinforcers.

Partial reinforcement   A schedule of reinforcement in which only some occurrences of the instrumental response are reinforced.

Partial-reinforcement extinction effect   Greater persistence in instrumental responding in extinction after partial (intermittent) reinforcement training than after continuous reinforcement training. Abbreviated *PREE*.

Perceptual concept   Responding the same way to a set of physically different stimuli (pictures of various types of dogs, for example) that all belong to the same category (dog).

Performance   An organism's activities at a particular time.

Persistence   The continued performance of an instrumental response after an extinction procedure has been introduced.

Positive occasion setting   Same as *Facilitation*.

Postreinforcement pause   A pause in responding that typically occurs after the delivery of the reinforcer on fixed-ratio and fixed-interval schedules of reinforcement.

Practice   Repetition of a response or behavior, usually with the intent of improving performance.

Predatory imminence   The perceived likelihood of being attacked by a predator. Different species-typical defense responses are assumed to be performed in the face of different degrees of predatory imminence.

Premack principle   Given two responses with different baseline probabilities of occurrence, the opportunity to perform the higher-probability response will reinforce or increase performance of the lower-probability behavior.

Primary reinforcer   A reinforcer that is effective without prior conditioning.

Proactive interference   Disruption of memory by exposure to stimuli before the event to be remembered.

Proprioceptive cue   An internal response feedback stimulus that arises from the movement of muscles and/or joints.

Prospective memory   Memory of a plan for future action. Also called *Prospection.*

Punishment   A type of instrumental conditioning procedure in which occurrence of the instrumental response results in delivery of an aversive stimulus.

Puzzle box   A type of experimental chamber used by Thorndike to study instrumental conditioning. The subject was put in the chamber and had to perform a specified behavior in order to be released and obtain the reinforcer.

R-S interval   The interval between the occurrence of an avoidance response and the next scheduled presentation of the aversive stimulus in a nondiscriminated avoidance procedure.

R-O association   An association between the instrumental response (R) and the reinforcer (O).

Radial maze   A maze consisting of a series of arms of the same length emanating from a central choice point. To go from one arm to another, the participant has to return to the central choice point each time.

Random control   A control procedure for Pavlovian conditioning in which the conditioned and unconditioned stimuli are presented at random times relative to each other.

Rate of extinction   How fast responding declines during the period of time when an extinction procedure is in effect.

Rate of responding   A measure of how often a response is repeated in a unit of time; for example, the number of responses that occur per hour.

Ratio run   The high and invariant rate of responding observed after the postreinforcement pause on fixed-ratio reinforcement schedules. The ratio run ends when the necessary number of responses has been performed and the subject is reinforced.

Ratio schedule   A reinforcement schedule in which reinforcement depends only on the number of responses the subject performs, irrespective of when these responses occur.

Reference memory   The retention of background information a subject needs in order to respond successfully in a situation. (Compare with *Working memory.*)

Reflex   A unit of elicited behavior involving a specific environmental event and its corresponding specific elicited response.

Reflex arc   Neural structures, consisting of the afferent (sensory) neuron, interneuron, and efferent (motor) neuron, that enable a stimulus to elicit a reflex response.

Rehearsal   A theoretical process whereby some information is maintained in an active state, available to guide behavior and/or the processing of other information.

Reinforcer   A stimulus whose delivery shortly following a response increases the future probability of that response; also called *Outcome.*

Reinstatement   Recovery of excitatory responding to an extinguished stimulus produced by exposures to the unconditioned stimulus.

Relative-waiting-time hypothesis   The idea that conditioned responding depends on how long the organism has to wait for the unconditioned stimulus (US) in the presence of the conditioned stimulus (CS), as compared to how long the organism has to wait for the US in the experimental situation irrespective of the CS.

Releasing stimulus   Same as *Sign stimulus*.

Reminder treatment   The presentation of a retrieval cue that reactivates a memory or facilitates memory retrieval.

Renewal   Recovery of excitatory responding to an extinguished stimulus produced by a shift away from the contextual cues that were present during extinction.

Renewal effect   Recovery of responding when subjects are returned to the training context after receiving an extinction procedure in a distinctively different environment.

Response deprivation hypothesis   An explanation of reinforcement according to which reduced access to a particular response is sufficient to make the opportunity to perform that response an effective positive reinforcer.

Response reserve   The idea that reinforcement of instrumental behavior leads to the buildup of response strength, which is then used up in extinction.

Retardation-of-acquisition test   A test procedure that identifies a stimulus as a conditioned inhibitor if that stimulus is slower to acquire conditioned excitatory properties than a comparison stimulus.

Retention interval   The period of time between acquisition of information and a test of memory for that information.

Retention stage   The second stage necessary for memory performance in which information is stored for later use.

Retrieval cue   A stimulus related to an experience that facilitates the recall of other information related to that experience.

Retrieval failure   A deficit in recovering information from a memory store.

Retrieval stage   The third stage necessary for memory performance in which information that has been retained is recovered from storage for use.

Retroactive interference   Disruption of memory by exposure to stimuli following the event to be remembered.

Retrospection   Same as *Retrospective memory*.

Retrospective memory   Memory of a previously experienced event.

Reward magnitude extinction effect   Less persistence of instrumental behavior in extinction following training with a large reinforcer than following training with a small or moderate reinforcer.

S^+   A discriminative stimulus that signals the availability of reinforcement for an instrumental response.

S^-   A discriminative stimulus that signals the absence of reinforcement for an instrumental response.

S-O association   An association between a stimulus (S) in the presence of which an instrumental response is reinforced and the reinforcer (O).

S-R association   The learning of an association between a stimulus and a response, with the result that the stimulus comes to elicit the response.

S-R learning   The learning of an association between a stimulus and a response, with the result that the stimulus comes to elicit the response.

S-R system   The shortest neural pathway that connects the sense organs stimulated by an eliciting stimulus and the muscles involved in making the elicited response.

S(R-O) association   A higher-order relation in instrumental conditioning situations, according to which a discriminative or contextual stimulus (S) activates an association between the instrumental response and the reinforcer (R-O).

S-S interval   The interval between successive presentations of the aversive stimulus in a nondiscriminated avoidance procedure when the avoidance response is not performed.

S-S learning   Same as *Stimulus-stimulus learning*.

Safety signal   A stimulus that signals the absence of an aversive event.

Salience   The quality of a stimulus that makes it effective in attracting attention and controlling behavior. More intense stimuli are typically more salient.

Schedule line   A line on a graph of different rates of instrumental and reinforcer behavior indicating how much access to the reinforcer activity is provided for various rates of instrumental responding on a particular schedule of reinforcement.

Schedule of reinforcement   A program or rule that determines which occurrence of an instrumental or operant response is followed by delivery of the reinforcer and how soon after the response the reinforcer is delivered.

Secondary reinforcer   Same as *Conditioned reinforcer*.

Selective associations   Associations that are formed more readily between one combination of conditioned and unconditioned stimuli than between other combinations.

Sensitization effect   An increase in the vigor of elicited behavior that may result from repeated presentations of the eliciting stimulus.

Sensory neuron   Same as *Afferent neuron*.

Sensory reinforcement   Reinforcement provided by presentation of a stimulus unrelated to a biological need or drive.

Sequential theory   A theory of the partial-reinforcement extinction effect according to which extinction is retarded after partial reinforcement because the instrumental response becomes conditioned to the memory of nonreward.

Shaping   Reinforcement of successive approximations to a target instrumental response, typically used to condition responses that are not in the subject's existing repertoire of behavior.

Short-term habituation   A habituation effect that lasts a relatively short period of time, sometimes less than a minute.

Short-term sensitization   A form of sensitization that lasts a relatively short period of time, sometimes less than a minute.

Shuttle box   An apparatus for the study of avoidance behavior consisting of two compartments connected end-to-end. The avoidance response involves moving from one compartment to the other (shuttling between the compartments).

Sign stimulus   A specific feature of an object or animal that elicits a modal action pattern.

Sign tracking   A form of appetitive classical conditioning in which a localized stimulus serves as the conditioned stimulus. As a result, the subject comes to approach (track) and sometimes manipulate the conditioned stimulus.

Simultaneous conditioning   A Pavlovian conditioning procedure in which the conditioned stimulus and the unconditioned stimulus are presented simultaneously on each conditioning trial.

Simultaneous matching to sample   A procedure in which subjects are reinforced for responding to a test stimulus that is the same as a sample stimulus. The sample and the test stimuli are presented at the same time.

Single-subject experiment   A type of experiment in which learning is investigated through extensive observation of the behavior of a single individual. The individual's behavior must be sufficiently well understood to permit accurate assumptions about how the subject would have behaved if he had not received the training procedure.

Skinner box   A small experimental chamber provided with something the subject can manipulate repeatedly, such as a response lever. This allows a subject to perform a particular response repeatedly without being removed from the experimental situation. Usually the chamber also has a mechanism that can deliver a reinforcer, such as a pellet of food.

Species-specific defense reactions   Species-typical responses animals perform in aversive situations. The responses may involve freezing, fleeing, or fighting.

Species-typical behavior   Behavior that is characteristic of most members of a species.

Spontaneous recovery   Recovery of a response produced by a period of rest after habituation or extinction.

SSDR   Abbreviation for *Species-specific defense reaction*.

Startle response   A sudden jump or tensing of the muscles that may occur when an unexpected stimulus is presented.

State system   Neural structures that determine the organism's general level of responsiveness or readiness to respond.

Stimulus   An event, external or internal to the organism, that activates sensory neurons and may elicit or cue behavior.

Stimulus dimension   The feature (color, for example) that distinguishes a series of stimuli in a test of stimulus generalization.

Stimulus discrimination   Differential responding in the presence of two or more stimuli.

Stimulus discrimination training (in classical conditioning)   One conditioned stimulus (the CS^+) is paired with an unconditioned stimulus, while another conditioned stimulus (the CS^-) is presented without an unconditioned stimulus.

Stimulus discrimination training (in instrumental conditioning)   A procedure in which reinforcement for responding is available whenever one stimulus (the S^+) is present and is not available whenever another stimulus (the S^-) is present.

Stimulus equivalence   Responding to physically distinct stimuli in the same fashion because of common prior experiences with the stimuli.

Stimulus generalization   The occurrence of behavior learned through habituation or conditioning in the presence of stimuli that are different from the stimulus used during training.

Stimulus generalization gradient   A gradient of responding that may be observed if subjects are tested with stimuli that increasingly differ from the stimulus that was present during training.

Stimulus generalization of habituation   See *Stimulus generalization*.

Stimulus-stimulus learning   The learning of an association between two stimuli, such that presentation of one of the stimuli activates a neural representation of the other.

Straight-alley runway   A straight alley with a start box at one end and a goal box at the other. Animals are placed in the start box at the start of a trial and allowed to run to the goal box.

Summation test   Same as *Compound stimulus test*.

Taste aversion learning   A type of Pavlovian conditioning in which the taste of a novel food serves as the conditioned stimulus and gastrointestinal illness serves as the unconditioned stimulus. Taste aversions can be learned even if the illness is delayed several hours after exposure to the taste.

Temporal coding   Learning not just that the CS is paired with the US but exactly when the US occurs.

Temporal contiguity   The simultaneous occurrence of two or more events.

Temporal cues   Stimuli related to the passage of time.

Time-out   A period during which the opportunity to obtain reinforcement is removed. This may involve removal of the participant from the situation where reinforcers may be obtained.

T-maze   A maze constructed in the shape of a T, with the start box at the end of the longest stem of the maze and goal boxes at the ends of the other stems. After leaving the start box, the subject can choose either the right or the left goal box.

Trace conditioning   A classical conditioning procedure in which the unconditioned stimulus is presented on each trial after the conditioned stimulus has been terminated for a short period.

Trace decay hypothesis   The theoretical idea that exposure to a stimulus produces changes in the nervous system that gradually decrease after the stimulus has been terminated.

Trace interval   The interval between the end of the CS and the beginning of the US in a trace conditioning procedure.

Trials-unique procedure   A matching-to-sample procedure in which a different stimulus serves as the sample on each trial.

Two-factor theory   A theory of avoidance learning involving two forms of conditioning: (1) Pavlovian conditioning of fear to a stimulus that signals aversive stimulation, and (2) instrumental conditioning of the avoidance response by fear reduction.

Two-way avoidance   A shuttle avoidance procedure in which trials can start in either compartment of a shuttle box, and the avoidance response consists of going from the occupied compartment to the unoccupied compartment.

Unconditioned response   A response that occurs to a stimulus without the necessity of prior training or conditioning.

Unconditioned stimulus   A stimulus that elicits vigorous responding in the absence of prior training.

Unpaired control procedure   A control procedure for classical conditioning in which the CS and the US occur but never together.

US devaluation   A procedure that reduces the effectiveness of an unconditioned stimulus in eliciting unconditioned behavior.

US inflation   A procedure that increases the effectiveness of an unconditioned stimulus in eliciting unconditioned behavior.

Variable-interval schedule   A reinforcement schedule in which reinforcement is provided for the first response that occurs after a variable amount of time from the last reinforcement.

Variable-ratio schedule   A reinforcement schedule in which the number of responses necessary to obtain reinforcement varies from trial to trial. The value of the schedule refers to the average number of responses needed for reinforcement.

Warning signal   Same as *Warning stimulus*.

Warning stimulus   The stimulus in a discriminated avoidance procedure that reliably precedes scheduled presentations of the aversive unconditioned stimulus.

Working memory   The retention of information that is needed only to accomplish the task at hand, as contrasted with reference memory, which involves background information that is also needed for future similar tasks.

REFERENCES

Adkins-Regan, E., & MacKillop, E. A. (2003). Japanese quail (*Coturnix japonica*) inseminations are more likely to fertilize eggs in a context predicting mating opportunities. *Proceedings of the Royal Society of London (B), 270,* 1685–1689.

Alcock, J. (2001). *Animal behavior* (7th ed.). Sunderland, MA: Sinauer.

Allison, J. (1983). *Behavioral economics*. New York: Praeger.

Allison, J. (1989). The nature of reinforcement. In S. B. Klein & R. R. Mowrer (Eds.), *Contemporary learning theories: Instrumental conditioning theory and the impact of biological constraints on learning* (pp. 13–39). Hillsdale, NJ: Erlbaum.

Allison, J., & Timberlake, W. (1974). Instrumental and contingent saccharin-licking in rats: Response deprivation and reinforcement. *Learning and Motivation, 5,* 231–247.

Amsel, A. (1958). The role of frustrative nonreward in noncontinuous reward situations. *Psychological Bulletin, 55,* 102–119.

Amsel, A. (1967). Partial reinforcement effects on vigor and persistence. In K. W. Spence & J. T. Spence (Eds.), *The psychology of learning and motivation* (Vol. 1, pp. 1–65). Orlando, FL: Academic Press.

Amsel, A. (1992). *Frustration theory: An analysis of dispositional learning and memory*. Cambridge, UK: Cambridge University Press.

Amsel, A., & Rashotte, M. E. (1984). *Mechanisms of adaptive behavior: Clark L. Hull's theoretical papers, with commentary*. New York: Columbia University Press.

Anger, D. (1963). The role of temporal discrimination in the reinforcement of Sidman avoidance behavior. *Journal of the Experimental Analysis of Behavior, 6,* 477–506.

Azorlosa, J. L., & Cicala, G. A. (1986). Blocking of conditioned suppression with 1 or 10 compound trials. *Animal Learning & Behavior, 14,* 163–167.

Azrin, N. H. (1959). Punishment and recovery during fixed-ratio performance. *Journal of the Experimental Analysis of Behavior, 2,* 301–305.

Azrin, N. H. (1960). Effects of punishment intensity during variable-interval reinforcement. *Journal of the Experimental Analysis of Behavior, 3,* 123–142.

Azrin, N. H., & Holz, W. C. (1961). Punishment during fixed-interval reinforcement. *Journal of the Experimental Analysis of Behavior, 4,* 343–347.

Azrin, N. H., & Holz, W. C. (1966). Punishment. In W. K. Honig (Ed.), *Operant behavior: Areas of research and application* (pp. 380–447). New York: Appleton-Century-Crofts.

Azrin, N. H., Holz, W. C., & Hake, D. F. (1963). Fixed-ratio punishment. *Journal of the Experimental Analysis of Behavior, 6,* 141–148.

Babkin, B. P. (1949). *Pavlov: A biography*. Chicago: University of Chicago Press.

Baerends, G. P. (1988). Ethology. In R. C. Atkinson, R. J. Herrnstein, G. Lindzey, & R. D. Luce (Eds.), *Stevens' handbook of experimental psychology* (Vol. 1, pp. 765–830). New York: Wiley.

Baker, T. B., & Tiffany, S. T. (1985). Morphine tolerance as habituation. *Psychological Review, 92,* 78–108.

Balaz, M. A., Kasprow, W. J., & Miller, R. R. (1982). Blocking with a single compound trial. *Animal Learning & Behavior, 10,* 271–276.

Balsam, P. D. (1988). Selection, representation, and equivalence of controlling stimuli. In R. C. Atkinson, R. J. Herrnstein, G. Lindzey, & R. D. Luce (Eds.), *Stevens' handbook of experimental psychology* (Vol. 2, pp. 111–166). New York: Wiley.

Balsam, P. D., & Tomie, A. (Eds.). (1985). *Context and conditioning*. Hillsdale, NJ: Erlbaum.

Barnet, R. C., Grahame, N. J., & Miller, R. R. (1993). Temporal encoding as a determinant of blocking. *Journal of Experimental Psychology: Animal Behavior Processes, 19,* 327–341.

Barnet, R. C., & Miller, R. R. (1996). Second-order excitation mediated by a backward conditioned inhibitor. *Journal of Experimental Psychology: Animal Behavior Processes, 22,* 279–296.

Baron, A., & Menich, S. R. (1985). Reaction times of younger and older men: Effects of compound samples and a prechoice signal on delayed matching-to-sample performances. *Journal of the Experimental Analysis of Behavior, 44,* 1–14.

Bashinski, H., Werner, J., & Rudy, J. (1985). Determinants of infant visual attention: Evidence for a two-process theory. *Journal of Experimental Child Psychology, 39,* 580–598.

Bechterev, V. M. (1913). *La psychologie objective.* Paris: Alcan.

Benedict, J. O., & Ayres, J. J. B. (1972). Factors affecting conditioning in the truly random control procedure in the rat. *Journal of Comparative and Physiological Psychology, 78,* 323–330.

Berlyne, D. E. (1969). The reward value of indifferent stimulation. In J. Tapp (Ed.), *Reinforcement and behavior.* New York: Academic Press.

Best, M. R., Batson, J. D., Meachum, C. L., Brown, E. R., & Ringer, M. (1985a). Characteristics of taste-mediated environmental potentiation in rats. *Learning and Motivation, 16,* 190–209.

Best, M. R., Dunn, D. P., Batson, J. D., Meachum, C. L., & Nash, S. M. (1985b). Extinguishing conditioned inhibition in flavour-aversion learning: Effects of repeated testing and extinction of the excitatory element. *Quarterly Journal of Experimental Psychology, 37B,* 359–378.

Bitterman, M. E. (1964). Classical conditioning in the gold fish as a function of the CS-US interval. *Journal of Comparative and Physiological Psychology, 58,* 359–366.

Blaisdell, A. P., Gunther, L. M., & Miller, R. R. (1999). Recovery from blocking achieved by extinguishing the blocking CS. *Animal Learning & Behavior, 27,* 63–76.

Blass, E. M., Ganchrow, J. R., & Steiner, J. E. (1984). Classical conditioning in newborn humans 2–48 hours of age. *Infant Behavior and Development, 7,* 223–235.

Boakes, R. A. (1979). Interactions between type I and type II processes involving positive reinforcement. In A. Dickinson & R. A. Boakes (Eds.), *Mechanisms of learning and motivation.* Hillsdale, NJ: Erlbaum.

Boakes, R. A. (1984). *From Darwin to behaviorism: Psychology and the minds of animals.* Cambridge, UK: Cambridge University Press.

Boakes, R. A., Poli, M., Lockwood, M. J., & Goodall, G. (1978). A study of misbehavior: Token reinforcement in the rat. *Journal of the Experimental Analysis of Behavior, 29,* 115–134.

Bolles, R. C. (1970). Species-specific defense reactions and avoidance learning. *Psychological Review, 71,* 32–48.

Bolles, R. C. (1972a). Reinforcement, expectancy, and learning. *Psychological Review, 79,* 394–409.

Bolles, R. C. (1972b). The avoidance learning problem. In G. H. Bower (Ed.), *The psychology of learning and motivation* (Vol. 6). Orlando, FL: Academic Press.

Bolles, R. C., & Riley, A. L. (1973). Freezing as an avoidance response: Another look at the operant-respondent distinction. *Learning and Motivation, 4,* 268–275.

Borovsky, D., & Rovee-Collier, C. (1990). Contextual constraints on memory retrieval at six months. *Child Development, 61,* 1569–1583.

Bouton, M. E. (1986). Slow reacquisition following the extinction of conditioned suppression. *Learning and Motivation, 17,* 1–15.

Bouton, M. E. (1988). Context and ambiguity in the extinction of emotional learning: Implications for exposure therapy. *Behaviour Research and Therapy, 26,* 137–149.

Bouton, M. E. (1993). Context, time, and memory retrieval in the interference paradigms of Pavlovian learning. *Psychological Bulletin, 114,* 80–99.

Bouton, M. E. (1994). Conditioning, remembering, and forgetting. *Journal of Experimental Psychology: Animal Behavior Processes, 20,* 219–231.

Bouton, M. E. (2001). Classical conditioning and clinical psychology. In N. J. Smelser & P. B. Baltes (Eds.), *Encyclopedia of the social and behavioral sciences* (Vol. 3, pp. 1942–1945). Oxford: Elsevier Science.

Bouton, M. E., & Bolles, R. C. (1980). Conditioned fear assessed by freezing and by the suppression of three different baselines. *Animal Learning & Behavior, 8,* 429–434.

Bouton, M. E., Mineka, S., & Barlow, D. H. (2001). A modern learning theory perspective on the etiology of panic disorder. *Psychological Review, 108,* 4–32.

Bouton, M. E., & Nelson, J. B. (1998). The role of context in classical conditioning: Some implications for behavior therapy. In W. O'Donohue (Ed.), *Learning and behavior therapy* (pp. 59–84). Boston: Allyn & Bacon.

Bouton, M. E., & Swartzentruber, D. (1989). Slow reacquisition following extinction: Context, encoding, and retrieval mechanisms. *Journal of Experimental Psychology: Animal Behavior Processes, 15,* 43–53.

Bouton, M. E., & Swartzentruber, D. (1991). Sources of relapse after extinction in Pavlovian and instrumental learning. *Clinical Psychology Review, 11,* 123–140.

Bower, G. H., & Hilgard, E. R. (1981). *Theories of learning* (5th ed.). Englewood Cliffs, NJ: Prentice Hall.

Bradshaw, C. M., & Szabadi, E. (Eds.). (1997). *Time and behavior: Psychological and neurobiological analyses.* Oxford: Elsevier Science.

Braveman, N. S., & Bronstein, P. (Eds.). (1985). *Experimental assessments and clinical applications of conditioned food aversions. Annals of the New York Academy of Sciences* (Vol. 443). New York: New York Academy of Sciences.

Breland, K., & Breland, M. (1961). The misbehavior of organisms. *American Psychologist, 16,* 681–684.

Brogden, W. J., Lipman, E. A., & Culler, E. (1938). The role of incentive in conditioning and extinction. *American Journal of Psychology, 51,* 109–117.

Brooks, D. C., & Bouton, M. E. (1993). A retrieval cue for extinction attenuates spontaneous recovery. *Journal of Experimental Psychology: Animal Behavior Processes, 19,* 77–89.

Burns, M., & Domjan, M. (2000). Sign tracking in domesticated quail with one trial a day: Generality across CS and US parameters. *Animal Learning & Behavior, 28,* 109–119.

Camp, D. S., Raymond, G. A., & Church, R. M. (1967). Temporal relationship between response and punishment. *Journal of Experimental Psychology, 74,* 114–123.

Campbell, B. A., & Randall, P. K. (1976). The effect of reinstatement stimulus conditions on the maintenance of long-term memory. *Developmental Psychobiology, 9,* 325–333.

Capaldi, E. J. (1967). A sequential hypothesis of instrumental learning. In K. W. Spence & J. T. Spence (Eds.), *The psychology of learning and motivation* (Vol. 1, pp. 67–156). Orlando, FL: Academic Press.

Capaldi, E. J. (1971). Memory and learning: A sequential viewpoint. In W. K. Honig & P. H. R. James (Eds.), *Animal memory* (pp. 115–154). Orlando, FL: Academic Press.

Charlop, M. H., Kurtz, P. F., & Casey, F. G. (1990). Using aberrant behaviors as reinforcers for autistic children. *Journal of Applied Behavior Analysis, 23,* 163–181.

Church, R. M. (1964). Systematic effect of the random error in the yoked control design. *Psychological Bulletin, 62,* 122–131.

Church, R. M. (1969). Response suppression. In B. A. Campbell & R. M. Church (Eds.), *Punishment and aversive behavior* (pp. 111–156). New York: Appleton-Century-Crofts.

Church, R. M., & Raymond, G. A. (1967). Influence of the schedule of positive reinforcement on punished behavior. *Journal of Comparative and Physiological Psychology, 63,* 329–332.

Clark, R. E., Manns, J. R., & Squire, L. R. (2001). Trace and delay eyeblink conditioning: Contrasting phenomena of declarative and nondeclarative memory. *Psychological Science, 12,* 304–308.

Cohen, L. B. (1988). An information processing view of infant cognitive development. In L. Weiskrantz (Ed.), *Thought without language* (pp. 211–228). Oxford: Oxford University Press.

Cole, M. R. (1999). Molar and molecular control in variable-interval and variable-ratio schedules. *Journal of the Experimental Analysis of Behavior, 71*, 319–328.

Cole, R. P., Barnet, R. C., & Miller, R. R. (1995). Temporal encoding in trace conditioning. *Animal Learning & Behavior, 23*, 144–153.

Colwill, R. M. (1994). Associative representations of instrumental contingencies. In D. L. Medin (Ed.), *The psychology of learning and motivation* (Vol. 31, pp. 1–72). San Diego: Academic Press.

Colwill, R. M., & Rescorla, R. A. (1986). Associative structures in instrumental learning. In G. H. Bower (Ed.), *The psychology of learning and motivation* (Vol. 20, pp. 55–104). San Diego: Academic Press.

Colwill, R. M., & Rescorla, R. A. (1990). Evidence for the hierarchical structure of instrumental learning. *Animal Learning & Behavior, 18*, 71–82.

Cook, R. G., Brown, M. F., & Riley, D. A. (1985). Flexible memory processing by rats: Use of prospective and retrospective information in the radial maze. *Journal of Experimental Psychology: Animal Behavior Processes, 11*, 453–469.

Cunningham, C. L. (1998). Drug conditioning and drug-seeking behavior. In W. O. O'Donohue (Ed.), *Learning and behavior therapy* (pp. 518–544). Boston: Allyn & Bacon.

D'Amato, M. R. (1973). Delayed matching and short-term memory in monkeys. In G. H. Bower (Ed.), *The psychology of learning and motivation* (Vol. 7, pp. 227–269). New York: Academic Press.

D'Amato, M. R., Fazzaro, J., & Etkin, M. (1968). Anticipatory responding and avoidance discrimination as factors in avoidance conditioning. *Journal of Comparative and Physiological Psychology, 77*, 41–47.

Dardano, J. F., & Sauerbrunn, D. (1964). An aversive stimulus as a correlated block counter in FR performance. *Journal of the Experimental Analysis of Behavior, 7*, 37–43.

Darwin, C. (1897). *The descent of man and selection in relation to sex.* New York: Appleton-Century-Crofts.

Davis, M. (1970). Effects of interstimulus interval length and variability on startle-response habituation in the rat. *Journal of Comparative and Physiological Psychology, 72*, 177–192.

Davis, M. (1974). Sensitization of the rat startle response by noise. *Journal of Comparative and Physiological Psychology, 87*, 571–581.

Davis, M., Hitchcock, J. M., & Rosen, J. B. (1987). Anxiety and the amygdala: Pharmacological and anatomical analysis of the fear-potentiated startle paradigm. In G. H. Bower (Ed.), *The psychology of learning and motivation* (Vol. 21, pp. 263–304). Orlando, FL: Academic Press.

Davison, M., & McCarthy, D. (1988). *The matching law: A research review.* Hillsdale, NJ: Erlbaum.

Dean, S. J., & Pittman, C. M. (1991). Self-punitive behavior: A revised analysis. In M. R. Denny (Ed.), *Fear, avoidance, and phobias* (pp. 259–284). Hillsdale, NJ: Erlbaum.

Deich, J. D., Allan, R. W., & Zeigler, H. P. (1988). Conjunctive differentiation of gape during food reinforced keypecking in the pigeon. *Animal Learning & Behavior, 16*, 268–276.

Denniston, J. C., Savastano, H. I., & Miller, R. R. (2001). The extended comparator hypothesis: Learning by contiguity, responding by relative strength. In R. R. Mowrer & S. B. Klein (Eds.), *Handbook of contemporary learning theories* (pp. 65–117). Mahwah, NJ: Erlbaum.

DeVito, P. L., & Fowler, H. (1987). Enhancement of conditioned inhibition via an extinction treatment. *Animal Learning & Behavior, 15*, 448–454.

Dickinson, A., Nicholas, D. J., & Macintosh, N. J. (1983). A re-examination of one-trial blocking in conditioned suppression. *Quarterly Journal of Experimental Psychology, 35*, 67–79.

Dinsmoor, J. A. (1952). A discrimination based on punishment. *Quarterly Journal of Experimental Psychology, 4*, 27–45.

Dinsmoor, J. A. (1977). Escape, avoidance, punishment: Where do we stand? *Journal of the Experimental Analysis of Behavior, 28*, 83–95.

Domjan, M. (1976). Determinants of the enhancement of flavored-water intake by prior exposure. *Journal of Experimental Psychology: Animal Behavior Processes, 2*, 17–27.

Domjan, M. (1977). Attenuation and enhancement of neophobia for edible substances. In L. M. Barker, M. R. Best, & M. Domjan (Eds.), *Learning mechanisms in food selection* (pp. 151–179). Waco, TX: Baylor University Press.

Domjan, M. (1985). Cue-consequence specificity and long-delay learning revisited. *Annals of the New York Academy of Sciences, 443*, 54–66.

Domjan, M. (1994). Formulation of a behavior system for sexual conditioning. *Psychonomic Bulletin & Review, 1*, 421–428.

Domjan, M. (1997). Behavior systems and the demise of equipotentiality: Historical antecedents and evidence from sexual conditioning. In M. E. Bouton & M. S. Fanselow (Eds.), *Learning, motivation, and cognition* (pp. 31–51). Washington, DC: American Psychological Association.

Domjan, M. (1998). Going wild in the laboratory: Learning about species typical cues. In D. L. Medin (Ed.), *The psychology of learning and motivation* (Vol. 38, pp. 155–186). San Diego: Academic Press.

Domjan, M. (2003). Stepping out of the box in considering the C/T ratio. *Behavioural Processes, 62*, 103–114.

Domjan, M., Blesbois, E., & Williams, J. (1998). The adaptive significance of sexual conditioning: Pavlovian control of sperm release. *Psychological Science, 9*, 411–415.

Domjan, M., Cusato, B., & Villarreal, R. (2000). Pavlovian feed-forward mechanisms in the control of social behavior. *Behavioral and Brain Sciences, 23*, 235–249.

Domjan, M., & Gillan, D. (1976). Role of novelty in the aversion for increasingly concentrated saccharin solutions. *Physiology & Behavior, 16*, 537–542.

Domjan, M., & Holloway, K. S. (1998). Sexual learning. In G. Greenberg & M. M. Harraway (Eds.), *Comparative psychology: A handbook* (pp. 602–613). New York: Garland.

Domjan, M., & Nash, S. (1988). Stimulus control of social behaviour in male Japanese quail, *Coturnix coturnix japonica. Animal Behaviour, 36*, 1006–1015.

Domjan, M., & Wilson, N. E. (1972). Specificity of cue to consequence in aversion learning in the rat. *Psychonomic Science, 26*, 143–145.

Edhouse, W. V., & White, K. G. (1988). Sources of proactive interference in animal memory. *Journal of Experimental Psychology: Animal Behavior Processes, 14*, 56–70.

Eisenberger, R., Karpman, M., & Trattner, J. (1967). What is the necessary and sufficient condition for reinforcement in the contingency situation? *Journal of Experimental Psychology, 74*, 342–350.

Estes, W. K., & Skinner, B. F. (1941). Some quantitative properties of anxiety. *Journal of Experimental Psychology, 29*, 390–400.

Fanselow, M. S. (1989). The adaptive function of conditioned defensive behavior: An ecological approach to Pavlovian stimulus-substitution theory. In R. J. Blanchard, P. F. Brain, D. C. Blanchard, & S. Parmigiani (Eds.), *Ethoexperimental approaches to the study of behavior* (NATO ASI Series D, Vol. 48, pp. 151–166). Boston: Kluwer Academic.

Fanselow, M. S. (1994). Neural organization of the defensive behavior system responsible for fear. *Psychonomic Bulletin & Review, 1*, 429–438.

Fanselow, M. S. (1997). Species-specific defense reactions: Retrospect and prospect. In M. E. Bouton & M. S. Fanselow (Eds.), *Learning, motivation, and cognition* (pp. 321–341). Washington, DC: American Psychological Association.

Fanselow, M. S., & Lester, L. S. (1988). A functional behavioristic approach to aversively motivated behavior: Predatory imminence as a determinant of the topography of defensive behavior. In R. C. Bolles & M. D. Beecher (Eds.), *Evolution and learning* (pp. 185–212). Hillsdale, NJ: Erlbaum.

Fanselow, M. S., Lester, L. S., & Helmstetter, F. J. (1988). Changes in feeding and foraging patterns as an antipredator defensive strategy: A laboratory simulation using aversive stimulation in a closed economy. *Journal of the Experimental Analysis of Behavior, 50,* 361–374.

Felton, M., & Lyon, D. O. (1966). The post-reinforcement pause. *Journal of the Experimental Analysis of Behavior, 9,* 131–134.

Ferster, C. B., & Perrott, M. C. (1968). *Behavior principles.* New York: Appleton-Century-Crofts.

Ferster, C. B., & Skinner, B. F. (1957). *Schedules of reinforcement.* New York: Appleton-Century-Crofts.

Foree, D. D., & LoLordo, V. M. (1973). Attention in the pigeon: The differential effects of food-getting vs. shock avoidance procedures. *Journal of Comparative and Physiological Psychology, 85,* 551–558.

Forestell, P. H., & Herman, L. M. (1988). Delayed matching of visual materials by a bottlenosed dolphin aided by auditory symbols. *Animal Learning & Behavior, 16,* 137–146.

Friedman, B. X., Blaisdell, A. P., Escobar, M., & Miller, R. R. (1998). Comparator mechanisms and conditioned inhibition: Conditioned stimulus preexposure disrupts Pavlovian conditioned inhibition but not explicitly unpaired inhibition. *Journal of Experimental Psychology: Animal Behavior Processes, 24,* 453–466.

Fudim, O. K. (1978). Sensory preconditioning of flavors with a formalin-produced sodium need. *Journal of Experimental Psychology: Animal Behavior Processes, 4,* 276–285.

Galbicka, G. (1988). Differentiating the behavior of organisms. *Journal of the Experimental Analysis of Behavior, 50,* 343–354.

Gallistel, C. R., & Gibbon, J. (2000). Time, rate, and conditioning. *Psychological Review, 107,* 289–344.

Garcia, J., & Koelling, R. A. (1966). Relation of cue to consequence in avoidance learning. *Psychonomic Science, 4,* 123–124.

Garcia, J., Ervin, F. R., & Koelling, R. A. (1966). Learning with prolonged delay of reinforcement. *Psychonomic Science, 5,* 121–122.

Gershoff, E. T. (2002). Corporal punishment by parents and associated child behaviors and experiences: A meta-analysis and theoretical review. *Psychological Bulletin, 128,* 539–579.

Gibbon, J., & Balsam, P. (1981). Spreading association in time. In C. M. Locurto, H. S. Terrace, & J. Gibbon (Eds.), *Autoshaping and conditioning theory* (pp. 219–253). New York: Academic Press.

Gillan, D. J., & Domjan, M. (1977). Taste-aversion conditioning with expected versus unexpected drug treatment. *Journal of Experimental Psychology: Animal Behavior Processes, 3,* 297–309.

Goodall, G. (1984). Learning due to the response-shock contingency in signalled punishment. *Quarterly Journal of Experimental Psychology, 36B,* 259–279.

Gordon, W. C., & Mowrer, R. R. (1980). An extinction trial as a reminder treatment following electroconvulsive shock. *Animal Learning & Behavior, 8,* 363–367.

Gormezano, I., Kehoe, E. J., & Marshall, B. S. (1983). Twenty years of classical conditioning research with the rabbit. In J. M. Sprague & A. N. Epstein (Eds.), *Progress in psychobiology and physiological psychology* (Vol. 10, pp. 197–275). Orlando, FL: Academic Press.

Graham, J. M., & Desjardins, C. (1980). Classical conditioning: Induction of luteinizing hormone and testosterone secretion in anticipation of sexual activity. *Science, 210,* 1039–1041.

Grant, D. S. (1976). Effect of sample presentation time on long-delay matching in the pigeon. *Learning and Motivation, 7,* 580–590.

Grant, D. S. (1988). Sources of visual interference in delayed matching-to-sample with pigeons. *Journal of Experimental Psychology: Animal Behavior Processes, 14,* 368–375.

Grant, D. S., & Soldat, A. S. (1995). A postsample cue to forget does initiate an active forgetting process in pigeons. *Journal of Experimental Psychology: Animal Behavior Processes, 21,* 218–228.

Green, L., & Freed, D. E. (1993). The substitutability of reinforcers. *Journal of the Experimental Analysis of Behavior, 60,* 141–158.

Green, L., & Rachlin, H. (1991). Economic substitutability of electrical brain stimulation, food, and water. *Journal of the Experimental Analysis of Behavior, 55,* 133–143.

Groves, P. M., Lee, D., & Thompson, R. F. (1969). Effects of stimulus frequency and intensity on habituation and sensitization in acute spinal cat. *Physiology & Behavior, 4,* 383–388.

Groves, P. M., & Thompson, R. F. (1970). Habituation: A dual-process theory. *Psychological Review, 77,* 419–450.

Gutiérrez, G., & Domjan, M. (1996). Learning and male-male sexual competition in Japanese quail (*Coturnix japonica*). *Journal of Comparative Psychology, 110,* 170–175.

Hall, G. (1991). *Perceptual and associative learning.* Oxford: Clarendon Press.

Hall, G., Kaye, H., & Pearce, J. M. (1985). Attention and conditioned inhibition. In R. R. Miller & N. E. Spear (Eds.), *Information processing in animals: Conditioned inhibition* (pp. 185–207). Hillsdale, NJ: Erlbaum.

Hallam, S. C., Grahame, N. J., Harris, K., & Miller, R. R. (1992). Associative structure underlying enhanced negative summation following operational extinction of a Pavlovian inhibitor. *Learning and Motivation, 23,* 43–62.

Hearst, E., Besley, S., & Farthing, G. W. (1970). Inhibition and the stimulus control of operant behavior. *Journal of the Experimental Analysis of Behavior, 14,* 373–409.

Hearst, E., Franklin, S., & Mueller, C. G. (1974). The "disinhibition" of extinguished operant behavior in pigeons: Trial-tempo shifts and novel-stimulus effects. *Animal Learning & Behavior, 2,* 229–237.

Hearst, E., & Jenkins, H. M. (1974). *Sign tracking: The stimulus-reinforcer relation and directed action.* Austin, TX: Psychonomic Society.

Heiligenberg, W. (1974). Processes governing behavioral states of readiness. In D. S. Lehrman, J. S. Rosenblatt, R. Hinde, & E. Shaw (Eds.), *Advances in the study of behavior* (Vol. 5, pp. 173–200). New York: Academic Press.

Herrnstein, R. J. (1969). Method and theory in the study of avoidance. *Psychological Review, 87,* 49–69.

Herrnstein, R. J. (1970). On the law of effect. *Journal of the Experimental Analysis of Behavior, 13,* 243–266.

Herrnstein, R. J., Loveland, D. H., & Cable, C. (1976). Natural concepts in pigeons. *Journal of Experimental Psychology: Animal Behavior Processes, 2,* 285–301.

Hogan, J. A. (1994). Structure and development of behavior systems. *Psychonomic Bulletin & Review, 1,* 439–450.

Holland, P. C. (1977). Conditioned stimulus as a determinant of the form of the Pavlovian conditioned response. *Journal of Experimental Psychology: Animal Behavior Processes, 3,* 77–104.

Holland, P. C. (1984). Origins of behavior in Pavlovian conditioning. In G. H. Bower (Ed.), *The psychology of learning and motivation* (Vol. 18, pp. 129–174). Orlando, FL: Academic Press.

Holland, P. C. (1986). Temporal determinants of occasion setting in feature-positive discriminations. *Animal Learning & Behavior, 14,* 111–120.

Holland, P. C. (1989). Feature extinction enhances transfer of occasion setting. *Animal Learning & Behavior, 17,* 269–279.

Holland, P. C. (1992). Occasion setting in Pavlovian conditioning. In D. L. Medin (Ed.), *The psychology of learning and motivation* (Vol. 28, pp. 69–125). San Diego: Academic Press.

Holland, P. C. (2000). Trial and intertrial durations in appetitive conditioning in rats. *Animal Learning & Behavior, 28,* 121–135.

Hollis, K. L. (1984). The biological function of Pavlovian conditioning: The best defense is a good offense. *Journal of Experimental Psychology: Animal Behavior Processes, 10,* 413–425.

Hollis, K. L. (1990). The role of Pavlovian conditioning in territorial aggression and reproduction. In D. A. Dewsbury (Ed.), *Contemporary issues in comparative psychology* (pp. 197–219). Sunderland, MA: Sinauer.

Hollis, K. L. (1997). Contemporary research in Pavlovian conditioning: A "new" functional analysis. *American Psychologist, 52,* 956–965.

Hollis, K. L., Cadieux, E. L., & Colbert, M. M. (1989). The biological function of Pavlovian conditioning: A mechanism for mating success in the blue gourami (*Trichogaster trichopterus*). *Journal of Comparative Psychology, 103,* 115–121.

Hollis, K. L., Pharr, V. L., Dumas, M. J., Britton, G. B., & Field, J. (1997). Classical conditioning provides paternity advantage for territorial male blue gouramis (*Trichogaster trichopterus*). *Journal of Comparative Psychology, 111,* 219–225.

Holloway, K. S., & Domjan, M. (1993). Sexual approach conditioning: Tests of unconditioned stimulus devaluation using hormone manipulations. *Journal of Experimental Psychology: Animal Behavior Processes, 19,* 47–55.

Holz, W. C., & Azrin, N. H. (1961). Discriminative properties of punishment. *Journal of the Experimental Analysis of Behavior, 4,* 225–232.

Homme, L. E., deBaca, P. C., Devine, J. V., Steinhorst, R., & Rickert, E. J. (1963). Use of the Premack Principle in controlling the behavior of nursery school children. *Journal of the Experimental Analysis of Behavior, 6,* 544–548.

Honey, R. C., & Hall, G. (1989). Acquired equivalence and distinctiveness of cues. *Journal of Experimental Psychology: Animal Behavior Processes, 15,* 338–346.

Honig, W. K., & James, P. H. R. (Eds.). (1971). *Animal memory.* New York: Academic Press.

Horne, P. J., & Lowe, C. F. (1996). On the origins of naming and other symbolic behavior. *Journal of the Experimental Analysis of Behavior, 65,* 185–241.

Horne, P. J., & Lowe, C. F. (1997). Toward a theory of verbal behavior. *Journal of the Experimental Analysis of Behavior, 68,* 271–296.

Hull, C. L. (1930). Knowledge and purpose as habit mechanisms. *Psychological Review, 30,* 511–525.

Hull, C. L. (1931). Goal attraction and directing ideas conceived as habit phenomena. *Psychological Review, 38,* 487–506.

Hulse, S. H. (1958). Amount and percentage of reinforcement and duration of goal confinement in conditioning and extinction. *Journal of Experimental Psychology, 56,* 48–57.

Humphreys, L. G. (1939). The effect of random alternation of reinforcement on the acquisition and extinction of conditioned eyelid reactions. *Journal of Experimental Psychology, 25,* 141–158.

Ishida, M., & Papini, M. R. (1997). Massed-trial overtraining effects on extinction and reversal performance in turtles (*Geoclemys reevesii*). *Quarterly Journal of Experimental Psychology, 50B,* 1–16.

Jenkins, H. M. (1962). Resistance to extinction when partial reinforcement is followed by regular reinforcement. *Journal of Experimental Psychology, 64,* 441–450.

Jenkins, H. M., Barnes, R. A., & Barrera, F. J. (1981). Why autoshaping depends on trial spacing. In C. M. Locurto, H. S. Terrace, & J. Gibbon (Eds.), *Autoshaping and conditioning theory* (pp. 255–284). New York: Academic Press.

Jenkins, H. M., & Harrison, R. H. (1960). Effects of discrimination training on auditory generalization. *Journal of Experimental Psychology, 59,* 246–253.

Jenkins, H. M., & Harrison, R. H. (1962). Generalization gradients of inhibition following auditory discrimination learning. *Journal of the Experimental Analysis of Behavior, 5,* 435–441.

Jitsumori, M., Wright, A. A., & Shyan, M. R. (1989). Buildup and release from proactive interference in a rhesus monkey *Journal of Experimental Psychology: Animal Behavior Processes, 15,* 329–337.

Kamil, A. C., & Clements, K. C. (1990). Learning, memory, and foraging behavior. In D. A. Dewsbury (Ed.), *Contemporary issues in comparative psychology* (pp. 7–30). Sunderland, MA: Sinauer.

Kamin, L. J. (1965). Temporal and intensity characteristics of the conditioned stimulus. In W. F. Prokasy (Ed.), *Classical conditioning* (pp. 118–147). New York: Appleton-Century-Crofts.

Kamin, L. J. (1969). Predictability, surprise, attention, and conditioning. In B. A. Campbell & R. M. Church (Eds.), *Punishment and aversive behavior* (pp. 279–296). New York: Appleton-Century-Crofts.

Kaplan, P. S., Werner, J. S., & Rudy, J. W. (1990). Habituation, sensitization, and infant visual attention. In C. Rovee-Collier & L. P. Lipsitt (Eds.), *Advances in infancy research* (Vol. 6, pp. 61–109). Norwood, NJ: Ablex.

Kazdin, A. E. (1985). The token economy. In R. M. Turner & L. M. Ascher (Eds.), *Evaluating behavior therapy outcome.* New York: Springer.

Kendrick, D. F., Rilling, M. E., & Denny, M. R. (Eds.). (1986). *Theories of animal memory.* Hillsdale, NJ: Erlbaum.

Khallad, Y., & Moore, J. (1996). Blocking, unblocking, and overexpectation in autoshaping with pigeons. *Journal of the Experimental Analysis of Behavior, 65,* 575–591.

Kimble, G. A. (1961). *Hilgard and Marquis' conditioning and learning* (2nd ed.). New York: Appleton-Century-Crofts.

Kremer, E. F. (1974). The truly random control procedure: Conditioning to the static cues. *Journal of Comparative and Physiological Psychology, 86,* 700–707.

Kremer, E. F. (1978). The Rescorla-Wagner model: Losses in associative strength in compound conditioned stimuli. *Journal of Experimental Psychology: Animal Behavior Processes, 4,* 22–36.

Lashley, K. S., & Wade, M. (1946). The Pavlovian theory of generalization. *Psychological Review, 53,* 72–87.

Lattal, K. M. (1999). Trial and intertrial durations in Pavlovian conditioning: Issues of learning and performance. *Journal of Experimental Psychology: Animal Behavior Processes, 25,* 433–450.

Lattal, K. M., & Nakajima, S. (1998). Overexpectation in appetitive Pavlovian and instrumental conditioning. *Animal Learning & Behavior, 26,* 351–360.

Lieberman, D. A., McIntosh, D. C., & Thomas, G. V. (1979). Learning when reward is delayed: A marking hypothesis. *Journal of Experimental Psychology: Animal Behavior Processes, 5,* 224–242.

Logue, A. W., Ophir, I., & Strauss, K. E. (1981). The acquisition of taste aversions in humans. *Behaviour Research and Therapy, 19,* 319–333.

LoLordo, V. M., & Droungas, A. (1989). Selective associations and adaptive specializations: Taste aversions and phobias. In S. B. Klein & R. R. Mowrer (Eds.), *Contemporary learning theories: Instrumental conditioning theory and the impact of biological constraints on learning* (pp. 145–179). Hillsdale, NJ: Erlbaum.

LoLordo, V. M., & Fairless, J. L. (1985). Pavlovian conditioned inhibition: The literature since 1969. In R. R. Miller & N. E. Spear (Eds.), *Information processing in animals: Conditioned inhibition* (pp. 1–49). Hillsdale, NJ: Erlbaum.

Lorenz, K. Z. (1981). *The foundations of ethology.* New York: Springer.

Lubow, R. E. (1989). *Latent inhibition and conditioned attention theory*. Cambridge, UK: Cambridge University Press.

Lubow, R. E. (1998). Latent inhibition and behavior pathology: Prophylactic and other possible effects of stimulus preexposure. In W. O'Donohue (Ed.), *Learning and behavior therapy* (pp. 107–121). Boston: Allyn & Bacon.

Lysle, D. T., & Fowler, H. (1985). Inhibition as a "slave" process: Deactivation of conditioned inhibition through extinction of conditioned excitation. *Journal of Experimental Psychology: Animal Behavior Processes, 11,* 71–94.

Mackintosh, N. J. (1974). *The psychology of animal learning*. Oxford: Academic Press.

Mackintosh, N. J. (1975). A theory of attention: Variations in the associability of stimuli with reinforcement. *Psychological Review, 82,* 276–298.

Mackintosh, N. J. (1977). Stimulus control: Attentional factors. In W. K. Honig & J. E. R. Staddon (Eds.), *Handbook of operant behavior* (pp. 481–513). Englewood Cliffs, NJ: Prentice Hall.

Mackintosh, N. J., Bygrave, D. J., & Picton, B. M. B. (1977). Locus of the effect of a surprising reinforcer in the attenuation of blocking. *Quarterly Journal of Experimental Psychology, 29,* 327–336.

Maki, W. S. (1979). Pigeon's short-term memories for surprising vs. expected reinforcement and nonreinforcement. *Animal Learning & Behavior, 7,* 31–37.

Maki, W. S., Beatty, W. W., Hoffman, N., Bierley, R. A., & Clouse, B. A. (1984). Spatial memory over long retention intervals: Nonmemorial factors are not necessary for accurate performance on the radial arm maze by rats. *Behavioral and Neural Biology, 41,* 1–6.

Marlin, N. A., & Miller, R. R. (1981). Associations to contextual stimuli as a determinant of long-term habituation. *Journal of Experimental Psychology: Animal Behavior Processes, 7,* 313–333.

Matzel, L. D., Gladstein, L., & Miller, R. R. (1988). Conditioned excitation and conditioned inhibition are not mutually exclusive. *Learning and Motivation, 19,* 99–121.

McAllister, D. E., & McAllister, W. R. (1991). Fear theory and aversively motivated behavior: Some controversial issues. In M. R. Denny (Ed.), *Fear, avoidance, and phobias* (pp. 135–163). Hillsdale, NJ: Erlbaum.

McDowell, J. J., & Wixted, H. M. (1988). The linear system theory's account of behavior maintained by variable-ratio schedules. *Journal of the Experimental Analysis of Behavior, 49,* 143–169.

McLaren, I. P. L., & Mackintosh, N. J. (2000). An elemental model of associative learning: I. Latent inhibition and perceptual learning. *Animal Learning & Behavior, 28,* 211–246.

McNish, K. A., Betts, S. L., Brandon, S. E., & Wagner, A. R. (1997). Divergence of conditioned eyeblink and conditioned fear in backward Pavlovian conditioning. *Animal Learning & Behavior, 25,* 43–52.

Medin, D. L. (1980). Proactive interference in monkeys: Delay and intersample interval effects are noncomparable. *Animal Learning & Behavior, 8,* 553–560.

Medin, D. L., Roberts, W. A., & Davis, R. T. (Eds.). (1976). *Processes of animal memory*. Hillsdale, NJ: Erlbaum.

Miller, D. B. (1985). Methodological issues in the ecological study of learning. In T. D. Johnston & A. T. Pietrewicz (Eds.), *Issues in the ecological study of learning* (pp. 73–95). Hillsdale, NJ: Erlbaum.

Miller, N. E. (1951). Learnable drives and rewards. In S. S. Stevens (Ed.), *Handbook of experimental psychology*. New York: Wiley.

Miller, N. E. (1960). Learning resistance to pain and fear: Effects of overlearning, exposure, and rewarded exposure in context. *Journal of Experimental Psychology, 60,* 137–145.

Miller, R. R., Barnet, R. C., & Grahame, N. J. (1995). Assessment of the Rescorla-Wagner model. *Psychological Bulletin, 117,* 363–386.

Miller, R. R., Kasprow, W. J., & Schachtman, T. R. (1986). Retrieval variability: Sources and consequences. *American Journal of Psychology, 99*, 145–218.

Miller, R. R., & Matute, H. (1996). Animal analogues of causal judgment. In D. L. Medin (Ed.), *The psychology of learning and motivation* (Vol. 34, pp. 133–166). San Diego: Academic Press.

Miller, R. R., & Matzel, L. D. (1988). The comparator hypothesis: A response rule for the expression of associations. In G. H. Bower (Ed.), *The psychology of learning and motivation* (Vol. 22, pp. 51–92). Orlando, FL: Academic Press.

Miller, R. R., & Matzel, L. D. (1989). Contingency and relative associative strength. In S. B. Klein & R. R. Mowrer (Eds.), *Contemporary learning theories: Pavlovian conditioning and the status of learning theory* (pp. 61–84). Hillsdale, NJ: Erlbaum.

Mineka, S., & Gino, A. (1980). Dissociation between conditioned emotional response and extended avoidance performance. *Learning and Motivation, 11*, 476–502.

Morris, R. G. M. (1974). Pavlovian conditioned inhibition of fear during shuttlebox avoidance behavior. *Learning and Motivation, 5*, 424–447.

Morris, R. G. M. (1975). Preconditioning of reinforcing properties to an exteroceptive feedback stimulus. *Learning and Motivation, 6*, 289–298.

Mowrer, O. H. (1947). On the dual nature of learning: A reinterpretation of "conditioning" and "problem-solving." *Harvard Educational Review, 17*, 102–150.

Mowrer, O. H., & Lamoreaux, R. R. (1942). Avoidance conditioning and signal duration: A study of secondary motivation and reward. *Psychological Monographs, 54* (Whole No. 247).

Neuringer, A., Kornell, N., & Olufs, M. (2001). Stability and variability in extinction. *Journal of Experimental Psychology: Animal Behavior Processes, 27*, 79–94.

Oberling, P., Gosselin, O., & Miller, R. R. (1997). Latent inhibition in animals as a model of acute schizophrenia: A reanalysis. In M. Haug & R. E. Whalen (Eds.), *Animal models of human emotion and cognition* (pp. 97–102). Washington, DC: American Psychological Association.

Olton, D. S., & Samuelson, R. J. (1976). Remembrance of places passed: Spatial memory in rats. *Journal of Experimental Psychology: Animal Behavior Processes, 2*, 97–116.

Papini, M. R., & Bitterman, M. E. (1990). The role of contingency in classical conditioning. *Psychological Review, 97*, 396–403.

Pavlov, I. (1927). *Conditioned reflexes* (G. V. Anrep, trans.). London: Oxford University Press.

Pear, J. J., & Legris, J. A. (1987). Shaping by automated tracking of an arbitrary operant response. *Journal of the Experimental Analysis of Behavior, 47*, 241–247.

Pearce, J. M. (1994). Discrimination and categorization. In N. J. Mackintosh (Ed.), *Animal learning and cognition* (pp. 109–134). San Diego: Academic Press.

Pearce, J. M., & Hall, G. (1980). A model for Pavlovian learning: Variations in the effectiveness of conditioned but not of unconditioned stimuli. *Psychological Review, 87*, 532–552.

Peeke, H. V. S., & Petrinovich, L. (Eds.). (1984). *Habituation, sensitization, and behavior*. New York: Academic Press.

Peele, D. B., Casey, J., & Silberberg, A. (1984). Primacy of interresponse-time reinforcement in accounting for rate differences under variable-ratio and variable-interval schedules. *Journal of Experimental Psychology: Animal Behavior Processes, 10*, 149–167.

Pelchat, M. L., & Rozin, P. (1982). The special role of nausea in the acquisition of food dislikes by humans. *Appetite, 3*, 341–351.

Perry, D. G., & Parke, R. D. (1975). Punishment and alternative response training as determinants of response inhibition in children. *Genetic Psychology Monographs, 91*, 257–279.

Premack, D. (1965). Reinforcement theory. In D. Levine (Ed.), *Nebraska symposium on motivation* (Vol. 13, pp. 123–180). Lincoln: University of Nebraska Press.

Rachlin, H. (1976). *Behavior and learning* (Chap. 3, pp. 102–154). San Francisco: W. H. Freeman.

Rachlin, H. C. (1978). A molar theory of reinforcement schedules. *Journal of the Experimental Analysis of Behavior, 30*, 345–360.

Reberg, D. (1972). Compound tests for excitation in early acquisition and after prolonged extinction of conditioned suppression. *Learning and Motivation, 3*, 246–258.

Reberg, D., & Black, A. H. (1969). Compound testing of individually conditioned stimuli as an index of excitatory and inhibitory properties. *Psychonomic Science, 17*, 30–31.

Repp, A. C., & Singh, N. N. (Eds.). (1990). *Perspectives on the use of nonaversive and aversive interventions for persons with developmental disabilities.* Sycamore, IL: Sycamore.

Rescorla, R. A. (1967). Pavlovian conditioning and its proper control procedures. *Psychological Review, 74*, 71–80.

Rescorla, R. A. (1969). Pavlovian conditioned inhibition. *Psychological Bulletin, 72*, 77–94.

Rescorla, R. A. (1972). Informational variables in Pavlovian conditioning. In G. H. Bower (Ed.), *The psychology of learning and motivation* (Vol. 6). Orlando, FL: Academic Press.

Rescorla, R. A. (1973). Effect of US habituation following conditioning. *Journal of Comparative and Physiological Psychology, 82*, 137–143.

Rescorla, R. A. (1985). Conditioned inhibition and facilitation. In R. R. Miller & N. E. Spear (Eds.), *Information processing in animals: Conditioned inhibition* (pp. 299–326). Hillsdale, NJ: Erlbaum.

Rescorla, R. A. (1988). Pavlovian conditioning: It's not what you think it is. *American Psychologist, 43*, 151–160.

Rescorla, R. A. (1993a). Inhibitory associations between S and R in extinction. *Animal Learning & Behavior, 21*, 327–336.

Rescorla, R. A. (1993b). Preservation of response-outcome associations through extinction. *Animal Learning & Behavior, 21*, 238–245.

Rescorla, R. A. (1996). Spontaneous recovery after training with multiple outcomes. *Animal Learning & Behavior, 24*, 11–18.

Rescorla, R. A. (1997). Spontaneous recovery after Pavlovian conditioning with multiple outcomes. *Animal Learning & Behavior, 25*, 99–107.

Rescorla, R. A. (1999). Summation and overexpectation with qualitatively different outcomes. *Animal Learning & Behavior, 27*, 50–62.

Rescorla, R. A. (2001). Experimental extinction. In R. R. Mowrer & S. B. Klein (Eds.), *Contemporary learning theories* (pp. 119–154). Mahwah, NJ: Erlbaum.

Rescorla, R. A., Durlach, P. J., & Grau, J. (1985). Contextual learning in Pavlovian conditioning. In P. Balsam & A. Tomie (Eds.), *Context and learning* (pp. 23–56). Hillsdale, NJ: Erlbaum.

Rescorla, R. A., & Freberg, L. (1978). The extinction of within-compound flavor associations. *Learning and Motivation, 9*, 411–427.

Rescorla, R. A., & Gillan, D. J. (1980). An analysis of the facilitative effect of similarity on second-order conditioning. *Journal of Experimental Psychology: Animal Behavior Processes, 6*, 339–351.

Rescorla, R. A., & Solomon, R. L. (1967). Two-process learning theory: Relationships between Pavlovian conditioning and instrumental learning. *Psychological Review, 74*, 151–182.

Rescorla, R. A., & Wagner, A. R. (1972). A theory of Pavlovian conditioning: Variations in the effectiveness of reinforcement and nonreinforcement. In A. H. Black & W. F. Prokasy (Eds.), *Classical conditioning II: Current research and theory* (pp. 64–99). New York: Appleton-Century-Crofts.

Reynolds, G. S. (1975). *A primer of operant conditioning.* Glenview, IL: Scott Foresman.

Richardson, R., Riccio, D. C., & Jonke, T. (1983). Alleviation of infantile amnesia in rats by means of a pharmacological contextual state. *Developmental Psychobiology, 16*, 511–518.

Rilling, M. (1977). Stimulus control and inhibitory processes. In W. K. Honig & J. E. R. Staddon (Eds.), *Handbook of operant behavior* (pp. 432–480). Englewood Cliffs, NJ: Prentice Hall.

Robbins, S. J. (1988). Role of context in performance on a random schedule of autoshaping. *Journal of Experimental Psychology: Animal Behavior Processes, 14*, 413–424.

Robbins, S. J. (1990). Mechanisms underlying spontaneous recovery in autoshaping. *Journal of Experimental Psychology: Animal Behavior Processes, 16*, 235–249.

Roberts, W. A., & Grant, D. S. (1976). Studies of short-term memory in the pigeon using the delayed matching to sample procedure. In D. L. Medin, W. A. Roberts, & R. T. Davis (Eds.), *Processes of animal memory* (pp. 79–112). Hillsdale, NJ: Erlbaum.

Roberts, W. A., & Grant, D. S. (1978). An analysis of light-induced retroactive inhibition in pigeon short-term memory. *Journal of Experimental Psychology: Animal Behavior Processes, 4*, 219–236.

Roitblat, H. L. (1980). Codes and coding processes in pigeon short-term memory. *Animal Learning & Behavior, 8*, 341–351.

Romanes, G. J. (1882). *Animal intelligence*. New York: Appleton.

Roper, K. L., Kaiser, D. H., & Zentall, T. R. (1995). True directed forgetting in pigeons may occur only when alternative working memory is required on forget-cue trials. *Animal Learning & Behavior, 23*, 280–285.

Rosas, J. M., & Bouton, M. E. (1996). Spontaneous recovery after extinction of a conditioned taste aversion. *Animal Learning & Behavior, 24*, 341–348.

Ross, R. T. (1983). Relationships between the determinants of performance in serial feature-positive discriminations. *Journal of Experimental Psychology: Animal Behavior Processes, 9*, 349–373.

Santi, A., & Roberts, W. A. (1985). Prospective representation: The effects of varied mapping of sample stimuli to comparison stimuli and differential trial outcomes on pigeons' working memory. *Animal Learning & Behavior, 13*, 103–108.

Sargisson, R. J., & White, K. G. (2001). Generalization of delayed matching to sample following training at different delays. *Journal of the Experimental Analysis of Behavior, 75*, 1–14.

Schachtman, T. R., Brown, A. M., & Miller, R. R. (1985). Reinstatement-induced recovery of a taste-LiCl association following extinction. *Animal Learning & Behavior, 13*, 223–227.

Schein, M. W., & Hale, E. B. (1965). Stimuli eliciting sexual behavior. In F. A. Beach (Ed.), *Sex and behavior* (pp. 440–482). New York: Wiley.

Schmajuk, N. A., & Holland, P. C. (Eds.). (1998). *Occasion setting*. Washington, DC: American Psychological Association.

Schneiderman, N., & Gormezano, I. (1964). Conditioning of the nictitating membrane of the rabbit as a function of the CS-US interval. *Journal of Comparative and Physiological Psychology, 57*, 188–195.

Schwartz, B. (1981). Reinforcement creates behavioral units. *Behavioural Analysis Letters, 1*, 33–41.

Shanks, D. R., & Dickinson, A. (1987). Associative accounts of causality judgment. In G. H. Bower (Ed.), *The psychology of learning and motivation* (Vol. 21, pp. 229–261). San Diego: Academic Press.

Shapiro, K. L., Jacobs, W. J., & LoLordo, V. M. (1980). Stimulus-reinforcer interactions in Pavlovian conditioning of pigeons: Implications for selective associations. *Animal Learning & Behavior, 8*, 586–594.

Sherry, D. F., & Schachter, D. L. (1987). The evolution of multiple memory systems. *Psychological Review, 94*, 439–454.

Shettleworth, S. J. (1975). Reinforcement and the organization of behavior in golden hamsters: Hunger, environment, and food reinforcement. *Journal of Experimental Psychology: Animal Behavior Processes, 1*, 56–87.

Shimp, C. P. (1969). Optimum behavior in free-operant experiments. *Psychological Review, 76*, 97–112.

Sidman, M. (1953). Avoidance conditioning with brief shock and no exteroceptive warning signal. *Science, 118*, 157–158.

Sidman, M. (1960). *Tactics of scientific research*. New York: Basic Books.

Sidman, M. (2000). Equivalence relations and the reinforcement contingency. *Journal of the Experimental Analysis of Behavior, 74*, 127–146.

Siegel, S. (1974). Flavor preexposure and "learned safety." *Journal of Comparative and Physiological Psychology, 87*, 1073–1082.

Siegel, S. (1975). Conditioning insulin effects. *Journal of Comparative and Physiological Psychology, 89*, 189–199.

Siegel, S. (1999). Drug anticipation and drug addiction. The 1998 H. David Archibald lecture. *Addiction, 94*, 1113–1124.

Siegel, S., & Allan, L. G. (1996). The widespread influence of the Rescorla-Wagner model. *Psychonomic Bulletin & Review, 3*, 314–321.

Siegel, S., & Allan, L. G. (1998). Learning and homeostasis: Drug addiction and the McCollough effect. *Psychological Bulletin, 124*, 230–239.

Siegel, S., & Ramos, B. M. C. (2002). Applying laboratory research: Drug anticipation and the treatment of drug addiction. *Experimental and Clinical Pharmacology, 10*, 162–183.

Simons, R. C. (1996). *Boo! Culture, experience, and the startle reflex*. New York: Oxford University Press.

Skinner, B. F. (1938). *The behavior of organisms*. New York: Appleton-Century-Crofts.

Skinner, B. F. (1953). *Science and human behavior*. New York: Macmillan.

Skinner, B. F. (1956). A case study in scientific method. *American Psychologist, 11*, 221–233.

Small, W. S. (1899). An experimental study of the mental processes of the rat: I. *American Journal of Psychology, 11*, 133–164.

Small, W. S. (1900). An experimental study of the mental processes of the rat: II. *American Journal of Psychology, 12*, 206–239.

Smith, J. C., & Roll, D. L. (1967). Trace conditioning with X-rays as an aversive stimulus. *Psychonomic Science, 9*, 11–12.

Smith, M. C., Coleman, S. R., & Gormezano, I. (1969). Classical conditioning of the rabbit's nictitating membrane response at backward, simultaneous, and forward CS-US intervals. *Journal of Comparative and Physiological Psychology, 69*, 226–231.

Solomon, R. L., Kamin, L. J., & Wynne, L. C. (1953). Traumatic avoidance learning: The outcomes of several extinction procedures with dogs. *Journal of Abnormal and Social Psychology, 48*, 291–302.

Spear, N. E., & Riccio, D. C. (1994). *Memory: Phenomena and principles*. Boston: Allyn & Bacon.

Spear, N. E., Smith, G. J., Bryan, R. G., Gordon, W. C., Timmons, R., & Chiszar, D. A. (1980). Contextual influences on the interaction between conflicting memories in the rat. *Animal Learning & Behavior, 8*, 273–281.

Spence, K. W. (1956). *Behavior theory and conditioning*. New Haven, CT: Yale University Press.

Staddon, J. E. R. (1979). Operant behavior as adaptation to constraint. *Journal of Experimental Psychology: General, 108*, 48–67.

Stewart, J., & Eikelboom, R. (1987). Conditioned drug effects. In L. L. Iversen, S. D. Iversen, & S. H. Snyder (Eds.), *Handbook of psychopharmacology* (Vol. 19, pp. 1–57). New York: Plenum.

Sulzer-Azaroff, B., & Mayer, G. R. (1991). *Behavior analysis for lasting change*. Fort Worth, TX: Holt, Rinehart, and Winston.

Tait, R. W., & Saladin, M. E. (1986). Concurrent development of excitatory and inhibitory associations during backward conditioning. *Animal Learning & Behavior, 14*, 133–137.

Testa, T. J. (1974). Causal relationships and the acquisition of avoidance responses. *Psychological Review, 81*, 491–505.

Theios, J. (1962). The partial reinforcement effect sustained through blocks of continuous reinforcement. *Journal of Experimental Psychology, 64*, 1–6.

Theios, J., Lynch, A. D., & Lowe, W. F., Jr. (1966). Differential effects of shock intensity on one-way and shuttle avoidance conditioning. *Journal of Experimental Psychology, 72*, 294–299.

Thomas, G. V., & Liebeman, D. A. (1990). Commentary: Determinants of success and failure in experiments on marking. *Learning and Motivation, 21*, 110–124.

Thompson, R. F., & Spencer, W. A. (1966). Habituation: A model phenomenon for the study of neural substrates of behavior. *Psychological Review, 73*, 16–43.

Thorndike, E. L. (1898). Animal intelligence: An experimental study of the association process in animals. *Psychological Review Monographs, 2* (Whole No. 8).

Thorndike, E. L. (1911). *Animal intelligence: Experimental studies.* New York: Macmillan.

Thorndike, E. L. (1932). *The fundamentals of learning.* New York: Teachers College Press.

Tierney, K. J. (1995). Molar regulatory theory and behavior therapy. In W. O'Donohue & L. Krasner (Eds.), *Theories of behavior therapy* (pp. 97–128). Washington, DC: American Psychological Association.

Timberlake, W. (1980). A molar equilibrium theory of learned performance. In G. H. Bower (Ed.), *The psychology of learning and motivation* (Vol. 14). Orlando, FL: Academic Press.

Timberlake, W. (1984). Behavior regulation and learned performance: Some misapprehensions and disagreements. *Journal of the Experimental Analysis of Behavior, 41*, 355–375.

Timberlake, W. (1994). Behavior systems, associationism, and Pavlovian conditioning. *Psychonomic Bulletin & Review, 1*, 405–420.

Timberlake, W. (2001). Motivational modes in behavior systems. In R. R. Mowrer & S. B. Klein (Eds.), *Handbook of contemporary learning theories* (pp. 155–209). Mahwah, NJ: Erlbaum.

Timberlake, W., & Allison, J. (1974). Response deprivation: An empirical approach to instrumental reinforcement. *Psychological Review, 81*, 146–164.

Timberlake, W., & Farmer-Dougan, V. A. (1991). Reinforcement in applied settings: Figuring out ahead of time what will work. *Psychological Bulletin, 110*, 379–391.

Timberlake, W., & Lucas, G. A. (1989). Behavior systems and learning: From misbehavior to general principles. In S. B. Klein & R. R. Mowrer (Eds.), *Contemporary learning theories: Instrumental conditioning theory and the impact of biological constraints on learning* (pp. 237–275). Hillsdale, NJ: Erlbaum.

Timberlake, W., Wahl, G., & King, D. (1982). Stimulus and response contingencies in the misbehavior of rats. *Journal of Experimental Psychology: Animal Behavior Processes, 8*, 62–85.

Tinbergen, N. (1951). *The study of instinct.* Oxford: Clarendon Press.

Tinbergen, N. (1952). The behavior of the stickleback. *Scientific American, 187*, 22–26.

Tinbergen, N., & Perdeck, A. C. (1950). On the stimulus situation releasing the begging response in the newly hatched herring gull chick (*Larus argentatus argentatus* Pont.). *Behaviour, 3*, 1–39.

Tomie, A., Brooks, W., & Zito, B. (1989). Sign-tracking: The search for reward. In S. B. Klein & R. R. Mowrer (Eds.), *Contemporary learning theories: Pavlovian conditioning and the status of learning theory* (pp. 191–223). Hillsdale, NJ: Erlbaum.

Tomie, A., Murphy, A. L., Fath, S., & Jackson, R. L. (1980). Retardation of autoshaping following pretraining with unpredictable food: Effects of changing the context between pretraining and testing. *Learning and Motivation, 11*, 117–134.

Turkkan, J. S. (1989). Classical conditioning: The new hegemony. *The Behavioral and Brain Sciences, 12*, 121–179.

Wagner, A. R. (1961). Effects of amount and percentage of reinforcement and number of acqui-sition trials on conditioning and extinction. *Journal of Experimental Psychology, 62,* 234–242.

Wagner, A. R., & Rescorla, R. A. (1972). Inhibition in Pavlovian conditioning: Application of a theory. In R. A. Boakes & M. S. Halliday (Eds.), *Inhibition and learning.* London: Academic Press.

Wallace, J., Steinert, P. A., Scobie, S. R., & Spear, N. E. (1980). Stimulus modality and short-term memory in rats. *Animal Learning & Behavior, 8,* 10–16.

Wasserman, E. A. (1990). Detecting response-outcome relations: Toward an understanding of the causal texture of the environment. In G. H. Bower (Ed.), *The psychology of learning and motivation* (Vol. 26, pp. 27–82). San Diego: Academic Press.

Wasserman, E. A., & Astley, S. L. (1994). A behavioral analysis of concepts: Its application to pigeons and children. In D. L. Medin (Ed.), *The psychology of learning and motivation* (Vol. 31, pp. 73–132). San Diego: Academic Press.

Wasserman, E. A., Franklin, S. R., & Hearst, E. (1974). Pavlovian appetitive contingencies and approach vs. withdrawal to conditioned stimuli in pigeons. *Journal of Comparative and Physiological Psychology, 86,* 616–627.

Weisman, R. G., & Litner, J. S. (1972). The role of Pavlovian events in avoidance training. In R. A. Boakes & M. S. Halliday (Eds.), *Inhibition and learning.* London: Academic Press.

Whitlow, J. W., Jr., & Wagner, A. R. (1984). Memory and habituation. In H. V. S. Peeke & L. Petrinovich (Eds.), *Habituation, sensitization, and behavior.* New York: Academic Press.

Williams, B. A. (1994). Reinforcement and choice. In N. J. Mackintosh (Ed.), *Animal learning and cognition* (pp. 81–108). San Diego: Academic Press.

Williams, D. A., & Overmier, J. B. (1988). Some types of conditioned inhibitors carry collateral excitatory associations. *Learning and Motivation, 19,* 345–368.

Winter, J., & Perkins, C. C. (1982). Immediate reinforcement in delayed reward learning in pigeons. *Journal of the Experimental Analysis of Behavior, 38,* 169–179.

Witcher, E. S., & Ayres, J. J. B. (1984). A test of two methods for extinguishing Pavlovian conditioned inhibition. *Animal Learning & Behavior, 12,* 149–156.

Wright, A. A., Urcuioli, P. J., Sands, S. F., & Santiago, H. C. (1981). Interference of delayed matching to sample in pigeons: Effects of interpolation at different periods within a trial and stimulus similarity. *Animal Learning & Behavior, 9,* 595–603.

Zamble, E., Hadad, G. M., Mitchell, J. B., & Cutmore, T. R. H. (1985). Pavlovian conditioning of sexual arousal: First- and second-order effects. *Journal of Experimental Psychology: Animal Behavior Processes, 11,* 598–610.

Zentall, T. R., Steirn, J. N., & Jackson-Smith, P. (1990). Memory strategies in pigeons' performance of a radial-arm-maze analog task. *Journal of Experimental Psychology: Animal Behavior Processes, 16,* 358–371.

Zimmer-Hart, C. L., & Rescorla, R. A. (1974). Extinction of Pavlovian conditioned inhibition. *Journal of Comparative and Physiological Psychology, 86,* 837–845.

Index